Difficult Rhythm

Difficult Rhythm

Music and the Word in E. M. Forster

MICHELLE FILLION

UNIVERSITY OF ILLINOIS PRESS
Urbana, Chicago, and Springfield

Manufactured in the United States of America
∞ This book is printed on acid-free paper.

The Library of Congress cataloged the cloth edition as follows:
Fillion, Michelle, 1949–
Difficult rhythm : music and the word in E.M. Forster /
Michelle Fillion.
p. cm.
Includes bibliographical references and index.
ISBN 978-0-252-03565-4 (hardcover : alk. paper)
1. Forster, E. M. (Edward Morgan), 1879–1970—Criticism
and interpretation. 2. Forster, E. M. (Edward Morgan),
1879–1970—Knowledge—Music. 3. Music in literature.
4. Music and literature. I. Title.
PR6011.058Z6539 2010
823'.914—dc22 2010037301
Paperback ISBN 978-0-252-07902-3

For Gordon Mumma

Contents

Abbreviations

ACF	Alice Clara ("Lily") Forster (1855–1945), Forster's mother.
AH	EMF, *Abinger Harvest* (San Diego: Harcourt Brace & Company [A Harvest Book], 1936).
AN	EMF, *Aspects of the Novel* (San Diego: Harcourt Brace & Company [A Harvest Book], 1927).
A-Wn	Austria, Music collection of the Austrian National Library (Österreichische Nationalbibliothek), Vienna.
BBCOH	*Benjamin Britten: Billy Budd,* ed. Mervyn Cooke and Philip Reed, Cambridge Opera Handbooks (Cambridge: Cambridge University Press, 1993).
BBLL2	*Letters from a Life: The Selected Letters and Diaries of Benjamin Britten, 1913–1976,* vol. 2, 1939–1945, ed. Donald Mitchell and Philip Reed (Berkeley: University of California Press, 1991).
BBLL3	*Letters from a Life: The Selected Letters of Benjamin Britten, 1913–1976,* vol. 3, 1946–1951, ed. Donald Mitchell, Philip Reed, and Mervyn Cooke (Berkeley: University of California Press, 2004).
BPL	Benjamin Britten-Peter Pears Library, Aldeburgh, U.K.
CB	EMF, *Commonplace Book,* ed. Philip Gardner (Stanford: Stanford University Press, 1985).
EMF	Edward Morgan Forster (1879–1970).
HE-D	EMF, *Howards End,* ed. from the Abinger Edition by Alistair M. Duckworth, Case Studies in Contemporary Criticism (Boston: Bedford Books, 1997).

HE-M	*The Manuscripts of Howards End,* ed. Oliver Stallybrass, Abinger Edition, 4a (London: Edward Arnold, 1973).
HE-NCE	EMF, *Howards End,* ed. Paul B. Armstrong, Norton Critical Edition (New York: Norton, 1998).
KCC	Archive Centre, King's College, Cambridge University, U.K.
L	Mary Lago, comp., *Calendar of the Letters of E. M. Forster* (London: Mansell, 1985).
LD	EMF, "Locked Diary" [a.k.a. "Locked Journal"], Ms. KCC (EMF/12/8).
LJ	EMF, *The Longest Journey,* ed. from the Abinger Edition, with introduction by Elizabeth Heine (London: Penguin, 1988).
LJ-A	EMF, *The Longest Journey,* ed. with introduction and commentary by Elizabeth Heine, Abinger Edition, 2 (London: Edward Arnold, 1984).
LN	*The Lucy Novels: Early Sketches for* A Room with a View, ed. Oliver Stallybrass, Abinger Edition, 3a (London: Edward Arnold, 1977).
MAU	EMF, *Maurice,* ed. with introduction by P. N. Furbank (London: Edward Arnold, 1971; rpt. London: Penguin, 1972).
MAU-A	EMF, *Maurice,* ed. with introduction and commentary by Philip Gardner, Abinger Edition, 5 (London: André Deutsch, 1999).
NG2	*The New Grove Dictionary of Music and Musicians,* 2nd ed., ed. Stanley Sadie and John Tyrrell (London: Macmillan Publishers Limited; and New York: Grove's Dictionaries, Inc., 2001).
NJ	EMF, "The Notebook Journal, 1903–09," Ms. KCC (EMF/12/7).
PI	EMF, *A Passage to India,* ed. from the Abinger Edition (1979), with introduction by Oliver Stallybrass (London: Penguin, 1979).
RV	EMF, *A Room with a View,* ed. from the Abinger Edition (1978), with introduction by Oliver Stallybrass (London: Penguin, 1978).
SL1	*Selected Letters of E. M. Forster,* ed. Mary Lago and P. N. Furbank, vol. 1, *1879–1920* (London: Collins, 1983).
SL2	*Selected Letters of E. M. Forster,* ed. Mary Lago and P. N. Furbank, vol. 2, *1921–1970* (Cambridge, Mass.: The Belknap Press of Harvard University Press, 1985).

TCD EMF, *Two Cheers for Democracy* (San Diego: Harcourt Brace & Company [A Harvest Book], 1951).

WAFT EMF, *Where Angels Fear to Tread,* ed. from the Abinger Edition (1975), with introduction by Oliver Stallybrass (London: Penguin, 1976).

Musical Examples

Figures

Preface

> Is there any effect in novels comparable to the effect of the Fifth Symphony as a whole, where, when the orchestra stops, we hear something that has never actually been played?
>
> —EMF, *Aspects of the Novel*

In 1927 E. M. Forster delivered the Clark lectures at Trinity College, Cambridge. His subject, aspects of the novel, was appropriate to the author of a string of celebrated novels ending with *A Passage to India* of 1924. Although Forster avoided examples from his own works, the talks are in many ways an exposé of his approach to writing. In the final sessions, he landed in the murky waters of prophecy and rhythm, by which a realist novel is enhanced through the elusive properties of music (*AN*, 125–69). If "prophecy" for Forster is the place where a novel "sings" and transcends the sum of its words, then "rhythm" is its song. At the apex of his literary metaphysics is the concept of "difficult rhythm," by which "great chords" resound below the verbal surface of a novel and echo after it has closed. Difficult rhythm springs from the capacity of sound, in the words of Marcel Proust's Swann, to "reflect, like water, like a mirror."[1] The effect is comparable to that experienced after Beethoven's Fifth Symphony is over, when "we feel that the notes and tunes composing it have been liberated, [and] have found in the rhythm of the whole their individual freedom" (*AN*, 169). In his 1945 essay "From the Audience," Forster reworked the concept of difficult rhythm as "the architectural emotion," which occurs "when a composition extending through time is suddenly apprehended as a whole."[2] Peter Burra observed famously that Forster "chose the novel because he had ideas to utter which needed a more distinct articulation than music could make."[3] I see it from another angle: music allowed Forster to transcend the precision of the word and, in his most visionary moments of "difficult rhythm," to open the novel to the timeless and the ineffable—and ultimately to the ambiguities of modern life.

For Forster the act of listening to music was always a balancing act between the "music itself" and its power to signify extramusical meaning. The unresolved debate between Helen and Margaret Schlegel in *Howards End* over how best to hear Beethoven's Fifth Symphony was very much Forster's own. The ambivalence at the heart of his musical aesthetics has its counterpart in the dialectics of gender, sexuality, class, politics, and nationhood that drive all his novels from *Where Angels Fear to Tread* (1905) to *A Passage to India* (1924). Each of these uses its layers of musical symbolism and allusion distinctively and purposefully to underscore its manifold conflicts and dilemmas, and to undercut their final resolution. North and South, Victorian optimism and Edwardian doubt, realism and symbolism, men and women, men and men, fin de siècle decadence and the novel of the future—Forster's music plays out these oppositions and sings a mysterious song of uncertainty beyond the final words of each novel. In the end, music becomes a prime contributor to Forster's qualified modernism, and to his ultimate failure to connect.

Music is woven in numerous ways into the plot, symbolism, narration, context, and structure of all his novels. When his years as a novelist were over, the tension between music and the word became a preoccupation of his critical essays of the 1930s and 1940s, especially "Word-Making and Sound-Taking" (1935), "Not Listening to Music" (1939), "The C Minor of That Life" (1941), and "The Raison d'Être of Criticism in the Arts" (1947). Musical matters also surface in *Goldsworthy Lowes Dickinson* (1934) and the 1953 memoirs of Forster's trips to India, *The Hill of Devi*. The most curious product of his musical enthusiasm was "Beethoven's Piano Sonatas," the unfinished project begun in 1939 to annotate all thirty-two sonatas. Forster's failure to complete it underscores the critical gap in his aesthetics between the signifying word and the resistance of music to signification. Finally, music recalled him from unwilling retirement to his last major project, the three-year collaboration with Benjamin Britten and Eric Crozier on the libretto of *Billy Budd* (1951). Herman Melville's elusive "song not without words" (*AN*, 142) provided Forster a last public occasion to confront the fraught relationship between word and music in the medium of opera.

Although the symbolic role of music in individual novels by Forster has been addressed selectively in a number of distinguished literary studies, this is the first comprehensive study of his musical world and its significant impact on his literary oeuvre from the perspective of a musicologist. I bring to this interdisciplinary study my own training in music history, analysis, and performance practices, amplified by the daunting wealth of literary criticism on Forster and English modernism. This book eschews any single literary methodology for a set of coordinated lenses, including recent perspectives from the fields of cultural history, narrative theory, biography, and gender studies, selected for their relevance to each chapter. These fields rub shoulders with the sociopolitical context of Forster's time and the reception of music in late Victorian and Edwardian England that formed his musical taste. My evidence also draws substantially from Forster's unpublished Locked Diary and Notebook Journal, sketches and drafts, and a major body of his voluminous (and still largely unpublished) correspondence, much of which is housed at King's College, Cambridge University. Philip Gardner's edition of Forster's literary journal, the *Commonplace Book* (1925–68), and the studies of the compositional drafts of the novels in the appendixes and companion volumes to the *Abinger Edition of E. M. Forster,* published by Edward Arnold and André Deutsch, provided valuable insights. The unpublished drafts of the libretto of *Billy Budd* and Britten's compositional sketches and drafts of the opera, housed at the Benjamin Britten-Peter Pears Library, Aldeburgh (U.K.), and the Austrian National Library, Vienna, provided indispensable evidence of Forster's major role in the project. The University of Victoria McPherson Library (British Columbia, Canada) possesses significant holdings of early twentieth-century English journals, magazines, and music literature known to Forster, which contributed valuable context for my study. The outcome is a fresh perspective on the familiar Forster and the musical themes that he developed purposefully and coherently throughout his literary life.

A note on citations: Frequently used sources are designated in the text by sigla as identified in the list of abbreviations (pp. ix–xi). Forster's letters are cited liberally throughout this study for the considerable insight into his musical experience and taste that they provide. Published letters are quoted from the two-volume *Selected Letters of E. M. Forster,* edited by Mary Lago and P. N. Furbank (*SL1,2*), while the numerous unpublished letters are identified with reference to Lago's indispensable *Calendar of the Letters of E. M. Forster* (L). Her inventory proceeds alphabetically by name of the recipient and then chronologically by number within each subset. Thus, Forster's letters to Britten correspond to her items B551–728, and the letter of 24 October 1948 would be identified in my text as L: B567. Although the definitive Abinger Editions were consulted at all stages of writing, for practical reasons the quotations from the novels and essays refer to the best available commercial editions more readily available to the reader and are embedded in the text. For the most part the paperback Penguin Editions, most of which derive from the Abinger texts, are used. An exception is Alistair M. Duckworth's 1997 edition of *Howards End* (*HE-D*), which corrects several errors in the Abinger Edition. Forster's *Aspects of the Novel* and the anthologies of essays *Abinger Harvest* and *Two Cheers for Democracy,* originally published by Edward Arnold, remain in print in paperback reprints by Harcourt Brace. For reasons of consistency, I have regularized the use of quotation marks to American style.

Chapter 1 provides the first biographical survey of the musical life of Edward Morgan Forster (1879–1970) and supplies the context for his musical world and the tastes on which it depends. It surveys his lifelong activities as amateur pianist, listener, and writer on music, from his childhood musical education in the late Victorian era to his collaboration on the libretto of *Billy Budd* (1951) and beyond. The next five chapters (Chapters 2–6) form a set of developing variations on Forster's manifold uses of music in his major novels. Chapter 2 proceeds from his discovery in Florence of Donizetti's opera *Lucia di Lammermoor* by way of an inspired singer. Forster embedded the voice, interpretation, and physical presence of soprano Luisa Tetrazzini into his first novel, *Where Angels Fear to Tread* (1905). As depicted there, her *Lucia* embodies the cultural divide between England and Italy and its life-changing impact on two English tourists, Caroline Abbott and Philip Herriton. Chapter 3 explores Forster's extravagant application of Wagner and Wagnerism in *The Longest Journey* (1907). Its numerous symbolic allusions to Wagner's *Ring* cycle, *Lohengrin,* and *Parsifal* situate the novel as a critique of English decadent Wagnerism of the 1890s, while its innovative adaptation of Wagner's structural principles to the novel reflects Forster's search for new literary forms. In the end, Wagnerism proves a dangerous source of self-delusion for Rickie Elliot and a problematic model for coherence in the novel.

Forster's Beethoven provides the musical centerpiece of the next two novels. *A Room with a View* (1908) eschews the heavily Wagnerian processes of *The Longest Journey* for psychosocial commentary through music. As discussed in Chapter 4, Lucy Honeychurch's choices of piano repertoire, from Beethoven and Wagner to Gluck and Henry Bishop, chart her downward course from aspiring "New Woman" to Victorian "piano girl." By contrast, Beethoven's last Sonata Op. 111 indicates her heroic potential and resounds in her ambiguous redemption at the novel's close. *Howards End* (1910), the subject of Chapter 5, applies the late-romantic debate regarding descriptive and absolute music among the followers of Wagner and Brahms to the study of a family and of England itself in the years before the Great War. How its protagonists hear Beethoven's Fifth Symphony—as organic whole or open-ended trajectory—will determine their success in resolving the dilemmas of modern life and finding the "connected" life at Howards End.

Music plays a unique role in *Maurice* (1913–14; completed 1959) as an emblem of homosexual desire and a perilous source of masculine self-knowledge. Chapter 6 addresses its use of Peter Ilyich Tchaikovsky's "Pathétique" Symphony and his brother Modeste's biography of the composer in the context of English writings on sexology and sexual identity at the turn-of-century. The musical techniques of the earlier novels persist with little further development in Forster's last novel, *A Passage to India*. Indeed, music plays a relatively minor symbolic role in its trenchant sociopolitical critique of colonialism in India—hence the perhaps surprising lack of a chapter of my book devoted to this much-discussed novel. The one stunning innovation in its musical world, however, will feature in my concluding Chapter 9.

Chapter 7 moves beyond the novels into the war years 1939–45 and a study of the fragmentary "Beethoven's Piano Sonatas," with a full first edition of the manuscript (King's College, Cambridge University). The project embodies both the growing tension between music and the word in Forster's critical essays of the time and the decline of his liberal humanism in the face of war and totalitarianism. In the *Billy Budd* project of 1948–51, Forster found a partial resolution to his aesthetic dilemma and an escape from the burden of isolation. Chapter 8 explores Forster's discovery of the joys and challenges of artistic collaboration by way of a case study of Claggart's monologue, "O beauty, o handsomeness, goodness." With evidence from the unpublished drafts of its libretto and musical score, this chapter clarifies Forster's role in the gestation of the opera and situates the *Billy Budd* project among his major literary achievements. Chapter 9 draws the conclusion of my book: that the musical flights of "prophetic song" in Forster's novels, though indeed a difficult sort of rhythm, are central to his characteristic voice as a writer. The compromised closures that contribute to the emergence of a qualified modernism in each of Forster's novels are dependent in part on their musical themes.

Forster is much admired by music lovers of all stripes, as much perhaps for his musical references as for the deep music of his prose. I hope that this book may be of interest to professional and general readers, including musicians and musicologists, literary scholars, cultural historians, and the multitude who continue to discover and revisit Forster's novels—perhaps by way of the successful feature film versions of them beginning with the 1985 releases of David Lean's *A Passage to India* and James Ivory's *A Room with a View*. For purposes of general accessibility, I have consciously avoided heavy-duty musical analysis and theoretical terminology; necessary musical vocabulary is defined in the text or notes. Musical examples have been kept to a minimum, are easily playable on the piano or recordings, and include commentary that should clarify their purpose for the nonmusician. Plot summaries unnecessary to the literary specialist should assist those whose Forster reading requires some brushing up. My study also suggests additional Forsteriana for the college classroom beyond the ubiquitous Fifth Symphony scene or the essay "Not Listening to Music." His musical scenes are a treasure trove of interdisciplinary material for instructors of humanities courses. In this context, the *Lucia* scene in *Where Angels Fear to Tread* provides a complementary source reading for the teaching of Italian romantic aria form or the patterns of opera consumption and international tourism in the late nineteenth century; Tchaikovsky in *Maurice,* for the study of homosexual subtexts and the culture of repression in Edwardian England; Lucy's music in *A Room with a View,* as a document in the study of women in turn-of-century society. Finally, Claggart's aria from *Billy Budd* furnishes a prime example of the collaborative creative process. In the end, however, my study aims to make an original critical contribution to the study both of English-language musical reception in the first half of the twentieth century and of a major writer on the cusp of literary modernism.

* * *

This study would have been impossible without the generous access to unpublished materials provided by numerous libraries and individuals. Chief among these is the Archive of King's College, Cambridge University, which holds the copyrights to Forster's letters and published and unpublished materials; these are cited with the kind permission of The Society of Authors (London) as agent for the Provost and Scholars of King's College Cambridge. The manuscript sources of the libretto and the compositional drafts of *Billy Budd,* as well as the Britten-Forster correspondence, are cited with permission of the Benjamin Britten–Peter Pears Library of the Britten-Pears Foundation (Aldeburgh) and the Britten Estate. Additional sketches of Claggart's aria are quoted courtesy of the Music Collection of the Austrian National Library (Österreichische Nationalbibliothek), Vienna. I am grateful as well to Boosey & Hawkes, Inc., for their permission to quote segments of the full score of Britten's *Billy Budd,*[4] and to their copyright administrator Bindiya Patel. For rights to quote from additional primary sources, I acknowledge with gratitude the following collections: the Harry Ransom Center (The University of Texas at Austin) for letters from Forster to Joe Ackerley, Malcolm Darling, E. H. W. Meyerstein, and Lady Ottoline Morrell; the Eda Kuhn Loeb Music Library of the Harvard College Library; the Master and Fellows of Trinity College Cambridge (for R. C. Trevelyan); Durham University Library (U.K.)

for Forster's letters to William Plomer (PLO/66); and for visual material, to the National Archive of the Richard-Wagner-Stiftung, Bayreuth (Germany) and the Iris & B. Gerald Cantor Center for Visual Arts (Stanford University). I am also indebted to the following individuals for allowing me to quote from documents in their ownership/stewardship: the Earl of Harewood; Eric Fletcher; John Edward Leigh (for Edward Leigh); and Edward Wilson of Johnson & Alcock Ltd., London (for Forrest Reid).

The major research was conducted at the McPherson Library (University of Victoria, British Columbia), the Doe Library and Jean Gray Hargrove Music Library (University of California, Berkeley), the University Library and King's College Library (Cambridge University), and the F. W. Olin Library (Mills College, Oakland, California), whose staff were immensely helpful. Above all, I owe a debt of gratitude for help, advice, and warm hospitality to the staffs of the Archive Centre of King's College Cambridge, including Librarian Peter Jones and Archivists Dr. Patricia McGuire and Dr. Rosalind Grooms, and of the Britten-Pears Library, Aldeburgh, especially Dr. Nick Clark (Librarian). My research stays in Cambridge and Aldeburgh are among the most cherished memories of this project. The musical examples were expertly prepared by David Archer of Soundstone Music (Victoria, B.C.) and Nicholas Piper, and the index by Audrey McClellan. I also wish to thank colleagues who commented on portions of this manuscript at its various stages, or who contributed in stimulating conversations or correspondence: Mark Evan Bonds, Philip Brett, Lynn Garafola, Dominic Gill and Julia Wilson-Jones, Lawrence Kramer, Nicholas Marston, Colin Matthews, Stephen McClatchie, Graham Smith, and Colin Tilney; and to Ruth Saxton, whose invitation to speak about Forster's Beethoven to her graduate seminar on the Modern English Novel at Mills College planted the first seeds of this book. Finally, it would never have seen the light of day without the wisdom, critical acumen, and encouragement of my editor at the University of Illinois Press, Willis G. Regier, or the invaluable contributions of Jennifer Reichlin, Kathleen Kornell, Copenhaver Cumpston, and my copy editor Nancy E. Albright. Working with them has been a pleasure.

This book is dedicated with love to my spouse, composer Gordon Mumma, whose unflagging enthusiasm for this long project saw me through its low points and whose own creative vigor has been my constant inspiration. The devoted springboard of my every idea, he read countless drafts, and never seemed to tire of the subject of a writer who crafted his words with the instincts of a composer in sounds.

Difficult Rhythm

1

E. M. Forster's Life in Music

Music has meant an enormous amount to me.
—EMF at eighty

Music was a pleasure, a companion, and a rich source of literary inspiration throughout E. M. Forster's life. In times of depression or loss, it provided him "light in the darkness, and because of the darkness," as he wrote to Aida Borchgrevink in May 1928 (L: B375). His musical activities peaked at several points in his life—his student years at Cambridge; his travels to Italy, India, and Egypt; and his emotional nadirs following both World Wars. Operas at Covent Garden, the *Ballets Russes,* concerts at the Queen's Hall and Aldeburgh Festivals, gramophone recordings and the "wireless," and his own amateur piano playing worked their way into his fiction, essays, literary theory, and reviews. The *Billy Budd* project was a unique musical experience that provided a fresh burst of creative energy in his later years. This chapter provides a biographical chronology of Forster as a musician and music lover. It is based on his unpublished letters, diaries, and papers in the archive of King's College Cambridge, with generous assistance of the biographies by P. N. Furbank, Mary Lago, Francis King, Nicola Beauman, and others, to which my selective account is gratefully indebted.[1]

Youth and Cambridge (1879–1901)

Edward Morgan Forster's musical life began sometime after 1883, when he and his mother moved to Rooksnest in Stevenage. His father had died of consumption in 1880, leaving Alice Clara ("Lily") a young widow after only three years of marriage. When Morgan was about six, she bought a piano. He received formal music lessons when he surpassed her teaching skills, using the popular Lebert-Stark piano method. Morgan was a precocious boy (having taught himself to read when he was four) and likely made swift progress. After she engaged a tutor in 1887, his performance was telling: "[Morgan] gets on well with his music, but with nothing else."[2] An early influence was his mother's friend, Mary ("Maimie") Aylward, whose husband, William Price Aylward, was a trained musician and choral director who also owned a music shop in Salisbury. A somewhat forbidding figure to the young Forster, he presided over Maimie and Lily's four-hand piano duets on the Érard piano in their Salisbury parlor until his death in 1890.

When Morgan entered the Kent House School in Eastbourne that year, his new piano instructor, Mr. H. Baillie, declared that he had "been very well taught" and dubiously agreed "that the scales do not matter" (L: F305). The issue of scales, likely a sore point with his mother, recurs elsewhere in the boy's early letters home; his technique would never be reliable. He was soon recruited to perform at the end-of-term concert, and he made his "debut" in November 1890 as the pianist in a trio by Stanislaus, with a further appearance on triangle in the Toy Symphony by Cornelius Gurlitt. He also studied singing, reporting to his mother that he was piping Shelley's "A Widow Bird" and had "sung the high B flat" (L: F324). The choral director took a dislike to Morgan, however, telling him that he "could not sing" (L: F332). He also had a brutish side, beating another boy with a stick and injuring Morgan in a "pinching" episode under his bedclothes.[3] By December of his first year, Morgan was acutely anxious and homesick. Two years later, however, his report card (see Fig. 1) shows "a much firmer grasp of his work," with firsts in classics, French, and scripture and commendations in piano and singing. His writing, however, was "still very weak."

The September 1893 move from his beloved Rooksnest was traumatic, and his early years as a day student at the Tonbridge School were miserable. There he found a mentor in the music master, Mr. Brewer, who advised him to continue his music, and enrolled him in the choir and chapel singers (L: F332). Classics and music provided safe haven until he found his footing, graduating in 1897 with prizes in Latin and English. In October of that year Morgan entered Cambridge University, a distinguished center for music since the mid–fifteenth century. Thus began the four halcyon years at King's College that both made and sustained him for the rest of his life.

Although Forster read classics there, music remained a strong interest. Under the professorship of Charles Villiers Stanford, music had flourished at Cambridge.[4] Stanford had also conducted the Cambridge University Musical Society from 1873 to 1893, building the chorus and orchestra into a renowned

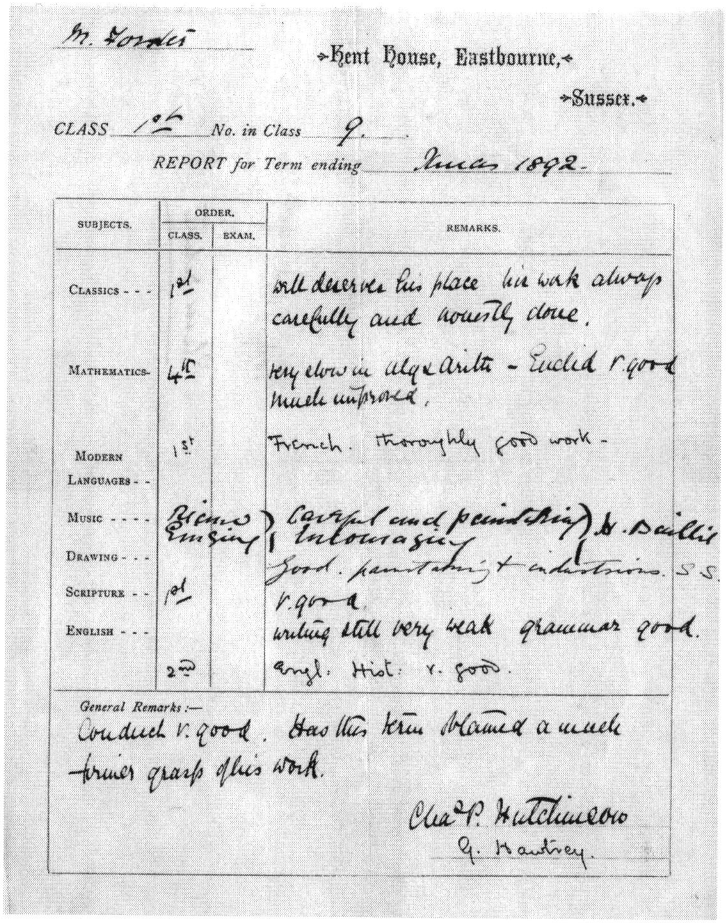
M. Forster

Kent House, Eastbourne,

Sussex.

CLASS 1st No. in Class 9.

REPORT for Term ending Xmas 1892.

SUBJECTS.	ORDER. CLASS.	ORDER. EXAM.	REMARKS.
Classics	1st		well deserves his place his work always carefully and honestly done.
Mathematics	4th		very slow in alg & arith – Euclid v. good much improved.
Modern Languages	1st		French. thoroughly good work.
Music	Piano / Singing		Careful and painstaking / Encouraging. H. Baillie
Drawing			Good. painstaking & industrious. S.S.
Scripture	1st		v. good.
English	2nd		writing still very weak grammar good. Engl. Hist: v. good.

General Remarks:— Conduct v. good. Has this term obtained a much firmer grasp of his work.

Chas P. Hutchinson

G. Hawtrey.

Fig. 1. Morgan Forster's Prep School Report, Kent House School, Eastbourne, Christmas 1892 (courtesy of KCC [EMF 18/188/1a])

ensemble and developing strong ties with major continental composers and performers. Under his successor as conductor of the series, Alan Gray, the Music Society mounted two large choral-orchestral concerts each spring, which Forster attended periodically. In May 1899, for example, he heard Verdi's *Stabat Mater,* Beethoven's *Christ on the Mount of Olives,* and Dvořák's recent Symphony in E minor, "From the New World" ("all the themes are negro songs, most cleverly worked in" [*SL1,* 28]). He also attended the 1901 memorial concert for Queen Victoria at the King's chapel, featuring Brahms's *German Requiem,* "which I much liked."[5] The chamber music series that Stanford had established also continued; Forster heard the likes of violinists Pablo de Sarasate and Joseph Joachim, the latter a frequent visitor to the university.

Forster made important musical contacts at King's. The colorful University Lecturer in history, Oscar Browning, took an immediate liking to him. "The O. B." was a passionate music-lover, an amateur singer and pianist with more panache than polish, and a resident eccentric characterized by E. F. Benson as a cross between a "great intellectual force" and a "buffoon."[6] Browning admired Beethoven and had attended the Beethoven Festival in Bonn in 1871, where he had crossed paths with Brahms and Joachim, George Grove, and William Sterndale Bennett. Browning was also a Wagnerite and a regular pilgrim to Bayreuth: he had witnessed the 1876 premiere of the *Ring* cycle and the 1883 *Parsifal* and had consorted with the Wagners at Villa Wahnfried.[7] Forster's growing enthusiasm for both Beethoven and Wagner were surely nourished by Browning. Forster also attended Browning's famous Sunday-evening musical soirées, where he may have first met Edward J. Dent, an advanced music student and future King's Fellow (1902–8) who ultimately became Cambridge Professor of Music (1926–41). Forster and Dent would remain friends for the next decade, although the connection waned as Forster's career as a novelist took flight. Until then, he took interest in Dent's research on Alessandro Scarlatti and Mozart's operas, which established him as the doyen of English musicologists.[8] The friendship had cooled by 1918, when Forster pegged him as an "absurd but somewhat wise old bird" (L: B85).

At Cambridge, music became for Forster an intellectual passion to be shared in the company of men, as it would for his Rickie Elliot and Clive Durham. As explored in Chapters 3 and 6, the role of music in homoerotic friendship was well developed in Edwardian intellectual circles. During his second year, he took rooms "in College" and in October 1898 joined the University Musical Club. At the weekly meetings he fraternized with Cambridge musical society and attended chamber music performances by its members. Forster's classics tutors Nathaniel Wedd and John Edwin Nixon were also deeply interested in music. Wedd was a Wagnerite, while Nixon, who had helped establish the King's Choir School, served as the auditor of the Musical Club.[9] Forster probably also attended the weekly quartet parties that Nixon hosted in his rooms. In his fourth year Forster was elected to the "Apostles," an exclusive conversation society dedicated, according to Leonard Woolf, to three passions: friendship, literature and music, and "what we called truth."[10] On such occasions the dominating musical figures of the day—Wagner, Strauss, and Brahms—and the future of English music may well have sparked lively discussion.[11] Forster's affectionate biography of moral philosopher Goldsworthy Lowes Dickinson reveals that Goldie's musical passions for Wagner, Beethoven, Bach, and Gluck duplicated Forster's own.[12] Although he did not share his friend's veneration for Mozart, Forster admired his 1920 *The Magic Flute,* which recasts Mozart's characters in a pessimistic "allegory of contemporary life and human destiny" that was also a veiled apologia for homosexual love.[13]

A single musical event of the Cambridge years deserves pause: Forster's first opera. On June 3, 1898, he was invited to Covent Garden to hear Wagner's *Tristan und Isolde* ("a difficult opera to start with," his host observed).[14] He cherished this performance into old age, with Milka Ternina in her London premiere as Isolde and Jean de Reszke as Tristan. Ternina was noted for her acting ability, "which imparts rare expressive power to the beauty of her voice," and the second-act love duet with de Reszke was highly praised in the press.[15] By the end of the evening, Forster had assimilated Wagner's style enough to appreciate the glory of Isolde's closing "Transfiguration" scene, where "Ternina sailed out of the mists and passed into the reality of darkness." His passion for Wagner was born that evening, and he would remain a Covent Garden patron for life.

Italy and Austria (1901–3)

On completion of Cambridge and with no employment in sight, Forster and his mother embarked on a one-year tour of Italy, with excursions into the Austrian Tyrol and Bavaria, followed by a return trip to Italy and Greece in 1903. There he discovered his voice as a writer and began drafting portions of a "Lucy Novel," later to become *A Room with a View.* Lucy's grand tour would duplicate many of his experiences. There, too, he crossed paths with Dent and gained a tentative appreciation of Italian opera, chipping away at his antipathy to the Italian bel canto style shared with other London Wagnerites. His first opera at the Teatro Verdi in Florence in November 1901 had been a disappointment to mother and son, as described tartly in a letter to Dent: "I do not think I shall ever enjoy the Italian opera. All the conventions are so irritating. . . . We had Rossini's *Cenerentola*—I believe not a great work, and after two hours of a Cinderella who was too fat to blow the pink paper fire, we retired. It may still be going on" (L: D256). It would take the combined influence of a stellar singer and the persuasions of Dent to change Forster's mind. Dent was then going through an uncharacteristic phase of enthusiasm for Donizetti, Bellini, and early Verdi (and didn't "wish ever to hear a note of Wagner again").[16] The occasion, again in Florence, was a performance on

May 12, 1903 of Donizetti's *Lucia di Lammermoor,* with Luisa Tetrazzini in the title role. "[W]e much enjoyed [it]," wrote Dent in his diary. "The Lucia (Tetrazzini) was excellent & the audience very noisy."[17] Forster would recall the performance in *Where Angels Fear to Tread* (see my Chapter 2).

On the whole the celebrated musical life of Italy disappointed them. Lily may have been echoing her son in announcing to her mother that: "Italian music is a delusion. Bands are all drum, & the Church music is not half as good as ours."[18] No wonder Morgan longed for a dose of Wagner in Rome in 1902 and spent all his pocket money on a ticket to *I maestri cantori di Norimberga* and a score of *Tannhäuser.* One of his goals of the 1903 trip, the *Ring* in Munich, fell through. As they cut a path from Tuscany to Sicily, however, Morgan made his own music on the pianos in the drawing rooms of their pensions—unless other guests complained. The piano proved a refuge from his mother's constant fretting and the overwhelmingly female company of the English tourists. From Rome Lily observed that Morgan "is always longing to be rid of the females so that he can play piano."[19] The passion of Italy had brought him full-face with his own sexual repression. His withdrawal eventually drove even him to worry that his "self consciousness" would, "if I'm not careful—drive me into books or the piano."[20] Forster would demonstrate the lure of aestheticism to the homosexual man in his characters Cecil Vyse and Clive Durham.

The Years of the Novels (1904–24)

The burst of writing that began on his return saved him, and he produced the four major novels *Where Angels Fear to Tread* (1905), *The Longest Journey* (1907), *A Room with a View* (1908), and *Howards End* (1910). To these can be added the fragmentary *Arctic Summer,* begun in 1911 and abandoned in 1912, and *Maurice* (1913–14), suppressed during Forster's lifetime because of its homosexual theme. Although he lived with his mother in Weybridge during these years, he made regular trips to London, where he taught Latin at the Working Men's College near Bloomsbury and attended operas and concerts with friends.

In autumn 1904, he secured a short-term appointment as tutor to the children of the Count and Countess von Arnim in Nassenheide (Pomerania). Forster set out in March 1905, stopping for the *Ring* cycle at the Dresden Court Opera from 28 March to 3 April. He found *Das Rheingold* and the first act of *Die Walküre* "more wonderful."[21] He heard the famous *Heldentenor* Karel Burrian as Siegfried, but it was Marie Wittich as Brünnhilde whose voice haunted him. In 1963 he reminisced: "She soared, she towered. Force, weight, majesty! She seemed to make history and we to embroider it by listening to her. After Ternina's hers is the voice I would most like to recall, though it hadn't the extra touch of the unearthly."[22] Otherwise the five months in Nassenheide were musically uneventful. The Count, a pianist who had studied with Liszt, intimidated Forster enough to keep him away from the piano during his brief visits, while himself refusing to play. Although disappointed by his progress in German, Forster likely gained enough skill to make his way through the libretti of German operas.

At some point after his return to England, Forster developed a passing interest in the British folk-music revival that was underway, enough so as to feature it accurately in his incomplete novel *Arctic Summer.* Dorothea Borlase, its only decent female character in an ensemble of harpies, is a pianist and a plucky folk-music researcher attached to the "Conservatoire." The latter probably refers to the Hampstead Conservatory, which from 1896 to 1905 had been directed by Cecil Sharp, the dean of English folk-music scholars.[23] Like the folksong researcher Lucy Broadwood, Dorothea tramps around the countryside, frequenting "queer places and rough men" and collecting carols and songs for use in schools. Dorothea sings the fourth stanza of "As I Sat on a Sunny Bank," which Forster had evidently located in Sharp's *English Folk-Carols* (1911).[24] The manuscript breaks off shortly after Dorothea's first appearance, so we can only speculate how her musical research and her love of Pergolesi might have played out in the novel.

The experiences of Forster's 1912–13 and 1921 trips to India were transferred accurately into *A Passage to India,* which he began writing in 1913 following his return from the first trip but completed only in January 1924.[25] Both were for him voyages into the musical unknown. His letters and Indian diary, which were assembled for his 1953 memoir *The Hill of Devi,* record his conflicted fascination with Indian music. Decades later he was still torn between intellectual appreciation and emotional distance from it. He never shed his western way of listening to its unfamiliar scale systems, which seemed "never to get further than the note below the keynote," or its apparent repetitiveness and lack of "any dramatic feeling" (*SL1,* 181). In comparison to the goal-directed strategies of Beethoven or Wagner, Indian music appeared static in its failure to "come to a crisis" (*SL1,* 171). The gendering of Indian music also puzzled him, with a "Nautch" or women's dance party in Lahore in November 1912 unfortunately representative: "the noise was often excruciating—the musicians seemed out [of] tune and playing in different keys, I could seldom follow the rhythm, and the ladies' voices went into my ears like battering rams" (*SL1*, 150). Several weeks later in Chhatarpur he witnessed a Vaishnava Mystery Play on the birth of Krishna, performed "at night on a terrace at the top of the Palace." He was relieved to discover that this music "was seldom uncouth—it is 'male music'—the actors being boys and different to the 'female' nautch music. . . . Much of this was in our own major & minor keys, whereas Heaven only knows what the 'female' was in" (*SL1*, 165).

The art of raga singing proved Forster's main inroad into Indian music. In Lahore in February 1913 he met a Brahman musician named Godbole, who took Forster "for a walk through the Public Gardens where he sang songs to me. There are scales appropriate for all hours of the day. That for the evening was the scale of C major, but with F# in it instead of F."[26] Godbole would return in *A Passage to India* to entrance and disturb Mrs. Moore and Miss Quested with his "song of an unknown bird" (*PI*, 95). This was, however, the beginning of Forster's appreciation of raga singing. Its tranquility refreshed him, as seen in his magical description of night music at the court of the Maharaja of Dewas, where Forster was engaged as secretary in 1921: "I went to bed at midnight, but at 3:00 a.m. something unusual aroused me—the music became beautiful. . . . I am as far as ever from understanding Indian singing, but have no doubt that I was listening to great art, it was so complicated and yet so passionate. The singer (man) and the drummer were of almost equal importance and wove round the chord of C major elaborate patterns that came to an end at the same moment; . . . it was like Western music reflected in trembling water."[27]

On his return from India, Forster's attempts to penetrate the mysteries of Indian music continued with limited success. In 1944, for instance, he wrote to Bob Buckingham: "Menon is coming to the flat at about 6:00 with his Vina. It will be an occasion to hear good Indian music and to wonder whether one likes it" (L: B1930). Indian music would remain as tantalizingly elusive for Forster as the possibility of friendship between cultures in *A Passage to India*. Accordingly, it plays only a vague symbolic role in his novel as an indicator of the inscrutability of India for the Westerner. Even European music, in the guise of low-class English music hall or band music, plays an incidental role that reflects the debased culture of Anglo India in the novel.

A very different set of musical experiences involved the London performances of Serge Diaghilev's *Ballets Russes,* which Forster attended between 1911 and 1919. There he joined ranks with members of royalty, London high society, and Bloomsbury literati and intellectuals, all swept up in the craze for the Russian ballet.[28] It is possible to identify at least fourteen ballets that he witnessed (see Appendix A). Besides some of the most celebrated dancers of the time, including Michel Fokine, Tamara Karsavina, Léonide Massine, Bronislava Nijinska, and the redoubtable Vaslav Nijinsky, he encountered recent work by the three stellar Diaghilev choreographers, Fokine, Nijinsky, and Massine. The musical experiences were no less vivid, including a healthy dose of Russian music and orchestrations. The postwar productions also exposed him to early examples of neoclassicism in Massine's "The Good-Humoured Ladies" and "La Boutique fantasque."

The *Ballets Russes* likely brought Forster's first taste of the music of Igor Stravinsky, beginning with two performances of *The Firebird* in June 1912. He also attended the 1919 *Petrouchka* shortly after his return from Alexandria. But a high point was undoubtedly his two viewings in July 1913 of *Le Sacre du printemps* (The Rite of Spring) in the famous Nijinsky choreography. As for many others, his first impression was one of shock (finding the music "hideous"), but by the next day he was already eager to get tickets for the last performance. "Thinking it over," he admitted to Malcolm Darling, "I am sure that much was very fine" (L: D69). As a result, Forster witnessed two of the scant nine documented performances of Nijinsky's *Le Sacre.*[29] Matched with Fokine's Polovtsian Dances from *Prince Igor* and Nijinsky's choreography of Debussy's *L'Après-midi d'un faune* on July 23, it formed one of the stellar programs of dance history. Nijinsky was the featured dancer in *Prince Igor* and *L'Après-midi.* His "naked" recreation of Debussy's "humourous and alarming animal" had entranced Bloomsbury homosexuals and threw Forster "into an intoxication greater than my youth's, so that I wanted to miss my train and have adventures all night. . . . There was a great deal to watch—mind on fire and body tinder—but the unsinking eye remained" (LD, 32). The performance may have served as a prelude of sorts to the events of the coming months, which witnessed Forster's private reflections on the primacy of the "life of the flesh" and a tentative sexual encounter (LD, 33). In September 1913, his visit with homosexual apologist Edward Carpenter and readings in the field of sexology initiated work on *Maurice.*

Alexandria (1915–19)

The need for employment during World War I led Forster to volunteer for the Red Cross in Egypt, a British protectorate and quiet front of the war with Germany. From November 1915 until January 1919 he was stationed in Alexandria and nearby Montazah, serving as a "Searcher" whose primary duty was interviewing the wounded for information on missing comrades.

He took well to the work, which left him ample free time, and he settled into one of the most enjoyable periods of his life. There he also took up journalism, writing occasional articles for the English-language newspapers the *Egyptian Gazette* and the *Egyptian Mail*. Among these were his first essays in light music criticism, which appeared under the pseudonym "Pharos" in 1917–18.[30]

Forster never felt fully at home in what he called "the pretentious, squalid, gutteral Levant."[31] His situation improved in March 1917 with the start of a friendship with Mohammed el Adl, a handsome young Alexandria tram-driver with whom Forster experienced his first mature sexual relationship. Although Mohammed took a new job in Cairo in late October of that year, he left Morgan "freed forever from the burden of loneliness and failure that has oppressed me for so many years" (L: C121). They met infrequently thereafter, and Mohammed died of tuberculosis in May 1922. Nicola Beauman asserts that Forster had inflated the relationship into a "great love";[32] regardless, Forster's musical activities in Alexandria swelled during the Mohammed affair.

Following a slow start, Forster slowly made other new friends who would figure in his musical experiences in Alexandria. There was Aida Borchgrevink, an American heiress and widow who had trained as an opera singer and was an astute reader of modern literature.[33] She adopted Morgan as a literary protégé, encouraged his piano playing, and found lodging for him with her retired maid, Irene. His landlady and her daughter Hélene were Italian-speaking Greeks who welcomed Morgan into their home, and many of his most colorful musical experiences took place in their parlor. He also met G. H. Ludolf, a fellow Red Cross Searcher and a musical connoisseur; music figures frequently in their later correspondence. Local composer Enrico Terni shared Forster's enthusiasm for Wagner and Franck, and hosted string quartet parties at his flat at which Forster heard Beethoven's Quartet in C# minor, Op. 131. Although Terni later wrote an atonal string quartet, his music at this time was gently modernist, and Forster took an active interest in it.[34] Through Terni he also met a coterie of local performers, and on occasion a wounded musician passed through the hospital. Such was the pianist, composer, and conductor Walford Hyden, who had studied with Ferruccio Busoni and toured with the great dancer Anna Pavlova from 1910 to 1930 as her rehearsal pianist, musical director, and biographer.[35] Finally Florence Barger, the wife of a Cambridge associate and herself an amateur pianist, developed into an epistolary confidante during these years. In 1915 Forster had shared the manuscript of *Maurice* with her, and later entrusted her with details of his intimacy with Mohammed.

Forster's musical experiences in Alexandria were those of a European imperialist; he never developed a taste for the indigenous music, which he considered "debased." The center of his musical life there was the Casino San Stefano, a concert hall in a seaside hotel that offered symphony and chamber concerts in season.[36] There he heard musical fare no different from that at the Queen's Hall—Beethoven's Fifth and Seventh Symphonies, *Coriolan* Overture, and "Kreutzer" Sonata for violin and piano; Schubert's "Unfinished" and Dvořák's "New World" Symphonies; and much César Franck. The venue itself was curious, as he discovered in November 1915 at his first concert, which featured Franck's Sonata for violin and piano: "The theatre was quite empty. . . . In the stalls a few Levantine ladies, most curiously shaped and coiffed, two Egyptians in fezzes, and one Arab in complete robes. He stood. In the Upper Boxes me, two Tommies, one Italian, three Greeks, and no one else at all. In the Gallery a sprinkled mixture of smokers and readers of newspapers. Everyone kept fairly quiet, the applause that interrupted the lovely music being not ours but wafted in from the adjacent cinema" (L: F492). Forster's letters maintain this wry tone until 1918, when the relentless war and Mohammed's illness brought new urgency to his musical experiences. In May 1918, he heard Beethoven's "Pastoral" Symphony, which inspired a plaintive outburst to Dickinson: "Will people be ever able to feel like that again? Those who write 'joyously' nowadays do so for educational reasons: that is to say they write not joyously but cheeringly" (L: D320). On October 1 he went to hear Franck's String Quartet, hoping for some solace for his nerves: "a little music should either make them or break them," he wrote Florence (L: B101).

The piano provided his "greatest consolation" (L: D318). By February 1918 he had tired of having to depend on the charity of friends for the occasional use of a piano, and fearing that he was losing his ability to play,[37] rented a "truly lovely instrument" from Italy. "The Piano" was installed in Irene's sitting room, provoking a vignette tailored for a mother's amusement:

> It had not been in the house an hour before it began to sprout horrors. —First of all Irene put a crochet mat with a vase of flowers upon it. Then Hélene brought a piece of music called "The Millions of Harlequin,"[38] and leant her mandolin against its side. Then Irene added a matchbox and a china cat. It was now Hélene's turn, and on returning from the post I found a second piece of music called "Rêve d'amour." However Irene owns the heavier artillery, and she now produced objects I had never seen in the house before—a gigantic shell with a clock upon its cheek, a naked terra cotta baby impressed into a cushion of crimson plush, another match box (smiling pig), two Dresden

> figures, and etc.—and trimmed the unhappy instrument from end to end. I was in despair—then said that one sometimes wanted to open a Piano, and the moving would be difficult. So now nothing stands upon it (L: F563).

Several days later he returned to find a party in full swing, and "had the shock of seeing beer glasses upon the instrument's top while a young gentleman played a valse without changing the bass" (L: F564). Forster took over at the piano, playing dances and accompanying a Greek singer in Iago's "Credo" from Verdi's *Otello,* which he sight-read to acclaim (*SL1,* 287). After retiring to bed, he awoke later to hear the company singing "God Save the King" in his honor.

Over the next two months (the piano had to be returned in April when Irene moved), his skills quickly returned. Florence and Lily received regular updates of his progress. He worked his way through his small music library, which included the Beethoven piano sonatas (perhaps in the Augener edition by Sigmund Lebert that was in his collection at his death) and Franck's Sonata for violin and piano and "Prelude, Aria, and Finale" for piano (L: F563). He also borrowed some Haydn sonatas, as well as "much Debussy whom I like mildly, some Vincent d'Indy whom I don't like, Ravel's *Valses Nobles et Sentimentales,* Strauss' *Salome; Tristan; Louise.* . . . I long to hear Hugo Wolf" (L: B88). To Florence he reported that he was playing the Introduction and Rondo of Beethoven's "Waldstein" Sonata, Schumann's *Carnaval,* and Chopin's Preludes, Op. 28 (Nos. 11, 17, 20, and 22) and the Rondos, Op. 1 and 5 (*SL1,* 287).

This degree of specificity is rare in Forster's papers; it provides telling information on his Franco-German tastes and pianistic ability. The Chopin Preludes, with the exception of the C-minor Prelude No. 20, are not among the shortest or the easiest of the cycle. No. 11 in B major, for example, is a *Vivace* etude in legato playing and voicing that features nimble cross-meters and appoggiaturas, while the G-minor Prelude No. 22, *Molto agitato,* is a bravura octave study for the left hand.[39] The Rondo from the Waldstein Sonata also demands a superior technique. Notable, too, is the recent French piano music by Debussy and Ravel. Forster repeatedly played Wagner for friends during this time, perhaps from this *Tristan* score (in spite of the distaste for such "Bosch-music" among British soldiers),[40] and once "lifted the roof . . . with heavy slabs of Salome" (L: F567).

A unique musical experience in Forster's life was the "Classical Concert" of April 18, 1917, which he organized with one day's notice for the military patients at Montazah. Forster also gave a preconcert lecture, attempting successfully "to talk sense about music instead of that damned superior art patronage" (L: C119). He wrote glowingly of the evening to family and friends, with Lily receiving the most extravagant report along with a little autograph sketch of the program (see Fig. 2):

> Your child here arose to address a howling mob of 700 Tommies on Classical Music—how they mustn't suppose it was dreary dull stuff written by old men who died 300 years ago and were mostly German. . . . The speech went well, almost too well, for they grew uproarious over the jokes. The curtain rose. I introduced each performer by name . . . and the pale patient [Walford Hyden] sat down to the piano, and boomed out the Rachmaninov Prelude in fine style. This was an enormous relief. Suares followed, and not only did the accompanist turn out all right for him, but he had a great success with the Handel Sonata—introduced by me as "a piece for the violin in four sections and please do not clap between the sections." After that all was well: the per-

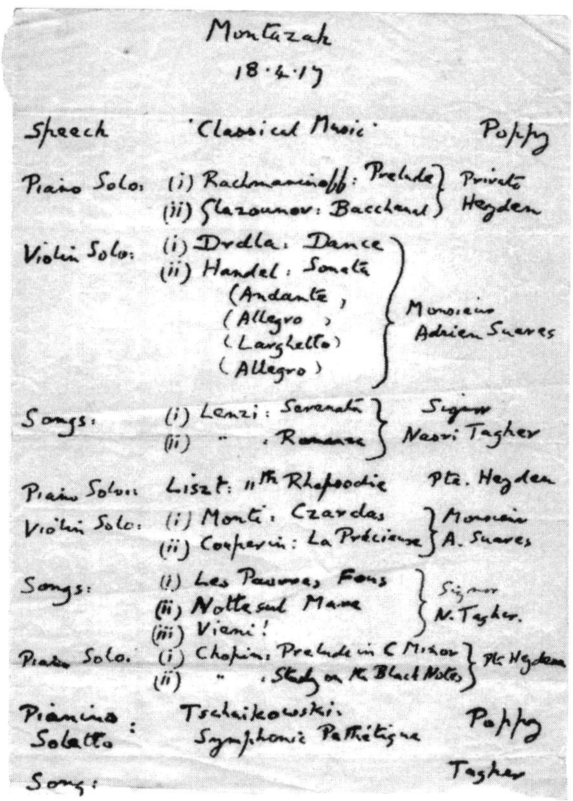

Montazah
18·4·17

Speech 'Classical Music' Poppy

Piano Solo: (i) Rachmaninoff: Prelude } Private Hyden
(ii) Glazounov: Bacchanal

Violin Solo: (i) Drdla: Dance } Monsieur Adrien Suares
(ii) Handel: Sonata
(Andante,
(Allegro,
(Larghetto)
(Allegro)

Songs: (i) Lenzi: Serenata } Signor Nasri Tagher
(ii) " : Romance

Piano Solo: Liszt: 11th Rhapsodie Pte. Hyden

Violin Solo: (i) Monti: Czardas } Monsieur A. Suares
(ii) Couperin: La Précieuse

Songs: (i) Les Pauvres Fous } Signor N. Tagher.
(ii) Notte sul Mare
(iii) Vieni!

Piano Solo: (i) Chopin: Prelude in C Minor } Pte Hyden
(ii) " : Study on the Black Notes

Pianino Solatto: Tschaikowski: Symphonie Pathétique Poppy

Song: Tagher

Fig. 2. Forster's ink sketch of the program of the Classical Concert at Montazah, 18 April 1917 (courtesy of KCC [EMF 18/188/1h])

> formances throughout quite first class, but I didn't seem to hear a single note what with comforting the performers whom the strangeness of the audience intimidated—, and what with "holding" the audience till the next performer appeared. They were awfully good—absolutely silent during the pieces—and the great majority stayed till the end (L: F535).

Toward the end of the program, Forster himself made a brief appearance in a "Pianino Soletto," playing an arrangement from Tchaikovsky's Symphony No. 6, "Pathétique." The concert left him elated; as he wrote to Edward Carpenter: "I felt that I had been burrowing under rubbish and touched something that was alive and had been trying to touch me" (L: C119). The "Pathétique," which had functioned as a symbol for homosexual desire in *Maurice*, likely had personal significance in these early weeks of his relationship with Mohammed. Revealing as well is the reversion to Lily's childhood nickname for him—"Poppy"—on the little program, attached to a covert acknowledgment of his growing adult affection.

Between the Wars

Forster returned to an England reeling from the Great War, and slid into a depression. Like others of the lost generation, he had fallen prey to the "puzzling and queer [feeling] that one's the last little flower of a vanishing civilisation" (L: L305). Unable to begin making headway on his India novel, or any major project, he feared that he had "failed as a creator, both from the popular and the spiritual standpoint" (L: R110). Virginia Woolf's diary captures the bleakness of his situation after the 1922 India trip: "To come back to Weybridge, to come back to an ugly house a mile from the station, an old, fussy, exacting mother, to come back having lost your Rajah, without a novel, & with no power to write one—this is dismal, I expect, at the age of 43."[41] Until the completion of *A Passage to India* in 1924, music supplied spiritual refreshment. As he wrote to Ludolf in March 1920: "music—or one's prostration before it—grows more profound" (L: L311).

At first it was Beethoven's String Quartet Op. 131, with its associations with Alexandria, which helped him turn "some spiritual corner or other" in January 1920 (L: L310). The music of Bach, "much of whom I have heard since," counteracted his post-India depression over the next several years (L: A31). The St. Matthew Passion, Brandenburg Concertos, Mass in B minor, and Goldberg Variations became favorites. He sought out Bach recitals by pianists Alexander Siloti (in 1920) and Harold Samuel (in 1924 and 1931), and by violinist Adolf Busch at the Queen's Hall in October 1935. His engagement with the piano also continued unabated during this decade. In 1924 he even began to take formal piano lessons again, practising seriously at a Bach Partita and Antonín Dvořák's *Legends,* Op. 59.[42] He also heard some of the greatest pianists of the era during these years, including Vladimir de Pachmann, Fanny Davies, Alfred Cortot, and Artur Schnabel. In 1927 he began a serious search for an instrument to replace his mother's old piano. He steered away from the English Broadwood, German Bechstein, and French Érard pianos that he had played in his youth, and settled on a Blüthner upright from Leipzig, an instrument known for its sweet, rounded tone. Its arrival in March 1928 was cause for serious household upheaval, as Lily had refused to part with her old instrument. The Blüthner went upstairs into Morgan's sitting room in their West Hackhurst home, next to his gramophone (L: B375). His mother's piano remained in the dining room and was later sold, while the Blüthner followed him to King's College and remained with him until the late 1960s, when deafness and infirmity made it impossible for him to play any longer. It features in several photographs of his rooms in College, including an evocative late photo by Edward Leigh, showing the near–ninety-year-old at his writing table, gazing dreamily into the distance and framed by his library, with his Blüthner piano at his right hand (Fig. 3).

In 1925 Forster took a flat in London for periodic escapes from his mother's watchful eye. He began developing a new circle of male friends, of whom Joe Randolph Ackerley and Robert Buckingham shared his interests in music. Ackerley was a minor novelist, BBC radio producer, and literary editor of *The Listener* from 1935 to 1959 (to which Forster would contribute numerous essays on music and other subjects); he supplied Forster with tickets to London concerts and recordings of classical music. Bob Buckingham, a handsome London policeman and amateur painter, met Forster in 1930 and entered into a passionate friendship with him that lasted for the rest of their lives. Their relationship survived the strain of Bob's marriage to May Hockey in 1932. At first a source of rivalry for Morgan, May eventually developed into a dear friend who accompanied him to concerts and the ballet, and nursed him through several serious illnesses, including his last. Bob attended concerts and operas with Morgan, and was also his frequent companion on trips to Aldeburgh in the *Billy Budd* years. The charmed circle around Britten also included William Plomer, a novelist and poet whom Forster had met in 1931; Plomer would be the librettist of *Gloriana* (1952–53), Britten's next opera after *Billy Budd,* and advised Forster in the course of the latter project. Several long-distance friendships also had musical significance. Charles Mauron,

Fig. 3. E. M. Forster in his King's College sitting room, 18 July 1968 (Edward Leigh; courtesy of KCC [EMF/27/861] and the Leigh family)

who prepared the French translations of Forster's novels and other writings, shared his enthusiasm for the piano and gramophone in their letters and during Forster's visits to his home in Provence. Mauron was the catalyst for the "Beethoven's Piano Sonatas" project and a witness of Forster's own playing of Beethoven (especially the Sonata Op. 111). The Belfast novelist Forrest Reid, with whom Forster had begun corresponding in 1912, was the recipient of Forster's most informative description of the project in a letter of September 1940 (*SL2*, 181–4).

Forster also shared with Ackerley an enthusiasm for the gramophone and recorded sound, which Forster would always prefer to the wireless associated with his mother (L: L331). It provided him space for solitary reverie and temporary peace for his "restless and feeble brain" (*CB*, 31). He owned his own gramophone by at least 1926 and began collecting recordings just as English firms such as The Gramophone Company began recording full classical works in their original scoring.[43] One of his earliest acquisitions was the famous 1926 Beethoven Violin Concerto with Fritz Kreisler and the Berlin State Opera Orchestra conducted by Leo Blech, which became a mainstay of his early listening. Its first movement was "something apart from all other music, [and] reaches into a room which nothing else has succeeded in entering" (L: D117). The recordings that he selected in 1926 for Josie Darling, the wife of his friend Malcolm in faraway Lahore, are indicators of Forster's musical enthusiasms during this time: "5 records Beethoven Violin Concerto [with violinist Isolde Menges], 2 [records] Brahms Quartet, the other three being Scheherazade, Wagner, and César Franck" (L: D113). Thereafter he would swap recordings and recommendations with friends.

Music provided private solace in Forster's growing depression as another war approached. His engagement with the piano revived in the late 1930s; by then approaching sixty, his technique had slipped and he no longer played for friends. Beethoven's piano music provided the focal point of his playing during this time and inspired his unfinished project begun in the early days of the war to annotate all of Beethoven's sonatas. As will be shown in Chapter 7, the project failed to provide the bulwark that he was seeking against the "tide of wickedness and rubbish" (L: R236). Supportive as well were Dame Myra Hess's National Gallery Concerts in London, which Forster attended regularly.[44] The series began in October 1939 in aid of the Musicians' Benevolent Fund, and in order to compensate for the closure of all London concert halls for the duration of the War. It was the fulfillment of Dame Myra's lifelong dream to found a populist chamber music series performed by top professionals and open to the general public at a price that all could afford.[45] There, Forster heard a broad range of repertoire, from piano recitals and vocal or instrumental ensembles to Indian music. Dame Myra also invited Forster to contribute a piece to the fifth-anniversary booklet issued in early 1945. The result was a short but significant essay entitled "From the Audience," in which he illumines the inner world of a concert scene much like that of *Howards End*: "There is the architectural emotion, when a composition extending through time is suddenly apprehended as a whole [Forster's "difficult rhythm"]. There is scholarship. But the vibrations are part of the truth. The flittering inattentive birds, the audience which looks so reliable and is really all over the shop, the trailing filaments of beauty—they are part of the complex set up by any public performance."[46]

The concert experience also had private meaning suitable for his diary alone. On August 14, 1945, he awoke to dark thoughts of the threat of atomic warfare and his mother's recent death. News of the surrender of Japan had not yet broken when he went to the National Gallery Concert. There he heard a lecture by Denis Matthews and Howard Ferguson on playing Mozart's four-hand piano music and a performance of the Sonata in F major, K. 497, "somber and fine and—the only time in the day—I had an external sensation." On leaving the concert, still trailing its "filaments of beauty," he heard the news. And yet "all through the day" he could not shake the "painful" feelings that "'I cannot go on, simply cannot,' and then 'surely [Mother] will give up being dead now'" (LD, 83).

The Postwar Period (1946–70)

Exacerbated by the death of his mother, advancing age, and the expulsion from his West Hackhurst home, this postwar period was even harder on Forster than the last. Again he saw himself as a "last survivor" of a failing liberal-humanist tradition (L: P215). King's College solved his housing problem unexpectedly with an offer of rooms in College, which he occupied until the end of his life. Then an invitation from Professor A. Tillman Merritt to participate in Harvard University's *Symposium on Music Criticism* (May 1–3, 1947) promised stimulating distraction. He accepted despite uncertainty that "he had anything pertinent to say to a symposium of musicologists," and in April 1947 he flew to New York.[47] He used the opportunity to connect with old friends and make new ones (including composers Aaron Copland and Roger Sessions), to travel extensively across country, and "to hear all the American music I can during my stay."[48] His exploration of the musical New World began with *Annie Get Your Gun* in its original Broadway run with Ethel Merman, "an Irving Berlin show of much vigour and some charm" (L: B2058). (Rodgers and Hammerstein's *Carousel* in Chicago paled by comparison as merely long and dull.) In far-off Berkeley, California, he had a pleasant meeting with Sessions (L: T334). Back in New York in July he also met with Gian Carlo Menotti and enjoyed his "remarkable" operas *The Telephone* and *The Medium*, then playing at the Ethel Barrymore Theatre on Broadway. On another front, he was approached by 20th-Century Fox concerning possible film rights to *A Room with a View,* which he emphatically rejected out of fear that consorting with Hollywood would "have broken my heart" (*SL2,* 227).

The Harvard Symposium was the musical high point of the trip. For many years afterward, he was proud to have been invited to speak there under "musical auspices" (L: P219).[49] The international conference—Merritt's brainchild—aimed to reexamine the role of music criticism in modern society. It brought together a large community of scholars, composers, critics, music publishers, broadcasters, and performers for three days of prepared lectures and public discussions. The participants included a veritable "who's who" of American music, including Copland and Sessions, Walter Piston, Virgil Thomson, Olin Downes, Alfred Frankenstein, Otto Kinkeldey, and Paul Henry Lang.[50] Forster opened the May 1 session before an audience of eight hundred with what would become one of his major musical essays, "The Raison d'Être of Criticism in the Arts" (*TCD,* 107–23).

As Forster approached his seventieth birthday, he was again in dire emotional straits. And again it was music that intervened in the shape of Benjamin Britten, who invited Forster to write the libretto for his next opera. The collaborative process with Britten and co-librettist Eric Crozier—and the host of long-term literary and musical contacts that the project sparked—proved revelatory to Forster. He would refer to the year 1949, which witnessed the bulk of the work on *Billy Budd,* as his "Annis Mirabilis" (LD, 91). The Aldeburgh community provided Forster with a new model of creative collaboration and sparked an interest in English contemporary music that persisted until his death.

In his last decades, Forster's musical corridors gradually narrowed as his hearing and vision failed. He continued to attend musical events at King's, rarely missing a Sunday evening concert in the College Hall. When he found himself no longer fit for travel to the continent, Aldeburgh provided a practicable summer goal with the Buckinghams (his last festival was in 1969, when he attended an event daily at the age of ninety).[51] The Britten circle continued to supply interesting musical contacts such as Imogen Holst, Michael Tippett, Erwin Stein, and Donald Mitchell. Forster also continued making friendships among King's music students such as future conductor John Eliot Gardiner, tenor Nigel Rogers, and music historian Philip Brett. But there was no question that he was failing, especially following a series of small strokes in his last years. A particularly poignant episode was one of his last concerts at the Cambridge Guildhall in 1969 when he fell asleep and awoke to find himself locked in the cold, dark hall until morning.[52] In the end, the Buckinghams nursed him in their Coventry home. There he would sit listening to his gramophone records, "mostly Beethoven, Bach, Brahms, Mozart and Haydn, waiting for Robert to come home."[53] Death arrived on June 7, 1970, and Forster's ashes were spread on the crematorium's rose garden as if to echo the Goethe text of one of his favorite lieder, Hugo Wolf's "Anakreons Grab." On his request there was no religious ceremony or memorial service; his life was celebrated at a Chamber Concert in the King's College Hall on November 22, 1970, featuring music by Beethoven, Vaughan Williams, Duparc, and Britten.

Forster's Musical Taste

Forster's likes and dislikes in music are key to its role as signifier in his fiction and essays. As a Cambridge student and budding novelist, Forster's musical taste was very much that of an educated fin de siècle Londoner, with Beethoven and Wagner as the twin poles, and thereafter, Chopin, Gluck, Dvořák, Russian music, and Tchaikovsky (especially his "Pathétique" Symphony, already threatening overexposure).[54] The music of Brahms, however, was still foreign to many English listeners at that time,[55] and Forster's appreciation would come slowly. He developed an interest in Bach in the 1920s, although his music had been undergoing a gradual revival in England since the mid-1870s.[56] The great musical discovery of his Egyptian sojourn was César Franck, immensely popular in England during the Great War, when German music—even Beethoven and Wagner—had become suspect. Years later Forster still associated his time in Alexandria with memories of "fresh air mixed with dust and troubles with large beetles . . . and the sound of César Franck played badly by myself on a good upright."[57] Of all the music of Franck mentioned in his letters, Forster granted pride of place to the Piano Quintet in F minor (1879). He set great store by the fact that it was composed in the year of his birth and once called it perhaps "the greatest human achievement during my lifetime" (*SL2*, 75).

Forster's indifference to Mozart was also a product of English taste in the early decades of the twentieth century.[58] It resurfaces in the musical symbolism of *A Room with a View.* Forster would remain "puzzled by his reputation" (L: M493), and in 1926 went so far as to claim that he was "Mozart-deaf" (L: D113). There is no reference to his ever having played any Mozart piano music. Although he derived pleasure from the occasional performance of a piano concerto,[59] even the "Jupiter" Symphony was deemed "a boring nursery sort of affair" (L: B1498). *Don Giovanni,* which he saw in March 1920, almost changed his opinion ("topping entertainment and not a bad play"), but his remarks in the same letter to G. H. Ludolf remain guarded: "I have never liked Mozart so well—my opinion of him has hitherto coincided with Terni's 'Why listen to Mozart? I have my children'" (L: L311). He had more sympathy with the symphonies and piano music of Haydn, and greatly admired *The Creation* (*CB*, 244). Yet in the end Haydn too fell short of true greatness by "shunning the tragic."[60]

English music also posed challenges. In his youth Forster had little positive to say about the music of Stanford, Edward Elgar, or Ethel Smyth, and in later years Ralph Vaughan Williams, his neighbor in nearby Dorking, rarely escaped without a poke. Not until Forster's association with Britten in the mid-1940s did he begin to seek out English contemporary music by William Walton, Michael Tippett, and others. Britten's music inspired an enduring interest, beginning with Forster's discovery of his recording with Peter Pears of the *Seven Sonnets of Michelangelo,* a gift from the pair in 1945 (L: B552). As explored in Chapter 8, the Britten circle opened him to "new music" and the role of the composer in modern society.

After the piano, opera provided the axis of Forster's musical world. Although he never kept a musical journal, it is possible to reconstruct an impressive, though certainly incomplete log of his opera attendance from references in his letters and diaries (see Appendix B). Covent Garden productions dominate, beginning with his first opera in 1898, *Tristan und Isolde,* and extending to the two-act revision of *Billy Budd* in January 1964.[61] His most intensive opera attendance took place during the years of the novels (1902–13) and of his active friendship with Britten (1947–64). The breadth and distinction of the operatic culture that Forster brought to Britten's worktable may help explain the composer's willingness to engage a nonpoet for the task of writing the libretto for *Billy Budd* and to take musical criticism, some of it pointed, from a writer twice his age.

German operas outnumber all the rest, with Wagner in the lead. The numerous references to Wagner in Forster's novels and critical essays were steeped in this experience. Besides the two complete cycles of the *Ring* in Dresden (1905) and Bayreuth (1954), he also attended isolated performances of the *Ring* operas, including several *Götterdämmerung* productions. One of these was from Hans Richter's famous 1908 cycle, sung in Frederick Jameson's English translation.[62] *Tristan und Isolde* was another favorite, although by 1954—and in spite of the presence of Wolfgang Windgassen in the title role—he had tired of the story ("a he and a she, and German ones at that, for four hours are *zu viel*" [L: C393]). Forster's August 1954 pilgrimage to Bayreuth was the climax of his Wagner experiences. He traveled with Florence Barger and her son Evert, who arranged the tickets and afterward wrote a memoir of their trip.[63] In a luxury unthinkable today, Evert had managed to purchase tickets for every performance for the three weeks of their stay; they sold back those they did not wish to attend. As a result, Forster heard at least one run of the entire *Ring* in Wieland Wagner's minimalist staging, featuring Hans Hotter as Wotan. He and Florence caught all the *Parsifal*s (with Hotter again as Amfortas and Martha Mödl as a resplendent Kundry), and a single *Lohengrin* in the new production by Wolfgang Wagner, with Birgit Nilsson as Elsa. Long and heated were their postperformance discussions about the merits of the "New Bayreuth," with Forster keenly disappointed at the darkness and "gloom" of Wieland Wagner's starkly symbolic productions: "Bayreuth hates light, hates colour, mistrusts movement, and identifies mysticism with mists," he quipped in an article in *The Listener*.[64]

Among the Covent Garden productions of German operas that he attended are a number of historic performances. He saw Richard Strauss's controversial *Elektra* twice in its first London run in March 1910, both performances conducted by the composer. Later that year he also attended the Thomas Beecham performance of Strauss's *Salome,* with its still scandalous libretto based on the play by Oscar Wilde. Although Forster found it "disappointing" due to the "squalor" and "baseness" of its subject (LD, 16), his judgment may have been clouded by the failure of his declaration of love to his companion, Syed Ross Masood, after the performance.[65] When Forster caught *Elektra* again in May 1938, it was in the brilliant production conducted by Beecham, with Rose Pauly as Elektra and Kerstin Thorborg as Klytemnestra.[66] He also witnessed the classic staging of Strauss's *Rosenkavalier* in 1924, with Bruno Walter at the podium and one of the most distinguished casts ever assembled for this work: Lotte Lehmann as the Marschallin, Elisabeth Schumann as Sophie, and Delia Reinhardt as Octavian.[67] In 1952 he sought out two performances of Alban Berg's *Wozzeck* in a stellar production considered "the crown of [conductor Erich] Kleiber's work at Covent Garden."[68] Forster found that the work "much improves upon second sight" (L: P267).

His enthusiasm for the *Ballets Russes* went hand in hand with his discovery of Russian opera, led by Musorgsky's *Boris Godunov* in the 1913 Drury Lane production directed by Diaghilev. With basso Fyodor Chaliapin in the title role, *Boris* galvanized the London audience with its new style of operatic acting and spectacular choral singing, creating a sensation matched only by the first performances of Wagner's *Ring* and *Tristan* in the 1880s.[69] When Forster again caught *Boris* with the Russian Opera at the Lyceum Theatre in

1931, the performance level had sunk considerably, but Chaliapin, by then approaching sixty, still shone with undiminished luster.[70] With this experience in place, Forster was primed to appreciate the début of Boris Christoff in this role, which he heard in November 1949 as a guest of Lord Harewood, the director of Covent Garden.

Margaret Schlegel of *Howards End* was speaking for the author in her dislike of Puccini's *Tosca* and Gounod's *Faust* (*HE-D*, 49). French and Italian opera was always an uphill battle for him. French operas include only three works seen in the prewar years 1909–13, none of which elicited an enthusiastic response: Charpentier's *Louise,* Saint-Saëns's *Samson et Dalila,* and Debussy's *Pelléas et Mélisande.* Notably absent is the *verismo* repertory of Puccini, Mascagni, and Leoncavallo that was immensely popular at the time. Ironically, one of his last operas was Puccini's *Girl of the Golden West* in English at Sadler's Wells in 1963, which he much liked, especially its "terrific third act—I had no idea Puccini could do so much" (L: F214). His discovery of Verdi came earlier, assisted by the 1931 *La forza del destino* conducted by Tullio Serafin, with Rosa Ponselle as Leonora. Two years later, *Aida* with Eva Turner "absolutely ravished" him. By the end of Forster's life, Verdi had joined Beethoven in his highest estimation.[71]

In a 1959 BBC interview with David Jones to celebrate his eightieth birthday, Forster emphasized: "I have got an enormous amount out of music."[72] Although listening to music was always for him a tug of emotion and intellect, of passive daydreams and cool observation, of messy dilettantism and trained insight, of public and private worlds, he was always "gathering something" from music and "carrying it away for future use."[73] Forster's musical biography establishes his credentials as a writer *with* music. His deep love and experience of the art counsel the reader to attend to every musical moment in his novels and essays. Forster knew what he was talking about, and that is why we should be listening.

2

"Creating" *Lucia*

The Voice of Luisa Tetrazzini in *Where Angels Fear to Tread*

I based this account on a performance I had heard at Florence at the beginning of the century where Lucia was sung by a little known soprano. Her name was Tetrazzini.

—EMF, "Three Countries," 1959

In December 1904, Forster laid aside his faltering "Lucy Novel" (later to become *A Room with a View*) to focus on his "Gino Novel." *Where Angels Fear to Tread* was all but finished by early 1905 and was published in October of that year. His first completed novel received excellent reviews as a work of refreshing originality.[1] Benjamin Britten's appreciation when he reread it in 1942 captures its strengths: "God—what a cruel book, but how funny, & how damnably real."[2] In it the dull respectability of Sawston, a fictional London suburb, collides with the raw vitality of Italy, with all its "beauty, evil, charm, vulgarity, [and] mystery" (*WAFT,* 104). Sawston owes much to the young Morgan's despised Tonbridge, while Monteriano is a thinly veiled transformation of the Tuscan tower-town of San Gimignano, which he had visited in June 1902 on his first Italian tour with his mother. As an emblem of Italy, opera makes a vivid entry in the sixth of its ten chapters, in which the main characters attend Gaetano Donizetti's 1835 tragic opera *Lucia di Lammermoor* in Monteriano (107–12).

Forster's scene captures his recollections of the May 12, 1903, performance of *Lucia* at the Teatro Verdi in Florence, where in the company of his mother and musicologist Edward J. Dent he heard soprano Luisa Tetrazzini in the title role. Tetrazzini (1871–1940) was then almost thirty-two years old and in her vocal prime. She was still four years from her 1907 Covent Garden debut that would galvanize London and make her an international star.[3] Yet she was far from "little known" in 1903. In the thirteen years since her Florence debut, Tetrazzini had toured heavily from St. Petersburg to Montevideo to great acclaim.[4] Her triumphant Florence homecoming in May 1903 included eleven performances of *Lucia* and Rossini's *Il barbiere di Siviglia,* cornerstones of her traditional bel canto repertory. Her *Lucia* had opened on May 11, the night before Dent and Forster's attendance.[5] The critic of the *Fieramosca* echoed their enthusiasm: "It was as if some magical power enabled her to manifest such perfection that those present who had heard [Adelina] Patti and other divas in their youth declared that this their very own Florentine nightingale surpassed them all."[6] Eyewitnesses of the Teatro Verdi performance have confirmed that Forster's fictional *Lucia* scene accurately recalls its details.[7] He admitted as much in a letter of March 31, 1959, to Lord Harewood, confirming that in his novel he had "created the work [*Lucia*], and Tetrazzini in it."[8] Tetrazzini's is the phantom voice of the novel, shadowing its characters like the disembodied flute in Lucia's famous song of madness, "Alfin son tua," the centerpiece of Forster's opera scene. Tetrazzini's three early recordings of this aria reveal the qualities of voice and presence that inspired Forster's novel and his lifelong memory of her song.[9]

The *Lucia* scene is the structural and symbolic pillar of the novel, comparable in this regard to the Fifth Symphony scene in *Howards End.* Yet Forster's *Lucia* is generally dispatched in the literature on the novel as a splash of local color. Wilfred Stone, for example, dismissed it as "pure comic opera . . . for the eye rather than the ear."[10] Even the literature on the Victorian and Edwardian culture of Italian travel in Forster's early fiction passes over this opera scene.[11] This neglect is consistent with English reception history of bel canto opera at the turn of the century. Although Tetrazzini's performances had sparked a temporary renewal of interest, a 1907 London critic confirmed that such "old-fashioned Italian operas" had "for the last dozen years . . . been steadily dropping out of the Covent Garden repertory." They had indeed "come to be regarded in some quarters as dead beyond the possibility of resuscitation."[12] Tetrazzini notwithstanding, the works of Rossini, Bellini, and Donizetti had been falling out of favor in England since at least 1850, replaced by French and German operas, with Wagner predominating after 1880. By the 1898 season, 50% of the Covent Garden repertoire was Wagner, with only 14% representing operas in Italian.[13] The contemporary English press was especially hard on "prima donna operas," which were deemed to favor facile ornamentation over dramatic substance.[14] This attitude persists in Dent's unsympathetic 1955 article on Donizetti, where *Lucia*'s tenuous survival is said to depend "on the momentary popularity of some one particular singer."[15] Until the bel canto revival in the late 1950s and 1960s, this repertoire remained in disregard. Moreover, until Joan Sutherland's historic *Lucia* at Covent Garden in 1959, the opera had disappeared entirely from its boards for the fifty years following Tetrazzini's recreations of the role in the 1907–9 seasons.[16] For the major Forster critics of the mid–twentieth century, who had received their literary training during the fallow years of bel canto opera, the *Lucia* scene must have appeared a quaint relic of a bygone era.

The novel recounts the failed sentimental education of Philip Herriton, a young Edwardian aesthete for whom Italy is a haven of "Romance" in his sterile upper-middle-class life, and of Caroline Abbott, a sensible young woman with a hidden streak of defiance. They would seem destined for one another, were it not for the culture of repression that has tainted their lives. His is a fatherless home, surrounded by domineering women: his hard and calculating mother, whom Philip characterizes as a "well-ordered, active, useless machine" (84); and his brittle unmarried sister, Harriet. Although admittedly inspired by the misogynistic Dent,[17] the character of Philip, beginning with his unimpressive appearance (70), owes much to Morgan Forster.

The novel begins with the first of three Italian trips. Lilia, the careless, merry widow of Philip's late brother, is packed off to Italy with Caroline as chaperone in the hope of averting a family embarrassment. Tuscany intervenes and the ploy fails miserably. Lilia falls in love with Gino Carella, the rakish and penniless son of a Monteriano dentist; Caroline, heady with freedom, encourages the match. Philip's arrival to forestall the marriage finds Gino and Lilia already wed and in sordid circumstances. His romantic illusion of Italy shattered, Philip returns to Sawston with a contrite Caroline to face Mrs. Herriton's ire. Lilia's marriage proves disastrous. Disowned by the Herritons, she cannot adjust to the antiquated Catholic town or her husband's blithe neglect. When Lilia dies giving birth to a son, Mrs. Herriton again dispatches Philip—this time fortified by Harriet—to rescue the "poor child" from his "devil" of a father and bring him back to Sawston. But Caroline, horrified at the prospect of the baby being brought up by Harriet, leaves for Italy with the intention of adopting the child herself. After the three meet up in the same pension in Monteriano, they decide to attend a local performance of *Lucia di Lammermoor* on the eve of their interviews with Gino.

Lucia was a likely choice for both an Italian touring company and an English novelist around 1904. A resounding success within several years of its composition, *Lucia* remained a holdout in the general decline of the bel canto repertoire in Victorian England (at Covent Garden alone, it had passed its 200th performance in 1902).[18] The opera's lifeblood is melody, its vehicle the embodied voice, its subject romantic passion at its most elemental. Based on Sir Walter Scott's *The Bride of Lammermoor* (1819), the opera recounts the tragic love between Lucia Ashton and Edgardo Ravenswood, separated by bitter enmity between their families. In the end Lucia, duped by her brother into a political marriage with Arturo Bucklaw, murders her new husband on their wedding night and withdraws into madness, provoking her climactic arias "Alfin son tua" and "Spargi d'amaro pianto." Grasping too late the sincerity of Lucia's love, Edgardo commits suicide when he hears of her death. The opera's marriage of an English literary source with an Italian libretto by Salvadore Cammarano echoes the novel's cultural antithesis of North and South. The religious-based enmity between the Protestant Ashtons and the Catholic Ravenswoods replicates the Herritons' disdain for Papists, intensified by Lilia's conversion to Catholicism. Finally, the novel's much-discussed cruelty resonates with *Lucia,* which closes with one of the iconic scenes of female madness in the nineteenth-century operatic repertoire. The opera scene also served Forster admirably as a meeting point of our English tourists with the hubbub of daily life in Italy, which they can experience with rapture or revulsion, but never call home.

In Monteriano with No Baedeker

The opera scene is the testing ground for English middle-class values in *Where Angels Fear to Tread.* The Monteriano Theatre lies outside the safe zone of anglicized Italy as defined in the Baedeker guidebook that accompanied almost every middle-class English traveler on the traditional tour. Ticking off its list of "must-sees" had become a grim obsession that limited contact with Italy to its cultural and historical landmarks, to the neglect of the daily lives of its people. The Theatre would have been out-of-bounds for the Baedeker tourist: Forster's fictive Baedeker entry for Monteriano (29) does not even mention its Theatre except as a practical orientation point for the adjacent post and telegraph offices. But Philip had lost his copy en route in Bologna (90), freeing him to experience the otherness of Italy and its people without his cultural mooring.[19]

The setting for the opera scene is itself operatic. On the afternoon of their arrival in Monteriano, Philip and Caroline notice an opera-bill plastered to the base of the tower across from their hotel (104–5). With its sunlit summit stretching "up to heaven" and its base "down to the other place," the tower epitomizes the moral ambivalence of the town. The placement of the opera poster in the lower shadows warns of the erotic dangers awaiting them at the performance. The description of the "hot red theatre" that conflates everything "majestic in the bad taste of Italy" (107–8) subverts the conventions of a guidebook entry. Redolent of the bordello, it had recently been renovated "in the tints of the beetroot and the tomato," with "terracotta draperies" to the boxes. "There was also a drop-scene, representing a pink and purple landscape, wherein sported many a lady lightly clad, and two more ladies lay along the top of the proscenium to steady a large and pallid clock." For Caroline and Philip, who admit to liking the theater "most awfully," it is the abode of "Romance" and the setting for metaphoric sexual release.

Unable to secure a box, the English party is seated in the lower-class stalls (108), poised to experience Italian operatic culture from the vantage point of the masses. Accustomed to the rigid code of behavior and the "Bayreuth hush" of the Covent Garden audience,[20] they encounter there a chaotic, embodied world of spontaneous emotion and sexual freedom. The marriageable Caroline also escapes the display case of the "opera box," a common literary trope in late-nineteenth-century novels beginning with Flaubert's *Lucia* scene in *Madame Bovary* (1857).[21] She is freed to assume the position of subject rather than object of passion, reversing the gendered role assigned her in England. This leaves the young men, led by the seductive Gino, to occupy Forster's box.

The novel's *Lucia* scene (108–12) captures small-town Italian opera culture with devastating wit. The audience is noisy and instinctive in its enthusiasm, tapping and drumming during the opening chorus and "swaying in the melody like corn in the wind." The narrator grows attentive only at Lucia's entry, not surprising given the opera's tradition as a one-woman vehicle. The reader shares with the audience the physical impact of her "stout and ugly" body during the harp introduction to her *Scena e cavatina* (No. 3), which serves to "fetishise Lucia's body, isolating it from her voice."[22] Its considerable length gives Philip the opportunity to identify the singer as the same "hot lady of the Apennines" who had disgusted Harriet in the train with her profuse sweating (90). The Italian body cannot be denied as easily as its English counterpart: Lucia's physicality challenges Philip and his party to transcend the tourist's Italy and confront what James Buzard calls "the refreshingly coarse and refractory heart of the living culture."[23] The account also demonstrates Forster's intimate knowledge of the opera and of the typical Italian aria form of the period.[24] A "moment's silence" precedes her plaintive recitative, "Ancor non giunse!—He has not yet come!" Through Lucia's cavatina "Regnava nel silenzio," "the theatre murmured like a hive of happy bees. All through the coloratura [in its closing cabaletta, "Quando rapito in estasi—When lost in ecstasy"] she was accompanied by sighs, and its top note was drowned in a shout of universal joy." Caroline would have been among those sighing to its closing words, which revive the dormant madness that had first led her to endorse Lilia and Gino's love.

As the opera proceeds, the intoxication roused by the "two great sextets" (the famous "Chi mi frena in tal momento?" and the fast, *stretta* close of Act 2, "Esci, fuggi, il furor") takes on an increasingly sexualized pitch. "The audience sounded drunk, and even Caroline, who never took a drop, was swaying oddly. Violent waves of excitement, all arising from very little, went sweeping round the theatre. The climax was reached" in the first aria of the mad scene [No. 14, *Scena ed aria*], the famous "Alfin son tua" that celebrates Lucia's imagined marriage night with Edgardo. Only the censorious Harriet, a conventional English tourist to the end, remains untouched.

The thunderous ovation following its closing vocal cadenza brings the performance to a halt, and restores the novel's comedic world. When the diva tosses a bouquet concealing a love-note back to a young man in a box, Harriet leaves the theater in disgust, dragging the reluctant Caroline with her. The audience by now has "exploded," the unabashed pleasure of the "divine creature" serving to "unloose the great deeps." Philip, "drunk with excitement," dutifully follows the ladies, the diva's bouquet in hand. When he attempts to deliver it, he discovers its source to be Gino, who with his friends pulls "Fra Filippo" up into their box. There, Philip is bathed in masculine warmth and is "enchanted" by the "light caress of the arm across his back." In their company, Philip hears Lucia's "song of madness and death," the concluding cabaletta "Spargi d'amaro pianto." It is passed over in the novel with barely a mention; indeed, Harriet and Caroline have already exited. It is "Alfin son tua" that has engaged everyone's attention, Forster's included.

The Critics' *Lucia*

Recent musicological discourse on Donizetti's *Lucia* is likewise focused on the mad scene, especially among feminist critics.[25] Fundamental to their revisionist view is Michel Foucault's notion of madness as politicized behavior situated on the fringe of society, offering both an outlet of resistance to conventional behavioral norms and an object of voyeuristic spectacle for the so-called "male gaze."[26] To this end, feminist critics beginning with Elaine Showalter have argued that madness was increasingly feminized throughout the nineteenth century, resulting in fin de siècle notions of insanity as a peculiarly female disorder traceable to the hysteria induced by sexual excess. Late-nineteenth-century artistic images of fallen women as well as the emerging fields of sexology and psychiatry confirm the association of excessive female eroticism with madness and death.[27] Yet the madwoman's alleged lack of sexual inhibition, while fascinating to her largely male observers, also posed a threat to social order and male supremacy. In order to prevent the further infection of decently socialized women, the madwoman was confined, her madness framed by institutional boundaries.

Beyond this common ground comes a parting of the ways. For critic Catherine Clément and musicologist Susan McClary, madness is a zone of freedom and female *jouissance* in an otherwise repressive patriarchal society;[28] for others, including Mary Ann Smart and Showalter, the end product of madness is the silencing of women in death. Yet all agree on the central importance of the burst of florid, ecstatic song that heralds the demise of an operatic madwoman such as Lucia. Smart speaks for all in observing that the freedom and power of her coloratura voice liberate her momentarily from "the confinement of music and of language: a syllable stretched beyond recognition is an escape from signification."[29] Unlike the madwoman in literature and the visual arts, however, the operatic *pazza per amore* is gloriously and unabashedly audible. In her voice and the coloratura of her cadenza resides her power. It may be her last gasp, but it is a moment of fullness and freedom.

Donizetti's *Lucia*

In its libretto Lucia's final *scena* begins with her sudden emergence from her marriage chamber, splattered with blood, dagger in hand. Pale, "as if emerging from the tomb," her hair in disarray and her eyes fixed in an icy stare,[30] she evokes gasps of terror and pity from the funereal chorus, which serves as both sympathetic witness and controlling frame. In form and harmonic design the scene is unusually free with the conventions of 1835, especially in its use of the technique of thematic reminiscence in the orchestra. As Emilio Sala has observed, such "reminiscence motives" are a common recourse for operatic madwomen, who "habitually relive happy moments from the past in their deliriums and return obsessively to the traumatic events that drove them over the edge."[31] The three fragmentary themes associated with Lucia's past joy take on new meaning in the horror of her present. The first invokes the warning ghost from her entry scene by the fountain ("Regnava nel silenzio"), both recalling her meeting place with Edgardo and invoking an earlier victim of a jealous Ravenswood. Then comes a reprise of the opera's most memorable tune, her love duet with Edgardo ("Verranno a te sull'aure"), broken off mid-theme by the warning ghost. Madness increasingly grips her as she hears a disembodied voice—"un' armonia celeste"—originally scored for glass harmonica in Donizetti's autograph, but replaced by the traditional flute for the first performance.[32] In the end, the memory of her signing of the marriage contract with Bucklaw pushes her over the edge. She interprets its mournful cadences as music for her imagined wedding to Edgardo ("Oh, me felice—How happy I am!"), signaling the first of her many mad flights into coloratura.

The stage is set for "Alfin son tua," the theme of which is anticipated in the orchestra while she is still caught up in her recitative. Lucia's failure to respond to this traditional instrumental cue is often seen as a mark of her distraction.[33] In her delusion the sacred candles are lit, the priest awaits, and Lucia and her Edgardo are wed. Only then can she yield to the organizing structure of the aria. Its traditional, compact two-part form belies her distracted mental state, signaled by the continued presence of the flute's phantom voice. The first section modulates to the dominant key ("At last I am yours, you are mine—a god gave you to me"), and transitions back ("every pleasure we shall share"). The second section ("Del cielo") returns to the opening theme in the home key ("our life together shall be a smile from a merciful heaven"). The vocal ornamentation intensifies throughout this second half, signaling the end of each phrase and expressing with rising passion the imagined joy of their life together. A marker for hysteria, Lucia's notated coloratura is extreme even by the standards of bel canto opera,[34] and would have been further embellished in performance. At last she abandons the word altogether, dissolving into the illusory freedom of pure tone in her cadenza.

Originally improvised by the singer, the *Lucia* cadenza had by Forster's time hardened into a written tradition. The customary cadenza with flute obbligato, still sung today, has recently been shown to have been written in 1889 by vocal pedagogue Mathilde Marchesi for her protégée Nelly Melba, and was published around 1900 in Marchesi's *Variantes et points d'orgue*.[35] It quickly became a highlight in all performances of *Lucia*. Thus any reading of Lucia's cadenza as an escape into freedom runs up against its fixed performance tradition. As Wayne Koestenbaum quipped: "If the ornamentation were improvised, not canned, we might feel that Lucia were at last coming to individual life."[36]

The novel's apparent lack of interest in the cabaletta "Spargi d'amaro pianto" is reflected in much of the musicological literature.[37] The stark contrast between Cammarano's words, foretelling Lucia's death and afterlife, and the jaunty waltz music and nightingale song of Donizetti's cabaletta suggests that she has lost all touch with reality. Death is imminent, signaled by the tolling bells that symbolize for Smart the final "silencing of Lucia." This is the stern warning that Caroline's early departure deprives her of hearing.

Tetrazzini's *Lucia*

When Forster and Dent entered the Teatro Verdi in May 1903, they were about to hear one of the greatest Lucias of the new century. Tetrazzini was a warm, outgoing performer with a fabled joie de vivre and impressive dramatic sense. She was also a notoriously sensual woman, known for her love affairs and passion for jewels and fine food. Hers was a richer voice than most coloratura sopranos of the time, with a renowned technique based on solid diaphragm support, an intense legato line, superb trills and staccatos, and a mastery of the tradition of coloratura ornamentation. As the last of the great nineteenth-century bel canto sopranos, her repertoire was decidedly old-fashioned—Rossini, Bellini, Donizetti, and early Verdi through *La traviata.* To that repertoire she brought a unique musical intelligence and emotional directness that made for a stellar Lucia. She was noted especially for her "Alfin son tua," which she recorded three times in 1904–11:[38]

1. Universal Talking Machine Company (Zon-O-Phone), New York (recorded 1904?): Rondo ["Alfin son tua"] with unidentified piano accompaniment and unaccompanied cadenza
2. The Gramophone Company, London (HMV) (recorded December 1907): "Splendon le sacre faci—Del cielo clemente" ["Alfin son tua" verse is cut], with accompanied cadenza (Alberto Fransella, flute); orchestra conducted by Percy Pitt
3. Victor Talking Machine Company, Camden, N.J. (recorded 16 March 1911): "Splendon le sacre faci—Alfin son tua," with accompanied cadenza (Walter Oesterreicher, flute); orchestra conducted by Walter Rogers

The obscure 1904 New York recording was likely Tetrazzini's first experience in the studio. The volume and range of her voice presented insurmountable challenges to early recording technology, and the unfamiliarity of the venue combined with the plodding pace of her pianist likely affected the results. The 1907 version is among the earliest professional recordings made in the wake of her London debut, and was conducted by Percy Pitt, then music director of Covent Garden. By 1911 she was a seasoned recording artist with a Metropolitan Opera contract; the easy mastery of her third recording, conducted by veteran opera conductor Walter Rogers, may most closely approximate the Lucia heard by Forster and Dent in 1903. Although she would also record "Regnava nel silenzio" with its cabaletta "Quando, rapito in estasi" once in 1909, as well as the "Sextet" with a rousing ensemble including Enrico Caruso in 1912,[39] Tetrazzini never recorded the cabaletta from the mad scene, "Spargi d'amaro pianto." Judging from the number and quality of recordings, "Alfin son tua" was the centerpiece of her *Lucia*: her recordings of it allow us to overhear the voice that launched *Where Angels Fear to Tread.*

Tetrazzini's cadenza (transcribed from her 1907 recording as Ex. 1) is the least original part of her performance. It differs from the version most performed in the twentieth century in omitting the poignant recall of the love duet "Verranno a te sull'aure" that is one of the most-discussed segments of the traditional cadenza.[40] She opts instead for the closure beginning at the asterisk, highlighting her signature trills before an ascent into the uppermost range, where her vibratoless tone mimics the glass harmonica of Donizetti's original phantom voice. Tetrazzini's three recordings of this cadenza are virtually identical. As an emblem for the alleged freedom offered the operatic madwoman in feminist criticism, her cadenza fails to deliver.

Ex. 1. Tetrazzini's cadenza for Lucia's "Alfin son tua," transcribed by the author from the 1907 recording

Tetrazzini's recordings of the aria itself are a different matter. Although the music is, as McClary and others have observed, bound by the melodic, harmonic, and formal conventions of Italian romantic opera, operatic performance practices at the beginning of the twentieth century continued the romantic vocal tradition of free ornamentation and improvisation.[41] This was especially true of Tetrazzini, for whom the act of performance was at once creative and re-creative. The security of her technique freed her to experiment with every musical parameter—ornamentation, rhythm and accent, tempo fluctuation and *rubato*, accentuation, dynamics (to the extent discernible within the recording technology of the time), intonation, color, and text placement. The *portamento* (the expressive slide connecting two successive pitches) and selective vibrato shared with the great violinists of the era are put to intelligent and expressive use. Some of these qualities are evident in Ex. 2, which compares the three recordings of the second strophe ("Del cielo clemente") with the notated vocal line from the Ricordi score of c. 1910.[42] It marks the highpoint of embellishment in the aria and the climax

Ex. 2. Tetrazzini's three recorded interpretations of Lucia's "Alfin son tua," strophe two (1904, 1907, 1911), transcribed by the author and compared to Ricordi ed. (c. 1910)

of her performance in all three versions. Its closing incantation on their "life to come" (mm. 31–8) displays her remarkable improvisational flexibility. See especially her persuasive interpretation of m. 35 in the 1911 version, with her shivering octave *portamento* on "ri-*so*," followed by a massive slowing down to legato triplets at the poignant "la vita a noi." The freshness of such choices, as if discovered in the moment of performance, gives Tetrazzini's interpretations the illusion of freedom and frees her "Alfin son tua" from the bounds of musical notation and the limitations of the genre.

Caroline's *Lucia*

Fresh from the tantalizing freedom of her "Alfin son tua," the aura of madness still adhering to her large, sweating body, Forster's Lucia is at her most dangerous. Her male observers, Philip and the rowdy band in Gino's box, are entranced. One also senses in the novel's narrator a palpable whiff of disgust elicited by her wild scream of pleasure, her animal embrace of the floral tributes, her public procurement of a lover, and the unabashed rejoicing in her female power over her audience. Yet in a switch on Foucault, it is the "female gaze" that predominates. Harriet, the unwilling witness to Caroline's sexualized enjoyment of the opera, snaps in the bestial atmosphere of the diva's ovation ("'It's not even respectable!'" she cries).[43] It is too late: Lucia's aria has already infected Caroline.

Lucia resounds the next morning, in one of the novel's most perplexing scenes. It is here in Chapter 7 of the novel that its tone begins to shift from ironic social comedy to something darker and less predictable, as if in response to the experience of Donizetti's opera. Caroline awaits Gino in his deserted parlor, which he has transformed into a makeshift mausoleum for his dead wife Lilia. The mood is eerily silent and foreboding, duplicating that of Lucia's "Regnava nel silenzio." Among the mementos in this "charnel-chamber" is an inlaid box that has become the novel's chief leitmotif. Belonging to Harriet, it had been "lent, not given" to Lilia to store her prim "handkerchiefs and collars" while in Italy (20). The entry of Gino, "singing fearlessly from his expanded lungs, like a professional" (after a night of passion with the diva?), is enough to shake her resolve (115). His song surely recalls "the torrents of music" that had "troubled" her dreams. Still singing, he passes by the parlor without noticing Caroline. She watches his performance dumbstruck from the next room as he lights a cigar and blows a "fat smoke-ring." It takes on a sinister life of its own, floating "vast and elliptical" through the landing and extending "its pale blue coils towards her." It surrounds and invades her as if with the power of music. "She lost self-control. It enveloped her. As if it was a breath from the pit, she screamed" (116). On first reading, I remember thinking how very odd her behavior was. (Apparently director Charles Sturridge thought so as well, for in the film version Caroline, played by Helena Bonham Carter, is stricken with a migraine when Gino strips to the waist, and faints.) In the novel it is as if Lucia's madness converges with Caroline's passionate awareness of Gino's body. Now beyond words, Caroline "sings"—hence her operatic scream.

Realism intrudes. Gino leads her out of the ghostly parlor and gives her a glass of wine, freeing her to heady new experiences. Her weakening resolve to rescue the baby is upset by Gino's palpable bond with his son; Philip arrives to find them bathing the child together in a curiously sacramental rite. Yet Caroline's vicarious role as wife and mother has no more reality than Lucia's imagined union with Edgardo in "Alfin son tua." Fertilized only metaphorically by a night at the opera, Caroline's maternity remains symbolic. The very real child is the fruit of Gino's sexual union with another woman. She flees in tears to the hotel, babbling incoherently. Harriet, the voice of Sawston convention, announces Caroline's assumption of Lucia's role: "'Mad!'" screamed Harriet—"'absolutely stark, staring, raving mad!'" (128).

Philip also abandons the adoption plan, but his fatal passivity stands in the way of decisive action. This leaves Harriet to her own mad devices. She secretly kidnaps the baby, who is killed that night in a carriage accident during the flight to the station. Philip assumes responsibility for his sister's actions; the inquest deems the death an accident and Harriet, after a cruelly brief "illness," recovers to chilling forgetfulness.

If Caroline is becoming Lucia, will her fate be similar? Perhaps: In the final scene in the train (157–60), just as the book gives every evidence of winding down to a conventional happy ending for Caroline and Philip, Forster throws another curve. Marriage will not be possible for them, for Caroline is "crudely" and unashamedly in love with Gino ("'Rather! I love him too!'" blurts out Philip). Her love—like his—was born during the *Lucia* performance, when she "saw him mixed up with music and light" (159). Yet spontaneity and passion come at a price that neither is willing to pay. Foreswearing operatic ardor for a benign friendship with Philip (whose "almost alarming intimacy" with Gino would surely have compromised the marriage [153]), she cuts short Philip's first foray into adult emotional commitment in the novel. Caroline soars out of his reach, a "goddess to the end" (160), while Philip retreats into his aesthetic shell, weaving a mythological web around Gino as the eternally beautiful youth Endymion (his supine, naked figure a recurring emblem of homoerotic desire in late-nineteenth-century British art).[44] The novel's closing gesture sees them rushing off to minister to Harriet's whims in a grim foretaste of their lives to come.

Italy has confounded rather than bolstered English middle-class values. Caroline has concealed her feelings from Gino, and intends never to return to Italy. She will resume her old life in Sawston ("'and if I mayn't speak about him to you sometimes, I shall die'"). Her untried and unfulfilled love trails behind: its illusory smoke ring had by then "wrapped [her] round," and will likely prevent her from marrying and having her own family. "'All the wonderful things are over,'" she mourns (157). Like Lucia, she will recall the themes from her past, occasionally unfolding her dusty, secret love for Gino from its inlaid box. Although a witness to the lesson of Lilia's mistake, Caroline had succumbed to the passionate but deceptive freedom of the diva's voice. She had left the theater before Lucia's "Spargi d'amaro pianto," missing the "song of madness and death" that could have saved her.

Philip's fate remains undetermined. His retreat into the hermetic world of Greek myth suggests that a shift of sexual identity may be in the offing for him, but he will need to develop some pluck if he is ever to move beyond the effete inclinations of *Maurice*'s Clive Durham. His intention to leave his mother's Sawston home and move to London is vaguely motivated by the loss of Caroline and the death of Gino's son, but one wonders whether his feelings for Gino have also played a role. Conceived in the company of men as voyeur and listener to the exhibitionistic cabaletta "Spargi d'amaro pianto," his widening emotional landscape may yet save him. In London Philip may find the companionship of like-minded men, and perhaps attend Wagnerian operas at Covent Garden in their company. Yet his future at the novel's close appears bleak—as bleak, perhaps, as the author's own emotional life in 1905. It would be well over a decade before Forster would experience his first mature relationship with a handsome, dark-skinned Mediterranean boy in Egypt. And not until 1925 would he take his first London flat and begin loosening the ties with his mother.

3

Wagnerism, "Decadent" Wagnerites, and Wagnerian Motives in *The Longest Journey*

I can remember writing [*The Longest Journey*] and how excited I was and how absorbed, and how sometimes I went wrong deliberately, as if the spirit of anti-literature had jogged my elbow.
—EMF, 1960

The Longest Journey (1907) was a bold step in Forster's development as a novelist. Unlike the compact *Where Angels Fear to Tread*, originally intended for magazine publication, *The Longest Journey* was a full-scale novel that tested all his emerging skills as a writer. It is a work of youthful exuberance, its alleged flaws often attributed to inexperience: looseness of structure, a surplus of motifs and a surfeit of sudden deaths, and the intrusion of fantasy and symbolism in a realist novel.[1] Even Forster admitted that the "whirling" array of themes in this, "the least popular of my five novels," might "well have impaired my sense of direction."[2] For Jeremy Tambling, *The Longest Journey* "does not seem to possess a unity of its own," while for Carola M. Kaplan it "collapses upon itself."[3] Yet for Elizabeth Heine, it is a work of richness and originality that owes much to its very "complexity of symbolism and subtlety of structure."[4] For Forster it would remain the novel "I am most glad to have written."

In his search for models for its symbolism and structure, Forster turned to the music dramas of Richard Wagner.[5] Wagner's influence is roundly implicated in the strengths and weaknesses of this novel. *The Longest Journey* is in several respects a Wagnerian *Gesamtkunstwerk* that far exceeds the qualified mixture of mode in *Where Angels Fear to Tread*. It boasts a phantasmagoria of references to *Lohengrin, Das Rheingold, Siegfried, Götterdämmerung, Tristan und Isolde,* and *Parsifal,* with the *Ring* predominating. Wagnerian opera also competes with several parallel symbolic worlds, which are developed with almost equal intensity: these include classical mythology, philosophy, art history, and even photography.[6] There is some justification for Lionel Trilling's belief that *The Longest Journey* simply flies apart with the force of "the too-much steam that blows up the boiler."[7]

The overexuberance of *The Longest Journey* is attributable in part to its multivalent appropriation of Wagnerism, the sprawling artistic, social, and political phenomenon founded on the music and ideas of Richard Wagner (1813–83).[8] Wagnerism functions at every narrative level of *The Longest Journey.* Its two Wagnerites, Rickie Elliot and his friend Stewart Ansell, do not simply listen to and talk about Wagner: in complicity with the Wagner-savvy narrator they interpret and misinterpret their world in Wagnerian terms, to ironic or visionary effect.[9] Were Forster's use of Wagner to end here, his novel would hardly transcend the referential Wagnerism of George Moore's recent novels *Evelyn Innes* (1898) and *Sister Teresa* (1901).[10] The most innovative impact of Wagner's music dramas on *The Longest Journey* concerns matters of structure, and here Forster himself is the Wagnerite. It marks his earliest and most extreme application of Wagnerian leitmotivic practice to the novel, creating a formal precedent that would persist with increasing subtlety in his novels through *A Passage to India* and the libretto for *Billy Budd.*

English Wagnerism had been born in the wake of the first performances of Wagner's operas in London in the 1870s and Wagner's triumphant visit in 1877, which inspired a surge of Wagner mania that continued unabated until World War I. Yet by the 1890s Wagnerism remained highly controversial in England. For some it had become the major driving force in European culture, and offered "a way of thinking and feeling that might resolve the contradictions of the times in a new social vision."[11] For many other late Victorians, Wagner and his music posed a pernicious threat to morality, health, social order, and the future of the arts. For Edmund Gurney in 1883, even Wagner's finest melodies suggested "a faint flower of disease, something overripe in its lusciousness and febrile in its passion."[12] Such discourse came to a head in the 1890s, when Wagner and Wagnerism were increasingly associated with the English decadent movement around Oscar Wilde and Aubrey Beardsley. Emma Sutton, in her outstanding study of *Aubrey Beardsley and British Wagnerism in the 1890s,* has documented the singular impact of Wagner on the construction of English decadence at the fin de siècle, and with it the increasingly strident conflation of Wagnerism with eroticism, degeneration, and homosexuality in the wake of the Wilde trials of 1895.[13]

Beardsley's illustrations of scenes from *Tannhäuser, Tristan und Isolde, Siegfried, Götterdämmerung*, and what he called *The Comedy of the Rhinegold* provide archetypal visual icons for the association of Wagnerism with English decadence. As analyzed by Sutton, Beardsley's female Wagnerites are exotic, sexually aware New Women, all hair and voluminous flesh, their eyes intense and knowing; his male Wagnerites, by contrast, are physically deformed, emaciated, withdrawn, and visibly exhausted by the emotion of listening to or—in the case of Beardsley's *Siegfried, Act II* (1892)—interpreting Wagner.[14] That the *Rhinegold* project of 1896–97 was left incomplete by Beardsley's death from tuberculosis a year later only fueled the popular association of Wagnerism at the fin de siècle with physical decline, pathology, and morbidity. This was the fraught psychosexual context for the nineteen-year-old Morgan Forster's first opera at Covent Garden in June 1898, Wagner's *Tristan und Isolde*.[15]

Forster's enthusiasm for Wagner took hold in Cambridge at the turn of the new century, at a time when the extreme subjectivity and emotionalism of decadent Wagnerism of the 1890s was giving way to a more modern, rational, and scholarly approach to Wagner's music in England.[16] Forster's Wagnerism would be nourished during his periodic return visits to Cambridge in 1902–4 to attend meetings of the Apostles (the "Brothers" to whom the novel is dedicated). During one of these, Forster burst in on musicologist Edward Dent in February 1904 and demanded that he play Wagner, which proved "strangely unfamiliar" to Dent's "awkward fingers."[17] Besides Wagner performances that he attended during these years, Forster had likely read or taken part in discussions of recent literature on Wagner's use of myth and legend, including Jessie Weston's *Legends of the Wagner Drama* (1896) and Alice Leighton Cleather and Basil Crump's *Parsifal, Lohengrin, and the Legend of the Holy Grail* (1904).[18] He may have studied Wagner's techniques of the recurring *Leitmotiv* as described in recent books by Ernest Newman, H. E. Krehbiel, Albert Lavignac, W. J. Henderson, and Houston Stewart Chamberlain.[19] Given Forster's admiration for Edward Carpenter and Arthur Symons, it is likely that he consulted their recent literary studies of Wagner's theories of the music drama.[20] A decisive influence on the *Parsifal* symbolism in *The Longest Journey* was his friend R. C. Trevelyan's *The Birth of Parsival* (1905), which Forster read in March 1905 before his departure to witness the Dresden *Ring*.[21]

The first sketch for the novel, dated July 17, 1904, projects another Anglo-Italian novel. Its only hint of the *Ring* is a closing immolation, in which two reunited half-brothers die in a fire.[22] In September 1904 Forster visited the Figsbury Ring, a prehistoric circular earthwork near Salisbury, renamed the "Cadbury Rings" in his novel. His imagination "caught fire up on the Rings" and *The Longest Journey* found its catalyst.[23] The heavy-duty Wagner references entered the project only when he resumed the novel after his return from Germany in August 1905, with the Dresden *Ring* still fresh in his ears. By March 1906 the draft was at least two-thirds complete, but Forster was already plagued: "Doubt whether novel's any good: all ingenious symbols: little flesh and blood."[24] Such misgivings may explain his reduction of the Wagnerian symbolism in the final draft, completed by the end of that year.[25]

The Longest Journey consists of three parts comparable to the three-act division of Wagner's later works. "Cambridge," which "sought for reality and cared for truth," introduces undergraduate Rickie and his university friends, led by philosophy student Ansell. "Sawston," the mediocre London suburb already featured in *Where Angels Fear to Tread*, is the moral slippery slope of the novel. It houses the shabby public school presided over by Herbert Pembroke and his sister Agnes, both unmarried and unmusical. "Wiltshire" in the English countryside near Salisbury is the home of Rickie's cruel aunt, Emily Failing, and her rough-edged ward Stephen Wonham. Surrounding it are the chalk hills of the Salisbury plain, dominated by monuments of Christian and prehistoric rites—the cathedral spire and the Cadbury Rings.

The common assertion that the novel is a *Bildungsroman* recounting Rickie's education as a writer is flawed on several counts. He dies an acknowledged failure at age twenty-five having learned nothing, and his modest posthumous success as a writer is cast as a fluke of fashion rather than an affirmation of merit. He is one of Forster's most complex characters and an unlikely protagonist: shy, weakly, and plain, with a deformed foot inherited from his father and a disabling emotional legacy from both parents. Theirs was a supremely unhappy marriage. Orphaned at fifteen, Rickie cherishes the memory of his beautiful mother with an ardor that has blinded him to her emotional coolness and self-absorption. He despises the memory of his father, who had abandoned his wife and their sickly son when Rickie was still a baby. Concealed until the novel's midpoint, however, is the repressed trauma of Rickie's early childhood: his mother's flight to Stockholm with Robert Wonham, a Rousseauian farmer, when Rickie was about two. Robert had died after only seventeen days together, leaving Mrs. Elliot grief-stricken and pregnant with Stephen. Under social pressure she had given her illegitimate baby over to the Failings, who bring him up in ignorance of his past.

Rickie retains no conscious memory of his mother's one-year absence, and along with the reader remains ignorant of his half-brother until the strategic thirteenth chapter. Yet the impact of early maternal neglect and displacement by a healthy sibling is palpable in his escapist tendencies. Rickie is a "decadent"

Wagnerite of the old school. His vivid imagination, inhabited by the gods and heroes of classical myth and Wagnerian music drama, nourishes his fragile artistic leanings while shielding him from reality. His physical deformity and his tendency to withdraw into a mystical dream world also mark him as a Beardsleyesque Wagnerite. Deceived by the illusory glow of Wagner's *Ring* in his "diseased imagination" (*LJ*, 17), Rickie is lured into a disastrous marriage with Agnes Pembroke and a dangerous idealizing of his half-brother. In both relationships, Wagner proves a siren song that lures the imaginative mind away from "the idea of Reality" and the "ethical idea that reality must be faced"—Forster's philosophical foundation for *The Longest Journey*.[26]

Ring Resounding: Flosshilde and Brünnhilde at Cambridge

The most overt Wagnerian allusions occur in the first nine chapters, set at Cambridge around 1900. The novel opens in Rickie's room during a meeting of a society much like the Apostles. The twenty-year-old Classics major is dozing through a sophomoric and pleasantly muddled philosophical debate. The aesthetic trappings of the room include a print of G. F. Watts's "Sir Perceval"[27] and a player-piano, in which a roll of the Prelude to Wagner's *Das Rheingold* lies in wait. The narrator immediately identifies Rickie as a "fool," suggesting a potential likeness to the *reiner Tor* Parsifal, who finds "enlightenment through compassion" in Wagner's music drama.[28] The ploy also situates Rickie in a hermetic male society with links to *Parsifal*'s Monsalvat, with its common association at the time with male homosexuality.[29] Meanwhile Ansell is playing with matches against the "dancing" flames of the fireplace like a latter-day Loge, the demigod of fire and deceit from *Rheingold*. If intended, this link would degrade Ansell's reliability as Rickie's advisor. Throughout the novel, the Wagner allusions will modulate freely from one source to another, shifting shapes with the ease of the bearer of Wagner's *Tarnhelm*. That Forster would call the magic cap from *Rheingold* a "shabby trick"[30] may alert the reader to beware—not the least of interpreting the novel as a parody of any single Wagnerian work.

Rheingold first prevails when Anderson "crawled" across the smoke-filled room to the piano and "timidly" began its Prelude[31] "with his knee upon the soft pedal," a physical impossibility on anything but a player-piano.[32] Agnes Pembroke's operatically staged entry interrupts the music and awakens Rickie from his daydreams of cows and tree nymphs. She switches on the electric light, and "like mists before the sun" the timid boys flee in her wake (6); only

Ansell lingers long enough to ignore her entirely. Rickie's response validates Agnes's presence with reference to Wagner's Prelude:

> "And I thought she came into the room so beautifully. Do you know—oh, of course, you despise music—but Anderson was playing Wagner, and he'd just got to the part where they sing
>
> *'Rheingold!*
> *Rheingold!'*
>
> and the sun strikes into the waters, and the music, which up to then has so often been in E flat—"
>
> "Goes into D sharp." [Ansell replies] (16–7).

The Prelude would have been sounding for at least fifteen minutes to have reached the Rhine-maidens' song beginning at m. 540. Like the Wagnerian orchestra, the background music reveals the emotional underpinnings of the visible world. Its Rhine-maidens inject a jarring female eroticism into the male circle of the Cambridge "brothers." It also warns the crippled Rickie to beware the fate of Wagner's loveless gnome, Alberich, at the hands of Wagner's "faithless band of nymphs." This is a parallel that does not escape the narrator: "Love in return—that [Rickie] could expect from no one, being too ugly and too unattractive" (66). Indeed, Rickie will succumb to female deceit and the social stigma of the "abnormal," and will foreswear the love of brother and friend for the entire Sawston period of the novel.

Rickie's appreciation of the "handsome" Agnes owes much to the music that had announced her entry: the transfiguration of the Rhine's gold (mm. 506–40) and the sudden illumination of its murky depths by a shaft of light. Here "the music, which up to then has so often been in E flat," shimmers softly before beginning its move to a triumphant C major. In hushed phrases the Rhine-maidens spin a ravishing allegory of the female sun ("*die Sonne*") awakening with a kiss the gold, which is cast as a male sleeper ("*der wonnige Schläfer*"). With the new key of C firmly established, they greet the gold with whoops of joy and their jubilant "*Rheingold! Rheingold!*" In Rickie's imagination Agnes is endowed with all the radiance of Wagner's sunbeam, with himself presumably cast in the role of the "ecstatic sleeper." Ansell will have none of it, not because he is unmusical but because he is both jealous and prescient. He derails Rickie's rapturous Wagnerian gloss with a left hook about its shift into "D sharp." As the enharmonic equivalent of E flat, Ansell's substitute tonic would create no audible change of harmony; as a modulation it is as unreal as the Rhine-maidens' offers of love—or as Agnes herself. "'She was not really there,'" he tells Rickie later, thereby reducing her to "'the subjective product of a diseased imagination'" that, "'to our destruction, we invest with the semblance of reality'" (17).

The narrative perspective of this scene is recognizably that of the 1890s. Both Wagnerites are social outsiders, the one by virtue of his physical disability, the other (an expert in Schopenhauer's philosophy, in which Wagner's later music-dramas are steeped) as a Jew and likely homosexual. Even the player-pianist is limp and collapsed (he crawls rather than strides to the instrument). The overemotional mysticism of Rickie's Wagnerian outpouring aligns him with French symbolism or English decadence, while the sexual matrix of immature and socially withdrawn men frightened away by the entry of a brash woman rings true with the discourse on the New Woman and her perceived threat to male hegemony in the 1880s and 1890s.

The scene is disposed like an operatic set, colored perhaps by Forster's memories of the hyperrealistic Romantic staging of the Dresden *Rheingold*. Another visual inspiration is likely: Beardsley's frontispiece to *The Comedy of the Rhinegold* (see Fig. 4), published in the London periodical *The Savoy* in December 1896 and reprinted in 1900 in a deluxe anthology of the *Later Work of Aubrey Beardsley*.[33] There, Beardsley's three Rhine-maidens Woglinde, Wellgunde, and Flosshilde are cast as fin de siècle sirens, diaphanously clad, breasts bared, eyes penetrating and heavy-lidded, hair a voluminous snare for hapless males. (Significantly, the "natural glory" of Agnes's hair is the only physical feature on which the narrator later dwells [67].) Beardsley captures his three Rhine-maidens at the very moment of transfiguration described by Rickie. The gold, depicted as interlocking rings on the river's dark bed, lies beneath the flowing waves whose surface is adorned with roses of love. The sun's tongues of flame have just touched the gold, drawing their rapt gaze.[34] At their center is the shrewd and seductive contralto Flosshilde, who taunts Alberich with the greatest cruelty. Beardsley singled her out for a separate illustration (see Fig. 5). With the breasts of a lactating animal, the poised arm of a pianist rather than a swimmer, and the searing glance of a sage, this nymph would have inspired both desire and fear in many male observers. If Agnes has assumed the role of Flosshilde in Rickie's Wagnerian allegory, he is indeed in trouble.

The *Rheingold* Prelude resounds in a prose orchestration several months later. On a visit with the Pembrokes, Rickie stumbles upon Agnes and Gerald Dawes making love in the garden. This scene is not without violence, owing to Gerald's crudity as a lover. Rickie is both transfixed and repulsed (39), and resorts to the Prelude to *Rheingold* to exorcize the trauma in an aesthetic vision:

Fig. 4. Aubrey Beardsley, *Frontispiece to The Comedy of the Rhinegold*, 1896 (courtesy of The Iris and B. Gerald Cantor Center for Visual Arts at Stanford University [1973.8])

Music flowed past him like a river. He stood at the springs of creation and heard the primeval monotony. Then an obscure instrument gave out a little phrase. The river continued unheeding. The phrase was repeated, and a listener might know it was a fragment of the Tune of tunes. Nobler instruments accepted it, the clarionet [*sic*] protected, the brass encouraged, and it rose to the surface to the whisper of violins. In full unison was Love born, flame of the flame, flushing the dark river beneath him and the virgin snows above.

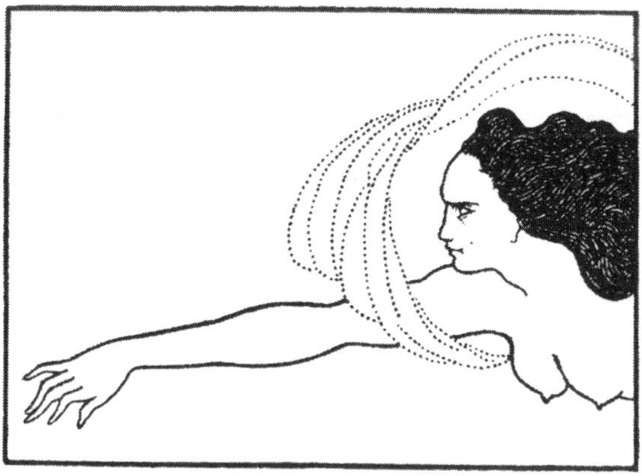

Fig. 5. Aubrey Beardsley, *Flosshilde,* 1896, published in *Savoy* 8 (December 1896): 45 (McPherson Library, University of Victoria)

> His wings were infinite, his youth eternal; the sun was a jewel on his finger as he passed it in benediction over the world. Creation, no longer monotonous, acclaimed him, in widening melody, in brighter radiances. Was Love a column of fire? Was he a torrent of song? Was he greater than either—the touch of a man on a woman? (40)

Critics have understandably dismissed this passage as overwrought,[35] but it is surely intentionally so. It mimics, likely with ironic intent on Forster's part, the emotionalism of decadent Wagnerism. Its mystical fog is no more extreme than that of G. L. Dickinson's Wagnerian allegory of a "Tower of Art" in *The Meaning of Good* (1901).[36] Elizabeth Heine accurately observes that Rickie's vision replays the pattern of instrumental entries of the *Rheingold* Prelude.[37] Forster had likely consulted the score to get the sequence right, beginning with the "primeval monotony"[38] of the open fifth in the bassoons and double basses (mm. 1–16) and the "little phrase" that first enters in the eighth horn in m. 17. The clarinets introduce the central diminution of the theme at m. 81, while the "brass" entry on four trumpets (m. 113) completes the ensemble. Meanwhile the coursing waters are evoked in the sixteenth-note figuration that builds from low to high strings, beginning in cello (m. 81) and progressing upward to the first violins (at m. 113). The entire *Rheingold* passage was a later insertion in the initial draft of the novel, and Forster's further revisions corrected the order of entry of the "clarionet" and "brass."[39] But Rickie's vision adds a new component to the *Rheingold* mythology: the birth of Love, the transcendent hero. The jewel on his finger identifies him as Siegfried, the subject of the third *Ring* opera. By making him the human product of the "touch of a man on a woman," Rickie unknowingly foretells the entry of the Siegfried-figure of the novel, his half-brother Stephen. Yet his Wagnerian flight to elevate and sanctify his first contact with rough, adult sexuality is ominous: this is Rickie's second delusion, and again Wagner is implicated.

Gerald is soon killed in a soccer accident (Rickie does not witness his cowardly death). Thereafter, Rickie transfigures the "gods and heroes" of his earlier fantasies into the myth of "a man who was dead and a woman who was still alive" (60), connecting Agnes momentarily with Wagner's widow-survivor Brünnhilde. Unaware of the connection of this tale with his own family romance, Rickie slips into guilty attraction to Agnes. Their engagement scene in the Madingley Dell is a riot of Wagnerian cross-references piled high by the narrator. Agnes arrives decked out like a Beardsley Rhine-maiden, sporting a "flowered muslin—something indescribably liquid and cool. It reminded him a little of those swift piercing streams, neither blue nor green, that gush out of the Dolomites" (66–7). Once there, "like a cataract again, she vanished pure and cool into the dell" (73). The sunlight flashes on her gold earrings, while her "face was clear and brown, like the face of a mountaineer" (67). Is this a comparison to Brünnhilde, who dwelled on the Glasberg before her long sleep on the summit of Brünnhilde's Rock? This parallel would appear forced, were it not bolstered by the narrator's immediate shift to the Forest Bird from Act 2, scene 3 of *Siegfried:* "A bird called out of the dell: 'Rickie!' A bird flew into the dell" (73).[40] Wagner's forest bird warns Siegfried of the treachery concealed behind Mime's flattering words, and leads him to the sleeping Brünnhilde. Yet Rickie is no Siegfried, and Rickie's *Waldvogel* lures him into the clutches of a very ordinary, deceitful woman. The bird also succeeds where Agnes had not: Rickie had stopped his ears when Agnes had called his name. The mythology has again shifted, now to the arch-seductress Kundry, whose searing summons "Parsifal!" precedes her maternal-demonic kiss. Rickie is no Parsifal either, but an Amfortas-figure who capitulates to seduction in a scene that the reader is spared.[41] When we rejoin the pair in the dell, they are engaged, and Agnes bends down to seal the bond with a kiss. Rickie is reclining like a child with his head in her lap.

The next morning Ansell, hung over from his Schopenhauer talk of the night before, is horrified to hear of the match. Their breakfast together is strained, despite Mrs. Lewin's uproarious tale of the near-death experience of her dove Parsival (77), a wry travesty of Parsifal's close shave in Klingsor's garden[42] and a mockery of Wagnerian interpretations of life-experience. Yet Rickie, who has by now invested Agnes with the heroic grandeur of Brünnhilde, is deaf to Ansell's pleas that she, like "Elsa in the question scene of

Lohengrin," is "not serious" and "not truthful" (82). The *Lohengrin* reference was honed through two stages of revision, with the early versions referring to "Ortrud" and then "Elsa," both "in the second act."[43] Forster had likely rejected the villainous Ortrud as too damning of Agnes before hitting on Elsa's questioning of Lohengrin in their bridal chamber in Act 3. The latter projects Ansell's distaste for curious, manipulative women intent on rooting out their husbands' secrets.[44] Rickie will have none of Ansell's predictions: the virginal Brünnhilde of *Siegfried* has now modulated into the loving wife of "the first scene of *Götterdämmerung*" (82), who grants her husband the freedom to live as he wishes.

Ansell's foresight is confirmed when Agnes tries "to run [Rickie], which a man won't pardon" (260). With an eye to Mrs. Failing's estate, she induces him to conceal Stephen's identity. She maneuvers him into postponing his dream of writing and accepting an offer as a teacher at the Sawston School, a vocation for which he is without skill or ability. His likeness to Amfortas of *Parsifal* is driven home in his hope to find healing for his "wound" at Sawston, perhaps even to "recapture the Holy Grail" of his Cambridge days (153).[45] His marriage proves a sham; Agnes separates him from Stephen and his friends; and their daughter is born lame and dies. Rickie's myth of compassionate love is destroyed, silencing the Wagnerian music in his life.

The Hero Ascendant: Siegfried in Wiltshire

The entry in Chapter 10 of a potential hero, Rickie's half-brother Stephen, opens the second stage of Wagnerian symbolism. Stephen's Wagnerian characteristics are entirely the creation of the narrator and of Forster: Stephen himself is a country workingman without experience or interest in sophisticated urban art. In the early drafts, Stephen's name was first "Siegfried," then the Byronic "Harold."[46] Having rejected both, Forster retained features of the epic and the romantic hero in his character. Stephen's love of nature, his preference for feeling over rational cognition, his flashes of brutality, and his homeless wandering through a corrupt world embody the isolated Byronic hero.[47] But it is the *epic* hero of his original namesake who predominates in Stephen's makeup. He resonates with Wagner's "free, untrammeled youth of all time," who in W. J. Henderson's words arrived "at the fundamental laws of life and love by observation, introspection, and the mighty workings of natural passion."[48] Stephen certainly looks the part of Wagner's "*rosiger Held,*" with his blond hair, "astonishingly blue eyes," florid complexion, and powerful frame. Like Siegfried, he was illegitimate and born in a distant northern land following the death of his father. Driven from his true home, he was brought up by a loveless, deceitful steward (the lame Mrs. Failing), who like the shambling Mime conceals his parents' identity. With similar cruelty she endows Stephen with the shattered fragments of his past (his mother's diary). Both Stephen and Siegfried grew up untutored and isolated,[49] with nature as their only teacher. Both have rejected the conventional gods (Stephen is described as a "pagan" and an "atheist") and can be thoughtlessly abusive, with a tendency to bully. They are men of the present whose fearlessness comes from their contempt for the past and freedom from its burden. At times Forster's noble savage sags under the burden of "*the* Teutonic hero, *par excellence,*"[50] and the sections of the novel in which he appears are among its most heavily revised.[51] Rickie remains blind to Stephen's potential until Chapter 27, when he learns his half-brother's true identity as the son of their mother and accepts Stephen's heroism at face value, oblivious to the narrative irony.

The reconciliation of Stephen and Rickie in Chapter 31 gave Forster considerable difficulty. One of its rejected drafts revisits the *Götterdämmerung* trope when the Sawston School catches fire, and Agnes (as Brünnhilde?) rushes into the flames to save the children while Stephen, Rickie, and Ansell escape.[52] In the final version it is the "heroic" Stephen who becomes the "symbol of redemption" for Rickie (249, 252). Stephen will have none of this. "'Come with me as a man,'" he urges, challenging Rickie to abandon Wagnerian myth for reality (257). Rickie complies. He leaves Agnes, takes up household with Stephen and Ansell, and recovers his inspiration as a writer. A happy ending for all but the novel's women seems afoot. The final sentence of Chapter 32 has all the ring of a convincing realistic closure. Agnes is left alone at the cemetery on the first anniversary of their child's death, pondering Gerald's adjacent grave: "There lay the athlete, and his dust was as the little child's whom she had brought into the world with such hope, with such pain" (261).

Perhaps critical response to the novel would be more positive had Forster called it quits at this point. But three chapters remain. Apparently dissatisfied with the tidy resolution, Forster opted for a closing surge into messy "prophecy" that revisits the decadent Wagnerian subtext and opens the novel to modernist ambiguity. Its point of departure is the visionary "mystic rose" scene (Chapter 33), which unshackles the plot from its realist moorings to float freely on the stream of gathering motifs. Stephen and Rickie are walking through the countryside at twilight. They reach a stream, and Stephen kneels in the swift current, lights a wad of paper, and sets it afloat. By its flickering light his face is "transfigured": "The paper caught fire from the match, and spread into a rose of flame. . . . [They] laid it flower-like on the stream.

Gravel and tremulous weeds leapt into sight, and then the flower sailed into deep water [before passing under a bridge, which] became a fairy tunnel, dropping diamonds. Then it vanished for Rickie; but Stephen, who knelt in the water, declared that it was still afloat, far through the arch, burning as if it would burn for ever" (272–3).

The mystic rose scene packs an unexpected punch, one source of which is its entanglement in *Ring* symbolism. It marks Stephen's ritual passage into manhood and his rebirth as Rickie's "transcendent hero." The ring becomes the "bar of gold" on his lips; the column of fire is the transfigured radiance of his face. Stephen is momentarily converted into a Siegfried who gets it right by restoring the gold and glow to the waters. Forster's "arch" suggests the underside of the Rainbow Bridge to Valhalla, transformed rather than destroyed by the passing flame. Forster's visionary image of the rose of flame may also be indebted to Beardsley's *Frontispiece to The Comedy of the Rhinegold,* with its prelapsarian river aglow with floating roses and tongues of fire (see Fig. 4).

The vision rekindles Rickie's illusions: "Stephen was a hero. He was a law to himself, and rightly . . . [Rickie] felt it worth while to sacrifice everything for such a man" (279). This he does that very night when he "wearily" sacrifices himself to save a drunken Stephen from being run over by a train. Yet Stephen's breach of promise not to drink again had marked for Rickie "the end of everything for a hero" (281). For a final time, his Wagnerian dream had "gone bankrupt": "That mystic rose and the face it illumined meant nothing. The stream . . . meant nothing. . . . The whole affair was a ridiculous dream" (282). Unlike the sacrificial Brünnhilde, who rides to her death to the triumphant swell of Wagner's orchestra, Rickie dies a mute failure, whispering that Mrs. Failing was "right" and negating everything he had learned about the value of compassion. Just as Forster was completing *The Longest Journey,* he tellingly observed: "We cannot believe in Siegfried as a hero."[53] In the end, the novel unexpectedly reinforces contemporary critiques of Wagnerism as a threat to social order, health, and life itself, and deflates the nineteenth-century heroic mythology on which Wagner's operatic world depends.

Too Much Wagner: The Problem of Structure

In contrast to Forster's largely cautionary, retrospective, and ironic use of Wagner in the narrative symbolism of *The Longest Journey,* his application of structural principles gleaned from Wagner's music and prose writings and contemporary Wagner criticism is innovative if controversial. Central to this novel is Forster's first thorough application of the Wagnerian leitmotif to the genre, a technique that would flower in the next generation of English modernist novels. *The Longest Journey* displays thorough understanding of Wagner's technique of the recurring "theme of reminiscence," as first realized in the *Ring* cycle and discussed in Wagner's *Opera and Drama* (1851) and his essay "On the Application of Music to the Drama" (1879). Both texts would have been available to Forster in recent English translations by William Ashton Ellis.[54] As described in *Opera and Drama,* Wagner's "prophetic or reminiscent melodic-moments" are "guides to feeling" that reside in the orchestra. They convey the unspoken thoughts and fundamental passions of a personage or dramatic situation by a motion into either "remembrance" or "foreboding."[55] In the words of Wagnerite Friedrich Stade, they reveal "the most private urges and impulses," allowing "the characterization to take on an extraordinary wealth of shadings and nuances."[56] Wagner's technique could thus have been deemed ideally suited to a modern psychological novel such as *The Longest Journey* in its capacity to suggest unconscious desires and repressed memories.

Wagner's most fundamental contribution to this novel, however, regards its structure.[57] Besides conveying "the profoundest secret of the poet's Aim," Wagner's "melodic-moments" form "the pillars of his dramatic edifice," which, in their "necessary play of repetition, will furnish . . . the highest unity of musical Form." When stretched "over the whole drama's self," the outcome should be a perfect union of "Form" and "Content."[58] Wagner's "On the Application of Music to the Drama" further defines this "Unity" as "a tissue of root-themes pervading all the drama, themes which contrast, complete, re-shape, divorce and intertwine with one another."[59] Again according to Stade, they promote "a unity which the old type of opera could never achieve."[60] Recent distinguished arguments against the "myth" of symphonic order in Wagner's music dramas aside,[61] English-language Wagnerian critics of Forster's generation vigorously promoted the form-generating properties of the so-called "leitmotif." Krehbiel considered it the "fundamental principle of [Wagner's] constructive scheme," while Henderson identified its pattern of repetition as "the only preservation of necessary musical method in a drama which had banished from its scheme the use of the established operatic forms." Chamberlain viewed the leitmotif as "a marvellous means of imparting both inward and outward unity to the work." For Carpenter "the underlying permanence of motive" gives "unity to his compositions."[62] Wherever he turned, Forster could well have been lured into the expectation that recurring motifs would have a parallel effect in a discursive novel, promoting an overarching unity of design.

Like Wagner, Forster resisted the term "leitmotif" in relation to his literary motives of reminiscence.[63] Forster's preferred term for the process was "rhythm," and his chief example of the technique Marcel Proust's *À la recherche du temps perdu* (for which Wagner also served as model).[64] Forster famously deemed that Proust's "chaotic, ill-constructed" novel, which "has and will have no external shape, . . . hangs together because it is stitched internally, because it contains rhythms" (*AN*, 165). The process for Forster is one of "repetition plus variation," and its effect lessens "our need of an external form." In Forster's eye, Proust's "rhythms" redeem his epic novel from the very looseness of construction for which *The Longest Journey* has been faulted.

The recurring themes in *The Longest Journey* seem to enter as with the tolling of a bell. At their simplest, they retain a consistent meaning throughout. Such is the motif of the "fool," by which every character is identified at least once. The structurally significant leitmotifs, however, develop new meanings across the novel, as do the "river" and "stream" that infuse Rickie's Wagnerian visions. The opening to *Rheingold* ripples in circles of reminiscence throughout *The Longest Journey,* in much the same way that Albert Lavignac claimed for the "Rhine" theme in Wagner's cycle.[65] Departing from the primal innocence of its first sounding in the utopian company of Apostles, Forster's "river" is tainted with seduction when Agnes enters; illumined by the kiss of Gerald and Agnes, it witnesses the birth of a redemptive hero; the "mystic rose" scene marks his baptism at its shores. By this point, however, the "stream" has already swelled into a river coursing to the sea of procreation, which denotes the transmission of life from one generation to the next. Rickie's flawed genetic code, manifest in the death of his crippled daughter, has removed him from this living stream ("'Let me die out,'" he murmurs [251]). It is Stephen who "would contribute to the stream; he, through his remote posterity, might be mingled with the unknown sea" (192). Thus Stephen alone, from his position in the stream, witnesses the course of the "mystic rose" beyond the bridge, "burning as if it would burn for ever." The novel's initial river of innocence has expanded into the sea of life and death for Stephen and Rickie.

Forster's postlude (Chapter 35) suggests that his model for closure may have been the final scene of Wagner's *Götterdämmerung.* Every listener perceives in Wagner's peroration a grand concatenation of reminiscences that collapses time and space in a cohesive moment—the essence of Forster's elusive "difficult rhythm." Forster's postlude rejoins Stephen several years later as a shrewd and competent farmer with wife and daughter; he is negotiating the posthumous publication of Rickie's stories. The future of England depends on such as Stephen, who has redeemed some measure of meaning for Rickie's life. The "ring-doves" are silent; Stephen's nameless wife, kept firmly "in line," is heard but not seen; the train-whistle sounds. Sweet peas, shattered knees, the Demeter of Cnidus, Herbert Pembroke's wish to reenact Hagen's stabbing of Siegfried, the outline of the Cadbury Rings, and the "rivulet that would in time bring its waters to the sea." One after another, these and the novel's other motifs sound in a "glittering web of counterpoint"—fitting words gleaned from Henderson's description of the close of the *Ring*.[66] Yet unlike Wagner's heroic resolution to *Götterdämmerung*, which in Henderson's words "knits for us the substance of the long tragedy into a perfect texture of poetry," Forster's final web of images is fractured. The shards of Stephen's life will not hold together. "'What am I to do?'" (289), he asks. His one recourse is simply to live and love the child who carries on his mother's name.

The Longest Journey is Forster's bold experiment in translating to the novel the symbolic depth and structural innovations of Wagner's *Ring*. As has been shown, the trajectory of Forster's Wagnerism in this novel points both backward and forward in time. His symbolism draws on the associations of decadent Wagnerism of the 1890s to motivate Rickie's tragedy. His structural use of the leitmotif, however, looks forward to the modernist novels of D. H. Lawrence, Virginia Woolf, and even James Joyce. Forster's purpose may have been to harness the alleged structural capacities of the leitmotif, as touted by Wagner and his English supporters, to promote unity in a large-scale and symbolically diffuse work. In this he may have overlooked the claims of Wagner's many detractors that the music dramas beginning with the *Ring* suffered from the very same alleged weaknesses that have been attributed to *The Longest Journey*: obscurity, formlessness, and excessive reliance on repeating motifs. At the very end, the Wagnerian structural ploy compromises the unity of *The Longest Journey,* pointing it toward modernist dissociation. That it met with mixed critical approval may explain Forster's retreat to a more controlled use of Wagnerian methods in his later novels.

Yet the finest moments in *The Longest Journey* soar like music itself. Rickie, himself a writer of fiction, was surely echoing Forster when he voiced envy for Wagner's medium: "'I can't soar; I can only indicate. That's where the musicians have the pull, for music has wings, and when she says "Tristan" and he says "Isolde" you are on the heights at once'" (141). Perhaps the novel soars too high. It is a difficult book, and like Virginia Woolf's Wagnerian fantasia, *The Waves* (1931), it requires multiple readings in order to hear its internal music. Perhaps *The Longest Journey* asks more of a reader than is justified. It is a scholar's book, meriting its dedication to the *Fratribus*. It is ultimately a musician's book, behind which hovers Richard Wagner, a goading spirit of "anti-literature" who served Forster as willful accomplice in its creation.

4

"New Woman" or "Piano Girl"

Lucy's Music in *A Room with a View*

She has marked the kingdom of this world,
how full it is of wealth, and beauty, and war—a radiant
crust, built around the central fires, spinning
towards the receding heavens.

—*RV*, 60

Forster's attitude toward *A Room with a View* (1908) was always slighting. Yet to the end of his life he retained affection for its heroine Lucy Honeychurch.[1] Forster made his Lucy an amateur pianist and a true musician whose abilities and conservative tastes duplicated his own, to become the only female character among his favorites in his own fiction (*CB*, 204). Like him, she values Beethoven's music and plays his piano sonata Op. 111 with insight, if not flawless accuracy. She has little enthusiasm for the piano music of Schumann or Mozart, has attended Gluck's *Armide* at Covent Garden, and knows Wagner's *Parsifal.* Although "no dazzling *exécutante,*" who like Forster "struck no more right notes than was suitable for one of her age and situation" (50), Lucy has the instincts of a serious pianist. Forster would return to her in his retrospective "A View without a Room" (1958), to reveal that Lucy would continue playing the piano and become a music teacher, and would even perform Beethoven on the radio during World War II.[2] At this point, however, she is merely an attractive girl with "a very pretty, pale, undeveloped face" (52) and a tendency to drift off into silence the moment a conversation turns to deeper things. Understandably, the critics who discount the musical content of the novel have also been hard on Lucy, dismissing her as "a two-dimensional heroine"[3] or "an average specimen of her kind—unoriginal, pretty and 'nice,' with second-hand opinions and borrowed enthusiasms."[4] Music rounds out her character and serves as a sounding narrator for the inarticulate girl, revealing her secret motives and self-deceptions, even when she appears unaware of them herself.[5] In *A Room with a View,* Forster revisits the genre of Anglo-Italian social comedy of *Where Angels Fear to Tread,* eschewing the Wagnerian heavy artillery of *The Longest Journey* for a medley of musical allusions with a serious social program. Lucy's piano becomes the battleground for her fate—and for that of modern woman at turn-of-century, striving for possession of the "kingdom of this world."

Lucy has undergone the standard Victorian rite of "girling at the piano." As recently discussed by Ruth A. Solie, Delia Da Sousa Correa, Jodi Lustig, Mary Burgan, and others, the piano had served generations of nineteenth-century girls and their parents as a rite of passage into decently socialized womanhood.[6] Playing the piano well enough to execute sentimental piano pieces or glittering salon etudes, waltzes or Turkish marches, and simple song accompaniments, was expected of any marriageable girl in an upwardly mobile family. Besides its function in courtship rituals, the piano was an agent of domestic harmony for harried fathers and rough-edged brothers, while developing in girls the virtues of industry, docility, and feminine grace. It also provided a sanctioned outlet for female self-expression and sexuality—within limits. To transcend them opened the Victorian woman and her male listener to the dangers of promiscuity and hysteria, a dire idée fixe for Victorian domestic manuals and pulp literature.

By these standards, Lucy's musical education has not been a success. At the novel's outset, she has been packed off on an Italian tour with her strait-laced maiden aunt, Charlotte Bartlett, presumably to ward off the inclinations that Lucy has been acting out at the piano. We learn from the voice of orthodoxy, the curate Mr. Beebe, that she had had the temerity to play the first movement of Beethoven's Sonata in C minor, Op. 111 at a rural church social. Her bold repertoire, redolent of "heavy winds, and vast panoramas," and other such unladylike "big things," signals her aspirations to the ranks of the "New Woman" (*RV,* 60). The term was coined in the late nineteenth century with reference to the ascendant breed of educated, sexually aware, and socially mobile women who were challenging the Victorian status quo.[7] But Lucy's liberation is only half-realized. At the start of the novel she occupies an uncomfortable middle ground between the conventional "piano girl" and the "new woman" represented by emerging female artist-musicians such as Clara Schumann, Ilona Eibenschütz, and Fanny Davies. Her challenge will not be to achieve professional status as a pianist, however, but to adapt her musical heroism to the daily life of a middle-class woman.

Lucy's educational process founders in the socially and emotionally charged world of courtship. As she navigates competing suitors and her own sexuality armed only with her musical skills, she slips progressively from her initial promise into a state of muddled, sterile convention. Lucy's musical choices and the social venues in which she plays them chart this downward course from aspiring New Woman to Victorian "piano girl." In Part One, her playing of a heroic Beethoven sonata in Florence situates her in a masculine domain and frames her brush with passion and death in the Piazza Signoria. In the context of Italian travel literature discussed in Chapter 2, Lucy's Beethoven also injects Germanic art into her Italian trip, marking her as a conventional English tourist immured in her dominant culture. Symptomatic of English taste at the time, Italian music is absent from the novel. The scene of George Emerson's first kiss in a field of violets over Fiesole is suffused with pastoral conceits suggestive of Beethoven's song "Adelaide," Op. 46. The heroic Beethoven falls from her repertoire in Part Two, following Lucy's rejection of George for a wealthy aesthete, Cecil Vyse. Romantic character-pieces by Robert Schumann, performed in an urban drawing room "with no view" (125), mark their inauspicious engagement. Easy operatic arrangements of Wagner and Gluck, played in a domestic setting, precede George's second kiss and Lucy's decision to end her engagement with Cecil. She accompanies her flight into celibacy with "tinkling" at Mozart's piano sonatas (198), with their aura of the girlhood schoolroom. Her nadir plays out in a Victorian setting to Lucy Ashton's song from Walter Scott's *The Bride of Lammermoor.* Yet Lucy's last-minute elopement with George restores her heroic potential, and distant echoes of Beethoven's last sonata accompany the newlyweds in Florence.

As depicted in *A Room with a View,* Lucy's piano-playing undercuts Victorian social conventions. It has become a liability to her feminine socialization, a distinct problem in a financially strapped and fatherless home. Her family finds nothing extraordinary in her playing (144). Her high-spirited, manly—and therefore unmusical—brother Freddy leaves his anatomy specimens lying on her piano (101) and kicks it vicariously at the news of her engagement to Cecil (104). Mrs. Honeychurch "disapproved of music" as a source of domestic discord, "declaring that it always left her daughter peevish, unpractical and touchy" (61). For Aunt Charlotte it is a mark of Lucy's narcissism, prompting the acid remark in the wake of the failed engagement: "'Lucy can always play'" (203).

The reader experiences Lucy's music exclusively by way of her three male listeners, Mr. Beebe, Cecil Vyse, and the intrusive narrator, who mirror Forster's interests. In the ideology of the time, their musicality helps identify them as veiled homosexuals and social outsiders whose marital potential is limited. Without their testimony, however, the reader would have no inkling of Lucy's musical ability or the untapped potential that it indicates. Mr. Emerson probably never hears her playing, and has only her comment that it is a "hobby," like Freddy's stamp collecting, by which to judge her commitment (48). Nor does music play a role in her relationship with George, who hears only a few faltering measures of Wagner's Flower Maidens' Song before she shuts the piano (174). And when Lucy tries to explain what music means to her, she gets no further than "'Music—'" before admitting defeat (52). In times of confusion she degrades it to "the employment of a child" (94, 175) or denies its sensual hold ("She liked music, but how much better tennis seemed. How much better to run about in comfortable clothes than to sit at the piano and feel girt under the arms" [175]).

Yet the narrator knows that for Lucy, music occupies a transcendent, wordless, and emphatically *masculine* realm that has little to do with manners, class, or courtship: "The commonplace person begins to play, and shoots into the empyrean without effort, whilst we look up, marvelling how *he* has escaped us, and thinking how we could worship *him* and love *him*, would *he* but translate *his* visions into human words, and *his* experiences into human actions. Perhaps *he* cannot; certainly *he* does not, or does so very seldom. Lucy had done so never" (50; emphases mine). Her playing is both self-absorbed and self-pleasuring rather than directed toward the male eye: "Like every true performer, she was intoxicated by the mere feel of the notes: they were fingers caressing her own; and by touch, not by sound alone, did she come to her desire" (51).[8] Lucy's admission that she liked her own playing best ("'Of course, I didn't mean that I played well'") is the insight of an active musician more concerned with the music itself than with its effect on a listener (52).

For all its centrality, the musical component was a relatively late addition to the novel. The earliest draft of 1901–2, now dubbed "Old Lucy," has her simply as an accompanist (*LN*, 8). Set exclusively in Italy, it revolves around a fund-raising concert for the English church in Florence, at which Lucy *Beringer* is a lowly accompanist. It is the novel's *hero* who is to play the solo at "The Concert," a telling detail at a time when male amateur pianists were rare and sexually suspect.[9] He downgrades Lucy's accompanying as a waste of time: "I shouldn't say you liked sitting in the drawing room most of the day and playing accompaniments to tenth rate songs" (*LN*, 45). The "New Lucy" draft, begun in December 1903 and abandoned a year later, is set in England. Although the Emersons and an identifiably homosexual Mr. Beebe appear in this version,[10] Lucy is no longer a musician. The musical symbolism reentered the project when Forster resumed the novel as *A Room with a View* in June 1907, arguably in response to his vivid exploration of musical allusion in the two previous novels.

"'Too much Beethoven'"

Beethoven dominates the first part of the novel and establishes Lucy's heroic potential. In this Forster was following a long-standing literary tradition, beginning with Lucy Audley in Mary Elizabeth Braddon's *Lady Audley's Secret* (1862), of placing Beethoven's music in the repertoire of rebellious, independent-spirited woman.[11] In Chapter 3, Mr. Beebe recalls the details of Lucy's earlier performance of the opening movement of Beethoven's Sonata Op. 111, as he again listens to her playing Beethoven in the Pension's parlor. His accurate recall of her church performance reveals close acquaintance with the sonata: "He was in suspense all through the introduction [*Maestoso,* mm. 1–16; see Ex. 3], for not until the pace quickens [at *Allegro con brio ed appassionato,* m. 17] does one know what the performer intends. With the roar of the opening theme [m. 19] he knew that things were going extraordinarily; in the chords that herald the conclusion [mm. 146–9; see Ex. 4 later in this chapter] he heard the hammer-strokes of victory. He was glad that she only played the first movement, for he could have paid no attention to the winding intricacies of the measure of nine-sixteen" [the second, final movement] (51).

At its close, Mr. Beebe had begun a manly round of "stamping" in a physical show of admiration, for Lucy "loved to play on the side of Victory. Victory of what and over what—that is more than the words of daily life can tell us. But that some sonatas of Beethoven are written tragic no one can gainsay; yet they can triumph or despair as the player decides, and Lucy had decided that they should triumph" (50). Together with the Beethoven work that Lucy played on the Pension piano, her music provokes Mr. Beebe's heady challenge: "'If Miss Honeychurch ever takes to live as she plays, it will be very exciting—both for us and for her'" (52). Lucy's Beethoven has primed her for easy moral victory in the novel.

One can imagine Forster's glee in having the Sonata Op. 111, among Beethoven's most difficult and profound works, share the stage of a country variety show with "the ladies and gentlemen of the parish," who "sang, or recited, or imitated the drawing of a champagne-cork" (51). In condemning the "sheer perversity" of Lucy's selection, the parish vicar had reflected both Victorian attitudes toward late Beethoven and Lucy's probable alienation of her rural audience. Even Mr. Beebe had expected the unidentified "Beethoven" listed on the program to be a piano arrangement favored by

Ex. 3. Beethoven, Sonata in C minor, Op. 111/i (Leipzig: Breitkopf & Härtel, c. 1865), mm. 1–22

marriageable girls, such as "*Adelaide* or the march of *The Ruins of Athens*" (51). Of these "Adelaide," a song to a pastoral text by Friedrich von Matthisson set to music in 1795–6, would have been an ideal feminine emblem, with its gentle, flowing rhythms, simple harmony, and Italianate melody. Although numerous piano solo and four-hand arrangements of the song existed,[12] Mr. Beebe's mention of a German art song without singer is curious, and may hint at unfinished business to come.

"Lucy never knew her desires so clearly as after music" (60). Irony prevails, however, when she steps out into Florence without a chaperone to Mr. Beebe's "'Too much Beethoven'" (59). Immediately, the tragedy in the Piazza Signoria transforms her in a manner suggesting a sexual awakening, a symbolic defloration, and a rebirth.[13] She faints into George's arms, and he throws her bloodstained print of Botticelli's *Birth of Venus* into the Arno. The river "roars" its response, suggesting "some unexpected melody to her ears" (66)—perhaps the "roaring victory" of her Op. 111.[14] On her return, Mr. Beebe's limp refrain "'Too much Beethoven'" (67) both reduces him in the reader's estimation and echoes the common Victorian correlation of passionate music and hysteria. Lucy awakens the next morning to an Arno like "a lion" (68), presumably roaring its melody of the previous night. Thus Beethoven frames this scene and emerges with increasing subtlety—and in combination with the currents of the Arno—to form an important motif in the novel.[15]

Lucy's Beethoven episode provides an ideal outlet for her frustrated yearning for freedom and other "strange desires" that Forster's narrator ascribes to the "modern woman" (60). It situates her in the empowering, sexually charged world of "wild, primal emotions that stretch out into the infinite," which Wagner had glimpsed in Beethoven's music.[16] It is also a *man's* world, over which Beethoven held sway as the musical paragon of masculinity for the turn-of-century listener.[17] Forster speaks eloquently about who Lucy *is* by associating her with Beethoven's last piano sonata, still rarely played in public recitals in 1908.[18] It was the last in the line of C-minor works that had forged the myth of defiant opposition to fate that was central to the "heroic" Beethoven.[19] In fact, Wilhelm von Lenz considered Op. 111 to be the piano equivalent of that paradigm of heroism, the Fifth Symphony.[20] For many musically literate readers at the time, a Beethoven work in C minor would be redolent of storm, battlefield, and all the trappings of epic resistance. Lucy's performance of the sonata Op. 111 marks her as a woman of substance holding her own in a man's musical world.

The first movement of the sonata is Promethean in its technical challenges, noted in almost all early reviews. A. B. Marx's fictive reviewer in the *Berliner Allgemeine musikalische Zeitung* (1824) was unable to play it.[21] The range is large, with quick shifts across the span of the keyboard, often with hand crossings advantageous to a woman's décolleté (the five-and-a-half-octave displacement at m. 115 is famous). Its spacious textures require of the pianist an erect posture with the chest open and exposed. It calls for a strong, flexible hand capable of spanning a minor tenth, accurately placing accented, disjunct chords, and maintaining relaxation during loud rotary patterns. The transcendental demands of Beethoven's late style—the octave chains, orchestral tremolos, large chords, and extended trills—are intensified by a relentless *fugato* texture that demands strength and athleticism. Lucy would have been hard-pressed to maintain a ladylike demeanor during her performance. Its formidable *musical* demands pose, however, the ultimate challenge. Beethoven dedicated the sonata to the Archduke Rudolph of Austria, his royal patron, student, and insightful interpreter. The 1823 review in the Berlin *Zeitung für Theater und Musik* identifies its ideal interpreters as "*denkende Spieler*"—players who can *think*.[22] Its rugged difficulty would seem predestined for the male performer of Forster's generation. As Edward Dannreuther observed in 1876, Beethoven's sonatas "call forth the men" to rise to the genius of their male creator, "no matter at what extravagant cost of time and labour."[23]

Forster's account of Lucy's performance focuses on two areas of the first movement, the *Maestoso* slow introduction and the spacious close of its coda. The opening gesture of the sonata (see Ex. 3 earlier in this chapter, m. 1) is both a musical and a physical emblem of daring in its double-dotted octaves played unassisted by the left hand.[24] The ensuing diminished-seventh chords are a fistful, and recur throughout the movement. In the continuation (mm. 5–10), the performer faces the challenges of chromatic linear counterpoint in contrary motion, numerous accidentals, and rhythmic and metric complications (its structural chords are placed on beat 2, with further rhythmic obfuscation of double-dotting). Once the home dominant is reached in m. 11, tension is further enhanced by the offbeat *sforzando* [*sfp*] accents in mm. 11 and 13, while the dissonant pitch clusters in mm. 12 and 14 (beat 4) dismayed an early English reviewer as a "crudity" attributable to the composer's deafness.[25] As the low left-hand trill enters in a *pianissimo* that is hard to control in this range (m. 16), it builds up intensity through a tricky tempo shift at m. 17, which must have the effect of a slight enhancement of pace.

Here, as the opening theme emerges from the "roaring" trill, Lucy's "magnificent" performance begins its excursion from "tragedy" to "triumph." To be triumphant, Lucy's performance would have needed to sustain the musical tension unbroken through the rest of the movement to its victorious resolution in mm. 146–9, which Forster singled out for special comment. This arresting passage (seen in Ex. 4) juxtaposes the three diminished chords in their original order and pitch, but placed now over a *tonic* C-pedal. They resolve through the major and minor subdominant to the movement's ultimate goal of C *major*, which is reinforced by an extended plagal cadence with minor coloration (iv-I) that almost effects a modulation to F minor (mm. 150–5). One easily forgets, however, that the close of Lucy's performance is not the end of Beethoven's Op. 111; nor is it a conventional tonal ending. The cadence places a diminished chord (vii°7) over a tonic pedal and subdominant minor harmony (m. 156), resolving directly to C major without recourse to the cadential dominant. The effect defers definitive tonal resolution of the first movement to the final measures of the magnificent *Arietta: Adagio molto semplice e cantabile* finale, making them an indissoluble pair.

Mr. Beebe's relief at having been spared the *Arietta* variation movement, which for most listeners is the prize, is puzzling. There is a long herme-

Ex. 4. Beethoven, Sonata in C minor, Op. 111/i, mm. 146–58

neutic tradition of interpreting the two-movement form of Op. 111 as a Hegelian synthesis of opposing forces, variously described as "resistance and submission" (Lenz), "Samsara and Nirvana" (Hans von Bülow), "action and reaction" (Paul Bekker), "worldly and otherworldly" realms (Edwin Fischer), "negation" and "triumph," or "becoming and being" (Wilfrid Mellers), "masculine and feminine principles" or "animation against repose" (Alfred Brendel), "*Schreckensfanfare* and contemplative vision" (William Kinderman).[26] By isolating the first movement from the second, Lucy would have associated herself with a heady sampling of masculine metaphors, while avoiding the passive, contemplative, and "feminized" *Arietta* finale. As Sanna Pederson has concluded, "the German tradition that valorizes Beethoven's narrative of overcoming has a tradition of viewing woman as an unchanging, eternal essence, as the polar opposite of the dynamically striving and achieving man."[27] The first movement of Op. 111 is an emblem for Lucy's yearning to escape this stranglehold of the *Ewig-Weibliche* and join the ranks of the New Woman in a man's world. Yet there may be another implication to which I will return in my conclusion: Lucy was not yet ready for the *Arietta*.

Beethoven No More

Although visibly more occupied with music than courtship, Lucy attracts two proposals within several months. Both are set in the idealized *locus* of the modern pastoral lyric, and both—at least initially—are unsuccessful. Otherwise, they could hardly be more dissimilar. George's advance is impulsive, wordless, and passionate, delivered by kiss in a sexually charged field of waving violets that "ran down in rivulets and streams and cataracts, irrigating the hillside with blue" (89). Lucy appears to the waiting George "as one who had fallen out of heaven," descending with "radiant joy in her face" from the empyrean to which Beethoven alone had previously granted her access. By contrast Cecil's second proposal of three occurs offstage and in hindsight, and is couched "in bald, traditional language" on the "margin of Italy, among the flower-clad Alps" (108). Both suitors had had the misfortune of choosing for their advances the very landscape of Beethoven's "Adelaide," present in the novel by its pointed exclusion from Lucy's repertoire as a musical relic of the Victorian past.

Beethoven's lyrical song resonates with the dangers that George's passion and Cecil's aestheticism would have represented to a young woman struggling to test her wings. Matthisson's swain wanders alone in a garden in springtime, bathed in a gentle, magical light that trembles among the swaying flowers.

The wind murmurs in the grasses, carrying with it the roar of distant waves. He sees his beloved's image "in the glittering cataracts and Alpine snow" and muses on the violet that will one day spring from his grave, each of its petals bearing her name. Yet he seems more bewitched with visions of his death than with the prospect of living with the real Adelaide. "Adelaide" is a male fantasy that objectifies the woman in an idealized pastoral tableau and reduces her to a projection of his artistic imagination. In the context of the emerging women's movement, the song projects the male "desire to govern a woman" (186) while bathing her image in beauty—the very matter of Cecil's intentions.

Although a brilliant catch by conventional standards, Cecil is a "feudal" aesthete bent on molding Lucy into a "Leonardesque" work of art, by teaching her Italian and plying her with ideas and "solid literature." He prizes her playing, in spite of its troublesome "Michelangelesque" greatness, as a manifestation of her mystery (107) and charm (173). Lucy's prime allure for Cecil is as a narcissistic reflection of self and adornment in a life devoted to culture and leisure. When he addresses her with the opening lines of Tennyson's "Come down, O maid, from yonder mountain height" (119), he places Lucy at the heart of his own pastoral idyll, while betraying an uncanny intuition of her very real scene among the violets:

> For Love is of the valley, come thou down
> And find him; by the happy threshold, he,
> Or hand in hand with Plenty in the maize,
> Or red with spirted purple of the vats[.][28]

Lucy's acceptance of Cecil's third proposal marks her capitulation to the regressive social forces of the romantic pastoral lyric.

Her initial rejection of the passionate, uncouth George, a Liberal and social outsider, is far more complex. "Too much Beethoven" would seem to have prepared Lucy for one such as him. It is tempting to conclude that, given her musical courage, she has simply not yet learned to "live as she plays." This is indeed Mr. Beebe's "pet theory" about Lucy, which he expounds with unwitting irony to Cecil moments before the announcement of the engagement: "'Does it seem reasonable that she should play so wonderfully, and live so quietly? I suspect that one day she will be wonderful in both. Her watertight compartments will break down, and music and life will mingle. Then we shall have her heroically good, heroically bad—too heroic, perhaps, to be good or bad'" (111). What Lucy herself cannot yet acknowledge is that George, while reenacting the motions of Victorian courtship, is offering her a new kind of equality in love (187). Rejecting his offer relegates the Beethovenian "'heroes—gods'" to "'the nonsense of schoolgirls'" (93). She will play Beethoven no more.

"'Schumann was the thing'"

By Chapter 11, set in London in Mrs. Vyse's "well-appointed flat," the project to overhaul Lucy in Cecil's image is under way. Her playing remains one of the few behavioral areas under her control. Accordingly, at a party of leisured "grandchildren of famous people" (141) she defies Cecil and plays Schumann. "'Now some Beethoven,' called Cecil, when the querulous beauty of the music had died. She shook her head and played Schumann again." Later, Cecil comments to his mother how "'wonderful'" Lucy's music has always been: "'How she kept to Schumann when, like an idiot, I wanted Beethoven. Schumann was right for this evening. Schumann was the thing'" (142). Still blind to Lucy's essence, Cecil had missed the wordless critique of his social circle embedded in her choice. Forster himself did not have much affinity for Schumann at the time. In March 1905 he had written to R. C. Trevelyan that Schumann was "a young person whom I don't yet take to. He isn't a tune and he isn't a noise, and I do like music to be one or the other" (L: T212). Implied is its vacillation between the lyric and heroic (the "tune" and the "noise"), reflected in the Eusebius-Florestan split between Schumann's introverted and extroverted musical personae.[29] Lucy apparently agreed, serving up Schumann to the languid assembly, who "launched into enthusiasms only to collapse gracefully, and pick oneself up amid sympathetic laughter" (141).

Although Lucy's Schumann piece is unidentified, Forster has provided rather specific indications of its contents: "The melody rose, unprofitably magical. It broke; it was resumed broken, not marching once from the cradle to the grave. The sadness of the incomplete—the sadness that is often Life, but should never be Art[30]—throbbed in its disjected phrases, and made the nerves of the audience throb. Not thus had she played on the little draped piano at the Bertolini, and 'Too much Schumann' was not the remark that Mr. Beebe had passed to himself when she returned" (141). Lucy had intuited that a piece lacking melodic continuity, harmonic resolution, and the ability to inspire courageous acts was just "'the thing'" for this audience. The effect arouses her listeners without delivering the ethical satisfaction of a resolution. The implication is that the work is an introverted, Eusebius-like piece and a "romantic fragment" in the sense defined by Charles Rosen, a circular piece without clear beginning or end, "an emblem of unsatisfied desire, of longing eternally renewed."[31]

"Warum?" from Schumann's *Fantasiestücke*, Op. 12, virtually replicates the details of the narrator's description (see Ex. 5). Its opening melody, harmonized by a dissonant applied dominant chord rather than the expected tonic triad, is no more fitting as a beginning than as an ending (cf. mm. 13–6). This melancholy gesture weaves ceaselessly and without issue through the piece, making "the nerves of the audience throb" with its unsettled, syncopated pulse. The second half sets up the expectation of an arrival by way of its increasing harmonic, dynamic, and rhetorical insistence (mm. 17–30). Yet the promised emphatic arrival dissolves into a *ritardando* and a soft return to the quizzical opening theme, its resolving E-flat7 chord undercut by a mysterious A-flat downbeat (m. 31; cf. also m. 13). The questioning theme returns repeatedly at its original pitch in the short reprise (mm. 31–42), but the piece does not cadence. Its final measures (39–42) recall the opening gesture (from mm. 1–4) before doubling back to the beginning of the second half for the repeat. In the absence of a more conclusive second ending, "Warum?" remains open-ended, the pianist seemingly enticed into infinite repetitions of its unanswered question.

Echoes from the Garden

In Chapter 15, Lucy's "disaster within" is again marked by music. From the upper-class urban drawing room and the sophisticated character-piece, Lucy now descends into the middle-class suburban milieu of feminized, domestic music-making, with two competing suitors in tow. She embraces the amateur piano arrangements that she had once avoided. Her pale performance fails by the standards of the marriage market, however, leaving her unattractively red-faced and awkward, her family bored and her fiancé irritated. The scene follows directly on a vision at the lunch table when, in the last breath of her childhood, Lucy's family and her pastoral Eden of Windy Corner stand transfixed in an eternal, golden present (173). After the meal, they ask her to play. Her choice is an ideal response to her epiphany at the table, "the music of the enchanted garden" from Act 2, scene 3 of Gluck's opera *Armide*,[32] "to which Renaud approaches, beneath the light of an eternal dawn, the music that never gains, never wanes, but ripples for ever like the tideless seas of fairyland" (173). With its chaste melody, pristine harmony, murmuring accompaniment, and aura of timeless repose, "Plus j'observe ces lieux" is a classic expression of the pastoral mode. Lucy had attended a Covent Garden production in French "that year" (173), probably with Cecil.[33] Her playing of the work "from memory" betrays repeated exposure, probably in an arrangement such as Friedrich Brissler's widely available piano-vocal transcription

Ex. 5. Schumann, "Warum?" from *Fantasiestücke,* Op. 12, ed. Clara Schumann (Leipzig: Breitkopf & Härtel, 1879)

(Ex. 6). Forster himself must have played it sufficiently to know that "such music is not for the piano" (173). Much of the beauty of the original comes of its ravishing orchestration for a quintet of woodwinds over muted strings,[34] considerably dulled in the piano reduction. Lucy's listeners grow "restive," finding the piece as soporific as did Renaud (he falls asleep during the extended postlude, mm. 108–26).

a. Mm. 1-24.

b. Mm. 108-26.

Ex. 6. Gluck, from Act 2, scene 3 of *Armide,* arr. Friedrich Brissler (Leipzig: Peters, 1882?): (a) instrumental introduction, mm. 1–24; (b) instrumental postlude, mm. 108–26

"Plus j'observe" fails Lucy as instrument of domestic concord, as vehicle of pianism, and as communication of erotic intent, but succeeds brilliantly as expression of her emotional state. Her memories of George's pastoral-lyric kiss in the field of waving violets converge in its text:

> Les plus aimables fleurs et le plus doux zéphyr
> Parfument l'air qu'on y respire.
> Non, je ne puis quitter des rivages si beaux:
> Un son harmonieux se mêle au bruit des eaux.
>
> (The fairest flowers and the softest breeze perfume the air that one there breathes. No, I cannot leave such beautiful shores: a harmonious sound mingles with the murmuring streams.)

Renaud's imagined imperviousness to Armide's charms finds its parallel in Lucy's bravado in the face of George's arrival mid-performance. Both Renaud and Lucy prove vulnerable to repressed sexuality, in spite of their armor (for Renaud, his thirst for "la gloire"; for Lucy, her engagement to a "fastidious" medieval saint [106] from whom she will expect few unrestrained advances). Lucy may have also resonated with Armide's own battle with forbidden love ("Faut-il que malgré moi tu règnes dans mon coeur?," the latter exclaims in Act 3, scene 1). Lucy's Gluck is a *private* performance responsive to her secret longings but unsuited to its social function.

"Cecil, sharing the discontent, called out: 'Now play us the other garden—the one in *Parsifal*'" (173), indicating the Flower Maidens' Song from Act 2 ("Komm'! Komm'! Holder Knabe!").[35] He has indeed upped the stakes: unlike Gluck's rococo garden, Wagner's is a topiary Venusberg heavy with late-romantic sexual guilt. And unlike Armide's spell, which will evaporate in the blinking of an eye when two of Renaud's cronies return to knock a little soldierly sense into him (Act 4, scene 3), Kundry's is powerful and ghastly, her punishment for sexual transgression an unspeakable wound. Lucy resolutely ignores Cecil's command and shuts the piano. Her burst of "undutiful" defiance rued, however, she looks up only to see that George has entered. Attempting to mask her confusion at the piano, she fixes on Wagner, intent on offering Cecil "the *Parsifal,* and anything else that he liked." She botches its opening measures and again closes the piano; at that, Freddy proposes tennis, "disgusted at the scrappy entertainment" (174).

Cecil's self-assured request suggests that they had attended one of the many concert performances of *Parsifal* (in 1907 the fully staged work was still the exclusive property of Bayreuth, but the concert version, which included the Flower Maidens' Song, was regularly performed in London). The Schott piano-vocal score, with English text by Margaret H. Glynn and simplified piano part by Liszt's student Karl Klindworth, was available in London after 1902, issued there by Novello.[36] If Lucy had attended a performance with Cecil, the latter's zeal to "improve" her might have led to some discussion of the Flower Maidens, especially given Cecil's affectation since his engagement of "a cosmopolitan naughtiness which he was far from possessing" (116).

Wagner's Flower Maidens, both the six soloists and the female choristers, had evolved since the first production of *Parsifal* into prime images of female sexuality. In January 1881 Wagner had commissioned singer Lilli Lehmann to help him find six female singers "of the highest quality, with similar voice and range, but also comely and slender, well-formed women" [hübsche schlank gewachsene Frauenzimmer], as well as at least "12 or 16 young, pretty [hübsche] female choristers of the highest quality."[37] He repeated his specifications to Ludwig II in September: "I require six [female soloists] with beautiful, matching high voices and the appropriate physical appeal" [das erforderliche angenehme Äußere].[38] Issues of Lehmann's success aside, the photograph of his first cast (Fig. 6) reflects Wagner's results. Though demure by today's standards, their costumes would have been daring in 1882, with swelling hips accentuated by fluttering petals that, cut to the knee, reveal bare legs and feet. Among them is Carrie Pringle, the pretty English soprano whose flirtations with Wagner caused Cosima great jealousy, and over whom the Wagners argued violently on the morning of Richard's fatal heart attack.[39] Encircling Parsifal in a tangle of exposed limbs, they create a *tableau vivant* of nymphomania. With that first performance, Wagner's Maidens entered the expanding iconography of woman as "flower of evil" at the fin de siècle. Although written in response to other predatory flower-women, Bram Dijkstra's perfervid "nightmare vision of woman as a palpitating mass of petals reaching for the male in order to encompass him, calling to him to be drained by her pistils yearning for fertilization," seems tailor-made for Wagner's maidens.[40]

In calling for Wagner's garden, Cecil may have been sharing with Lucy a naughty reference that would have been lost on the others. She is annoyed. Perhaps the Gluck has left her in a romantic reverie, making Wagner's heavily charged sexuality repugnant. Perhaps Lucy is resisting Cecil's invitation to join ranks with other Victorian literary "sirens at the piano," manipulative beauties such as Blanche Ingram from Charlotte Brontë's *Jane Eyre* (1847) or Rosamond Vincy from George Eliot's *Middlemarch* (1871–72), whose music lures men into ruinous marriages.[41] Wagner's garden also sadly underscores the gap between its rich sensuality and Cecil's repressed aestheticism, which

Fig. 6. Wagner's Flower Maidens with Parsifal (Hermann Winkelmann) in the 1882 Bayreuth production (courtesy of the Nationalarchiv der Richard-Wagner-Stiftung, Bayreuth [N1851-II])

John Lucas identifies as the essential problem in their relationship.[42] Lucy's stumbling performance is perhaps the most revealing detail, especially if she were playing from the Klindworth arrangement. She would have to have been confused indeed to bungle the elementary opening measures (Ex. 7), when we know that she could keep her head during a performance of Beethoven's Op. 111. Forster knew his *Parsifal,* and would surely have known that the Flower Maidens' words could have overwhelmed Lucy as soon as she began playing in George's presence: "Come! Come! Dear boy! / Come! Come! Let me blossom for you! / Dear boy! For your delight and refreshment / I offer my loving care!" Before our eyes, Lucy's garden of pastoral bliss is transmuting into a dark Eden about to be lost.

Ex. 7. “Flower Maidens’ Song” from Act 2 of Wagner’s *Parsifal,* arr. Karl Klindworth (Mainz: Schott, 1902), mm. 1–21

That night Lucy ends her engagement on the pretext that Cecil is an aesthete who wraps himself up “‘in art and books and music, and would try to wrap up me’” (192). Too late she has become for him “a living woman, with mysteries and forces of her own, with qualities that even eluded art” (191). Now it is Lucy who hides behind words, protesting that she “‘won’t be stifled, not by the most glorious music, for people are more glorious’” (192). Lest her manifesto be misinterpreted as an emancipation from art, it conceals more than a trace of duplicity. The problem for Lucy is not aesthetic but ethical, and her betrayal of music leaves her ravaged: “She gave up trying to understand herself, and joined the vast armies of the benighted, who follow neither the heart nor the brain, and march to their destiny by catchwords. . . . They have sinned against passion and truth” (194). The Wagnerite will hear a faint echo of the closing lines of the Flower Maidens’ Song: “If you cannot love and cherish us, we will fade and die thereby.”

"Easy live and quiet die"

The next morning finds Lucy “tinkling at a Mozart sonata” when Mr. Beebe enters (198). “‘How delicate those sonatas are!’ said Mr. Beebe, though, at the bottom of his heart, he thought them silly little things. Lucy passed into

Schumann" (200). She soon hatches her escape to Greece with the elderly Misses Alan, after which she returns to her "tinkling of a Mozart sonata" (203). The weather turns stormy as Mr. Beebe leaves, relegating Lucy to her Mozart after having abandoned Mrs. Honeychurch to her ravaged dahlias with the telling aside: "'It is terrible, this havoc among the flowers'" (199).

Although paired with the ambiguous Schumann, Mozart's piano sonatas emerge more negatively still. As seen in Chapter 1, Forster was no great admirer of Mozart; in this perspective, he and Mr. Beebe reflect English opinion of the time. C. F. Pohl's Mozart article, translated with additions by W. H. Hadow in the 1907 edition of *Grove's Dictionary,* dispatches Mozart's solo piano music in a few dismissive phrases as "thoroughly suited to the instrument—grateful, and for the present state of technique, easy." Hubert Parry's dismissal of Mozart in the same source as "not naturally a man of deep feeling or intellectuality" would not have endeared the composer to Forster.[43] Still many years from their rehabilitation by Artur Schnabel, Dame Myra Hess, and Clara Haskil, Mozart's piano sonatas were nothing more than scenes from childhood for many in 1907.

On Mr. Beebe's return toward evening, he is surprised to find Lucy singing a song that Cecil had given her, Lucy Ashton's song of renunciation from Scott's *The Bride of Lammermoor.* Forster interpolates its text throughout the scene (208–9):

> Look not thou on beauty's charming,
> Sit thou still when kings are arming,
> Taste not when the wine-cup glistens,
> Speak not when the people listens,
> Stop thine ear against the singer,
> From the red gold keep thy finger,
> Vacant heart, and hand, and eye,
> Easy live and quiet die.

Forster's Lucy shares much with her namesake. The latter's "Look not thou" is deemed "particularly adapted to her character," notably her "peace of mind, serenity, and indifference to the tinsel of worldly pleasure."[44] Yet appearances are deceptive for Scott's Lucy, for "left to the impulse of her own taste and feeling, [she] was peculiarly accessible to those of a romantic cast." Her romantic inclinations emerge in her life-and-death struggle to marry Edgar of Ravenswood. Lucy Ashton's capitulation to her parents' desire to see her married to a competing suitor "rich enough to supply her with every comfort" has tragic consequences. On the day of her marriage to Bucklaw Hayston (who is as awkward with women as Cecil), Lucy stabs her bridegroom and dies in a fit of insanity. This very scene in Donizetti's operatic setting had served Forster as the passionate musical centerpiece of *Where Angels Fear to Tread;* in *A Room with a View,* it warns against betraying one's heart for material security.

Donizetti's operatic libretto does not include this song text. In Lucy's stage of repressed, suburban English conformism the heady, sexualized, and dangerously foreign world of Donizetti's *Lucia* would have been a jarring note. Oliver Stallybrass has located one musical setting of Scott's text by Sir Henry Bishop (1786–1855), the composer of "Home, Sweet Home" (*RV,* 253–4). Hailed by his contemporaries as "the English Mozart," Bishop was a hugely prolific commercial composer of songs and operatic arrangements for domestic use. His star had set by 1902, when J. A. Fuller Maitland tartly dismissed his "so-called operas" in which "the low taste of the public was pandered to in each and all of them."[45] "Lucy Ashton's Song" places our Lucy in a Victorian setting, singing and playing for her family and the visiting curate.[46] A gift from Cecil, the song summarily dismisses the pursuits of the New Woman in the "kingdom of this world" with its "wealth, and beauty, and war," for a stultifying convention.

"A love more mysterious"

Lucy's stunning reversal in marrying George saves her, and fulfills Mr. Beebe's prediction of "living as she plays." Her "watertight compartments" have broken; music and life have come together. She chooses the hard path of the modern woman with her lower-middle-class man, the path predicted by her playing of Beethoven's Op. 111 and obscured by her regressive forays into the world of the Victorian piano girl. In choosing George, she forfeits Windy Corner and alienates her family and Mr. Beebe. Lucy's triumphant nonconformism will persist, if we are to believe Forster's plans for her in the 1958 essay "A View without a Room": she and George will become conscientious objectors during World War I, when she expresses her political stance by again playing Beethoven, bringing the police to her door for pro-German activities.

Literary scholars have voiced concern about the credibility of the novel's sudden conclusion,[47] especially the curious transformative power of the kiss from Mr. Emerson senior: "He gave her a sense of deities reconciled, a feeling that, in gaining the man she loved, she would gain something for the whole world." As Lucy would say in later years, "'It was as if he had made her see the whole of everything at once'" (225). Its timeless synthesis suggests the essence of "difficult rhythm." The effect is a harbinger of the hard-won goal in *Howards End,* "to see life steadily and to see it whole" (*HE-D,* 63, 148). Yet

Lucy seems to have attained this wisdom by osmosis rather than by spiritual toil, and from the lips of a character given to pompous proselytizing. Nevertheless, by the closing sentences of *A Room with a View,* something intangible but fulfilling has indeed happened, something more momentous than a marriage and return to Florence. The "Room" of the title has somehow been reconciled with its "View,"[48] and with it the rich interplay of dialectical oppositions in the novel: "Youth enwrapped them; the song of Phaethon announced passion requited, love attained. But they were conscious of a love more mysterious than this. The song died away; they heard the river, bearing down the snows of winter into the Mediterranean" (230).

It is a magical coda filled with sound. As the lovers yield to their passion, the song of a Florentine driver announces Lucy's personal fulfillment of "gaining the man she loved," while the transcendent roar of the Arno proclaims in its "love more mysterious" something "for the whole world," something that bears an unworldly burden of "deities reconciled."[49] Is the roar of Beethoven's Op. 111 concealed beneath the water's course? And if so, which part of the sonata would convey the palpable resolution delivered in the closing lines of the novel? The end of the first movement, as seen above, had failed to achieve the closure of a definitive dominant-tonic cadence. This pattern of cadential evasion continues throughout the entire *Arietta* second movement, in spite of the emphatic falling fourths and fifths and tonic-dominant fixation of its theme. The theme and each of its variations end on a tonic (I) chord with the *third* degree of the tonic scale in the upper voice, making for an *imperfect* authentic cadence that presses forward.[50] Full resolution is avoided until the closing measures of the movement (Ex. 8), where the music descends from the glacial heights of its high trills to attain its final resting point in the piano's low register. There the rising fourths that invert the falling fourths of the *Arietta* theme deliver the definitive dominant-tonic perfect cadence withheld since the end of the first movement.

Ex. 8. Beethoven, Sonata in C minor, Op. 111/ii, mm. 174–7

In married bliss, Lucy has at last claimed the right to the sonata as a whole. If distant echoes of Op. 111 murmur in the river's final course, it would appear that Forster may have sought a firm closure for this, his most intractable novel, in Beethoven's haunting conclusion to his final sonata. Yet Forster's repeated misgivings about its anachronistic resolution in conventional marriage led him to doubt the artistry of *A Room with a View* in the rapidly changing world of 1908. That year in Vienna, Arnold Schönberg's controversial String Quartet No. 2, with its atonal "air from a different planet," called into question the system of tonality on which Beethoven's sonata depends.

5

Not Listening to Beethoven and Brahms at the Queen's Hall

Music as Vision in *Howards End*

Only connect . . .

Forster's famous epigraph to *Howards End* has provided generous fuel for debate in the century of critical response since its 1910 publication. In his fourth novel, Forster turned from Wagner's music drama, as explored in *The Longest Journey*, to the classical tradition of Beethoven and Brahms as his primary musical model of internal logic. Yet R. A. Scott-James's early assessment of it as a "*connected* novel"[1] has proven the minority position. Virginia Woolf's 1927 critique established the dissenting view that since then has rippled through the steady waves of criticism on the novel. For Woolf, the "baffling and evasive" nature of Forster's literary gifts undercuts the "cohesion" of *Howards End,* promoting an ambiguous disconnection between its realist and visionary impulses.[2] Woolf's guarded assessment of the novel has gradually turned to Forster's benefit, its "rich ambiguity . . . [and] fundamental *irresolution*" now widely viewed as a bracing modernist challenge rather than the mere by-product of authorial muddle.[3] Regardless of theoretical perspective, the literature on *Howards End* since 1975 agrees on little else but its grand failure to "only connect . . ."[4] In his virtuoso essay for the *Cambridge Companion to E. M. Forster* (2007), David Bradshaw has summarized this position in concluding that *Howards End* "spotlights not the sturdiness of Forster's liberal values, but their relative frailty. Patently a novel of contrasts, *Howards End* is no less fundamentally a novel of contradictions" (171).

In *Howards End* Forster's music serves a broader social program than that of *A Room with a View.* Fundamental to its many contradictions is the crisis within the Edwardian middle class over "who shall inherit England" at a time when its traditional owners—the Liberals of the Victorian past—are "being dispossessed."[5] The contest for ownership plays out in the fifth chapter of the novel, the Sunday Concert at the Queen's Hall featuring Beethoven's Fifth Symphony and Johannes Brahms's *Four Serious Songs* (*Vier ernste Gesänge*, Op. 121). Beethoven's symphony, renowned as a masterpiece of musical integration, and Brahms's song cycle, with its dialectical progression from despair to hope, provide fitting musical analogies to the "connected" life for Forster's concert-goers. How they listen—or do *not* listen—to the music will help determine their inheritance in a prewar England up for grabs.

The dialectic of opposition in *Howards End* begins with its cast of characters. The Schlegel siblings, Margaret (age 29 at the start of the novel), Helen (21), and Tibby (16) are upper-middle-class gentlefolk, offspring of an English mother and an idealistic German father who had fled Bismarck's Germany when he was almost forty. The women dominate their ineffectual brother Tibby, who languishes in the woodwork of their comfortable life. They are holdouts of Victorian liberalism—literate, mildly Socialist, and musical, and make it a point to hear Beethoven's Fifth almost every time it is performed (*HE-D*, 111).[6] The sisters are devoted to "human relations" and the life of the mind, a trait inherited from their intellectual father (who was identified in an early draft as "a distant relation of the great critic"[7]). They are divided in their ways of living and loving: Margaret's is realistic "prose" and Helen's, visionary "romance." At the other end of the spectrum are the Wilcoxes, a powerful family of parvenu businessmen attached to the Imperial and West African Rubber Company. Successful venture capitalists such as the Wilcoxes may have been the backbone of the British Empire, but they are woefully inadequate in their dealings with people, especially the lower classes. One such is Leonard Bast, a struggling clerk clinging to the bottom rung of the middle class by a tattered umbrella. Leonard will be destroyed by his aspirations to art, learning, and romance, with an added push from the Wilcoxes. The Wilcox family has little place for books or music and is dominated by its men, led by the forceful Henry. His wife Ruth, by contrast, is gentle, artistic, and retiring (and promptly dies). Her legacy is her country home, Howards End, which becomes the focal point for the traditional rural England threatened by the imperialist forces of men and money (or of "panic and emptiness," as Helen is wont to say). Henry's eventual marriage to Margaret will provide an opportunity for connecting the families there.[8]

Forster's concert cunningly reflects the social layers of *Howards End*. The Sunday Concert at the Queen's Hall was a cultural meeting place for up to three thousand of the middling classes in Edwardian London. The immensely popular series was the brainchild of Henry J. Wood, conductor of the Queen's

Hall Orchestra. The concerts took place every Sunday at 3:30 from October to May, and offered a mixed program of symphonic music, concerti, and vocal excerpts at a price attractive to music-lovers of modest means. The presence of the Schlegels at the Sunday Concert (rather than the more exclusive Saturday Afternoon Concerts of the Queen's Hall Orchestra) reflects both their Socialist leanings and the limits of their financial means.[9] Forster had probably attended many such Sunday Concerts there, including one in spring 1908 that may have featured the Fifth Symphony.[10] The concert program in Chapter 5 of the novel, which appears to have been crafted by Forster rather than cribbed from any specific program, is typical of the fare of the Queen's Hall Sunday Concerts in the years before 1910.[11] Its miscellaneous character, bringing together highbrow symphonic music, a German song cycle with piano, and a popular English march, is a throwback to concert programming of the mid–nineteenth century,[12] and is no different in this regard from most programs in the Sunday series at the time except in its reduced length. The Queen's Hall Sunday Concerts regularly opened with an overture and ended with another overture or a festive march. Forster's opens with an unidentified work by Felix Mendelssohn that merits a curt dismissal from Margaret (47), probably one of the three Mendelssohn overtures that were regularly programmed at the Sunday Concerts. Most likely it would have been the *Ruy Blas Overture*[13] (for what would there be not to like about the *Hebrides* or *Midsummer Night's Dream* overtures?). His program closes with "Pomp and Circumstance," one of several military marches by that most English of composers, Sir Edward Elgar.[14] The surge of British patriotism in the years following the disaster of the Boer War (1899) had found enthusiastic expression in Elgar's marches.[15] One of them was featured at least once per season at the Sunday Concerts, always to end the program. The reactions of Forster's English and German listeners suggest that he may have had in mind the first march of 1901, that paean to British imperialism to which the words of A. C. Benson's "Land of Hope and Glory" were later attached. Forster cannot avoid pecking at its chauvinism ("'Ugh!'" exclaims Margaret, while the visiting Germans flee in its wake). Elgar's march plays out the contest between England and Germany for cultural hegemony in the years before World War I.

At the heart of the program are two German masterpieces by Beethoven and Brahms. Because of the shortness of Forster's fictive program, they can be performed without the expected intermission. Beethoven's Fifth Symphony in C minor, Op. 67, a regular on Queen's Hall programs, dominates Forster's scene and the literature on it.[16] The Brahms songs, however, are underplayed in the text and overlooked in every commentary on the novel. The *Four Se-*

rious Songs for low male voice and solo piano are an unexpected entry in a populist symphonic concert, but are not without historical basis. The Queen's Hall Sunday Concert occasionally featured vocal soloists in German lieder, usually short and well-known songs such as Beethoven's "Adelaide," Schubert's "Gretchen am Spinnrade," or Richard Strauss's "Ständchen." Nevertheless, on Sunday December 15, 1907, the distinguished English baritone Frederic Austin had indeed performed Brahms's *Four Serious Songs* (in the august company of Bach's Orchestral Suite No. 3 and Schubert's "Unfinished" Symphony). As a prelude to Elgar's rousing march, however, they are perverse. The cycle was Brahms's last major work, composed in 1896 to pessimistic Biblical texts on mortality in anticipation of the impending death of Clara Schumann. The composer considered them "damnably serious," and more than once voiced concern that the police would block their publication on religious grounds.[17] Their German texts would have been incomprehensible to any but the intelligentsia and German visitors or immigrants such as the Schlegels. And no one seems to be listening: Helen leaves the concert before the songs begin, Margaret dismisses them as "'grumbling and grizzling'" (47) and retreats into daydreams about social injustice and stolen umbrellas, and Tibby is lost in the score. The specific allusions to the *Four Serious Songs* later in the novel, however, suggest that both Forster and his narrator are attentive: the songs work in tandem with Beethoven's Fifth in the struggle for spiritual ascendancy in the world of *Howards End.*

For the moment Beethoven's symphony is the focal point. Although the narrator emphasizes the power of the Fifth to speak to "all sorts and conditions" (43), Forster's six listeners are exclusively middle class, and they can barely begin talking about it without arguing (43–4). Their reactions betray the cultural, social, and gender differences that divide rather than connect people, and summarize the multiple perspectives of Beethoven reception at the beginning of the twentieth century. Forster brings his lifelong testiness toward musicologists such as Edward Dent to bear on the hapless Tibby, a lifeless aesthete who "is profoundly versed in counterpoint, and holds the full score open on his knee." Mrs. Munt (Aunt Juley) is the naive British listener who loves to tap "when the tunes come," and for whom the potboilers on the Sunday Concert programs are a welcome treat. Yet for all her dottiness, Aunt Juley has the advantage of Forster's later endorsement of love as the critic's ultimate authority.[18] Frieda Mosebach, their visiting German cousin, represents the nationalist camp: her appropriation of Beethoven as "'*echt Deutsch*'" sounds the battle cry of the new German state and its increasingly shrill exploitation of Beethoven to justify Teutonic superiority.[19] Leonard Bast is a pragmatic listener who represents prewar Socialism. Beethoven's symphonies were often featured in workers' concerts in Germany, with the goal, according to Socialist Kurt Eisner, of alleviating the "darkness and viciousness of the daily lives of the little people."[20] The English had similar projects, such as the Working Men's College where Forster taught Latin for at least twenty years, beginning in 1903; it catered to men such as Leonard, eager to improve themselves at a Beethoven concert. The uncultured Wilcoxes are absent, missing the chance to learn something about life at a Sunday concert.

This leaves the sisters, Helen and Margaret, to occupy the twin poles of Forster's own aesthetics as expressed in his essay "Not Listening to Music" of 1939 (*TCD*, 127–30). How they listen to the Fifth—as Forster's "music itself" (Margaret) or "music that reminds me of something" (Helen)—reflects the realist and visionary perspectives that the novel attempts to reconcile. Their competing positions also replay the central dilemma facing the nineteenth-century music critic, between the claims of what Eduard Hanslick called "dry technical designations" and "poetic fictions."[21] The conflict had reached its apogee in the German critical debate between the followers of Brahms and Wagner after 1880, on which the aesthetics of Forster's generation depended.[22] Margaret prizes the "absolute" music, "untrammeled and untainted by reference," that Forster would guardedly endorse in "Not Listening" (*TCD*, 129). Her perspective disconnects music from its sociopolitical context and aligns her with the aesthetics of the Brahmsian Hanslick or German music theorists such as August Halm, Ernst Kurth, and Hugo Riemann.[23] For all her fundamental agreement with Tibby's stance, Margaret resists the connection with her brother ("'He treats music as music, and oh, my goodness! He makes me angrier than anyone, simply furious'" [50]).

Forster's sympathies in both essay and novel lie with the visionary Helen. His later admission that "only a purist would condemn all visual parallels, all emotional labellings, all programmes" (*TCD*, 128) and his penchant for mixing metaphors from painting, literature, and music reveal their kinship in matters of aesthetics. Helen is a Wagnerian referentialist who imposes on the symphony a poetic narrative of heroes and goblins that resonates with her secret emotional life. Her reading of the Fifth (44–6) is well known and frequently anthologized, and needs only to be summarized. It begins after the famous first movement has already been played. She dismisses the feminized "sweetness" of the *Andante con moto* second movement for "disconnecting" the masculine "heroes and shipwrecks of the first movement from the heroes and goblins of the third," and daydreams through most of it. (Grove too had dismissed the second movement as "wanting in the spur."[24]) With the beginning of the scherzolike third movement, Helen and the narrator snap to attention. Their comments highlight the two pathbreaking musical events of the scherzo-finale pairing as identified by Grove: the connecting timpani transition between the movements, and the recall of the scherzo theme at the close of the development section of the finale.[25] They weave around Beethoven's music a metaphorical gloss based on a century of hermeneutic interpretation of the Fifth, of which Forster's major sources appear to have been E. T. A. Hoffmann's 1810 review of the Fifth Symphony, Sir George Grove's *Beethoven and His Nine Symphonies* in its third edition of 1898, and Edward Dannreuther's 1876 "Beethoven and His Works," the last of which had transmitted the ideas of Wagner's 1870 essay on Beethoven to an English audience.[26]

Helen focuses on the threatening "goblins" of the scherzo and their stubborn resistance to both humor (the trio of "elephants dancing"[27] [m. 141]) and heroism (Beethoven's titanic interventions in the transition and finale). By denying the possibility of "splendour or heroism," her goblins uncover the "panic and emptiness" in a world in which liberalism was rapidly losing ground. Beethoven enters to the beating of the drum in the transition (iii, mm. 324–73), and to the blaring "gusts of splendour" of the finale, he leads his army of "gods and demigods" in battle against the increasingly menacing hoard (iv, mm. 1–152). His initial victory is fragile: "They might return," Helen observes, "and they did." In the unexpected reprise of the scherzo theme (iv, m. 153) she hears a "terrible, ominous note and a goblin, with increased malignity, walked quietly over the universe from end to end. Panic and emptiness!" This time the "flaming ramparts of the world" threaten to fall, but Beethoven again intervenes, bolstered by symbolism culled from Wagner's *Ring*:[28] "He built the ramparts up [reentry of the timpani, iv, mm. 203–6]. He blew with his mouth for the second time, and again the goblins were scattered [recapitulation, m. 207]. He brought back the gusts of splendour, the heroism, the youth, the magnificence of life and of death, and, amid vast roarings of a superhuman joy, he led his Fifth Symphony to its conclusion."

Taken at face value, Helen's tableau appears to affirm the masculine tropes of aggression and conquest—the very metaphors she will later claim to abhor.[29] Indeed, the symphony had embodied the idea of heroic resistance to tragic fate since the famous metaphor of fate knocking at its door attributed to Beethoven by the unreliable Anton Schindler.[30] Helen's resolving victory at the end of the symphony also seems to shore up the tenets of liberal-humanism, with its trust that the moral philosopher-statesman will prevail over the forces of prejudice and violence. On a wider front, her interpretation validates the male domains of German philosophical idealism and

Hegelian dialectics. Beethoven is a logical fit with this philosophical core, for his Fifth Symphony had been cast as an embodiment of idealist epistemology in nineteenth-century German music criticism from A. B. Marx to Hugo Riemann. By their standards the Fifth Symphony had been elevated to a model of organic wholeness and internal coherence,[31] musical attributes that promote the moral ideal of the unified life to which the novel aspires.

As Forster later observed in relation to the modern novel, the "rhythms" of the Fifth are "stitched internally" by a process of "repetition plus variation," to create the proselike continuity of the "symphony as a whole" (*AN*, 164–8). At the time of its 1808 premiere, the Fifth Symphony would have appeared unprecedented to Beethoven's contemporaries in the sheer power of its dialectical argument. Although Joseph Haydn had made significant forays into cyclic coherence in a number of his symphonies beginning with the Symphony No. 45 of 1772,[32] Beethoven's Fifth was the earliest symphony to demonstrate the full potential of long-term integration, thematic recall, and end-weighted form across a multimovement work. The famous "and-Two-and-ONE" motive is obsessively present throughout the first movement [see Ex. 9 (a)], and recurs in the three subsequent movements. Significant to Helen's Fifth is its reincarnation as the "goblin" theme of the scherzo [Ex. 9 (b)], now marching in triple meter ("And-and-and-ONE"). The "goblins"

Ex. 9. Beethoven, Symphony No. 5: Cyclic recurrences of the opening rhythmic motive

recur at least once in the varied reprise of the scherzo (twice, however, in Beethoven's first version),[33] and spawn the drumbeat of the transition [Ex. 9 (c)]. Rhythm (b) recurs in diminution (shorter rhythmic values) in the second theme of the finale [at (d)], which in turn dominates the long development section (mm. 90–144). Rhythm (a) makes a last stand in the closing *Presto* of the coda [at (e)].

By dialectical standards, Helen's "vast roarings of a superhuman joy" resolve the heroic confrontations of her symphony no less definitively than does Beethoven's coda. Although the coda fills over one-third of the movement (mm. 294–444), its harmonic framework is astonishingly basic: a massively expanded three-chord cadential formula that ends with an eighty-measure *Presto* tonic prolongation studded with V-I cadences (see Ex. 10). It piles high the tonal ramparts against the resurgence of the C-minor goblins with their "drumbeat of fate." The idealist listener hears in this "absolute and unequivocal closure" a "C major that *cannot be followed.*"[34]

But Beethoven's final cadence is not the end of Helen's Fifth. The reprise of the scherzo theme in the finale opens the symphony to the potential of endless cycles of returns. If it is always possible to go back, how *can* one make an end? Helen's Fifth has a subversive after-beat: "But the goblins were there. They could return. He had said so bravely, and that is why one can trust Beethoven when he says other things" (46). Suddenly her reading expands from schoolgirl romance to modernist uncertainty, as if to say along with Forster that heroism consists in merely "eating and working and loving" and "breathing" in a world over which a flaming twilight of the gods looms.[35] Her Fifth calls into question a German idealism (or an English liberalism) that is no longer viable.[36] It is a timeless moment in which she apprehends the "difficult rhythm" of the "symphony as a whole," and hears "something that has never actually been played" (*AN*, 168). In 1810 E. T. A. Hoffmann, who had witnessed the failure of the republican ideals of the French Revolution,

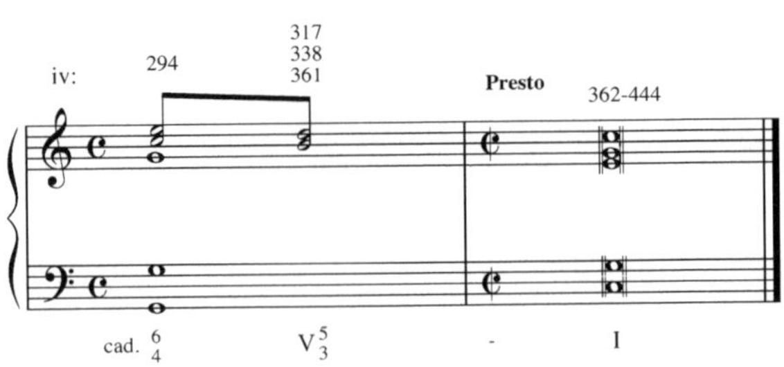

Ex. 10. Beethoven, Symphony No. 5/iv, mm. 294–444 (background)

also heard the uncanny music beyond Beethoven's closure of the Fifth: "The heart of every sensitive listener . . . is certain to be deeply stirred and held until the very last chord by *one* lasting emotion, that of nameless, haunted yearning. Indeed for many moments *after it* [my emphasis] he will be unable to emerge from the magical spirit-realm where he has been surrounded by pain and pleasure in the form of sounds."[37] *Howards End* would be rather straightforward were its philosophical base to end here. But Helen's flash of insight fails her almost immediately. Her "sloppy" and "muddled" aesthetics come under attack from Margaret, both in conversation with Leonard after the concert (50–1) and later at a luncheon party (79). And Helen flees the concert, missing Brahms's *Four Serious Songs*—surely more than a simple ploy to get her out of the theater with Leonard's umbrella.

The songs of Brahms's cycle are themselves internally divided. The first two, "Denn es gehet" and "Ich wandte mich," are settings of nihilistic texts from Ecclesiastes (3:19–22 and 4:1–3). For Helen, they would lay bare the "panic and emptiness" sown by the "goblins" of this world, against which heroic resistance is futile. Both songs gaze unblinking at the sordidness of life and the inexorability of death that ends all for man and beast alike. The third song, "O Tod, wie bitter bist du" (Ecclesiasticus, 41:1–2) reaches a nadir for the wealthy and powerful before yielding to a grim consolation that belies Helen's "magnificence of life and of death": "O death, acceptable is thy sentence unto the needy, and unto him whose strength faileth, . . . and to him that despaireth." The final song, "Wenn ich mit Menschen und mit Engelszungen" (Corinthians I, 13:1–13), is St. Paul's famous apostrophe to love as the greatest of the virtues: "Though I speak with the tongues of men and of angels, and have not love, I am become as sounding brass, or a tinkling cymbal." Its radiant B-major middle section looks beyond the visible world as seen "through a glass darkly" to the promise of an eternal moment in which, "face to face, . . . shall I know even as I am known." The triumphant E-flat coda lingers on love as the greatest of the virtues ("Aber die Liebe ist die größte unter Ihnen").

Helen's insight after the Fifth would likely have paled if confronted with the stark realism of the first three of these songs, for which she was not yet prepared. Only after she has broken with her sister and engineered the catastrophe at Oniton does Helen in effect hear their message. In Chapter 27, Forster engineers her bizarre love duet with Leonard to replay Brahms's song cycle, beginning with the "Imperial" entry of "Death" that "cries out" against wealthy and powerful oppressors like the Wilcoxes (209). "'We are all in a mist,'" she cries, before her "'panic and emptiness'" trope (206) yields to her prophetic aphorism, "'Death destroys a man; the idea of Death saves him'" (210). The latter duplicates Brahms's progression from lamentation to grim consolation in "O Tod" for those such as Leonard. Immediately, the narrator introduces the idea of Love in a move that duplicates the narrative of Brahms's final song: "Men of the world may recoil from the charnel-house that they will one day enter, but Love knows better. Death is his foe, but his peer, and in their age-long struggle the thews of Love have been strengthened, and his vision cleared, until there is no one who can stand against him." Her resolution falls short of the novel's endorsement of real-life "personal relations," however, when she uses Love to resolve the paradox of the "Visible and Invisible" in favor of the unseen (210).

The flesh is not so easily discounted. Helen's aphorism serves as prelude to her night with Leonard, which creates new life while setting the wheels of tragedy in motion. In their brief coming-together, death triumphs over love. Leonard will lie dead at Howards End in a recreation of Brahms's "O Tod": "Death alone still charmed him, with her lap of poppies, on which all men shall sleep" (272). This prophetic glimpse takes place, of course, at St. Paul's, a place of "echoes and whispers, *inaudible songs*."[38] Helen's phantom rehearing of the Brahms songs has uncovered her central failing in the moral world of this novel: her inability to hear Brahms's cycle to its conclusion, and thus to follow St. Paul through to his final paean to love. For all her talk of love, Helen sleeps with Leonard, then tries to pay him off, and finally forgets him. He dies ignorant of his unborn child, and is dispatched to the grave with relief. Hers is thus a failure to connect.[39] Margaret has already taken Helen to task for brooding on the "superiority" of vision over reality ("'of the unseen to the seen'"): "'Our business is not to contrast the two, but to reconcile them'" (102). When Margaret later confronts "Death," it is "stripped of any false romance; whatever the idea of Death may contain, the process can be trivial and hideous" (239). Margaret may have daydreamed during the Brahms at the Queen's Hall, but she has heard the realist message of its first three songs. It is the last song with its message of love that in the end will elude her as well.

For the moment Margaret emerges as the apparent moral spokesperson of *Howards End*. She heeds the call to balance reality with vision and to "see life steadily and to see it whole" (63). Although she had started out in fundamental agreement with the visionary Helen in choosing to see "modern life . . . whole" (148), her love for Henry Wilcox leads her to a truer insight: "Only connect the prose and the passion, and both will be exalted, and human love will be seen at its highest" (168). This suggests a possible completion of Forster's epigraph, whereby connection is not synthesis in the Hegelian sense, but a temporary moment of "proportion" in the dynamic flux of opposing states, "only to be found by continuous excursion into either realm" (174). Margaret's insight is a natural outgrowth, therefore, of Forster's way of listening to the "two sorts of music" that "melt into each other all the time" (*TCD*, 127).

The narrator spoils it all with his image for this balanced state as a "rainbow bridge" (167), which reverts to Helen's metaphoric response to music and life. Wagner's *Regenbogen-Brücke* is the triumphal passageway of the gods into Valhalla in Scene 4 of *Das Rheingold*. Froh enjoins the gods to "tread undaunted its terrorless path," as Wotan salutes the fortress as haven from "panic and dread" (*"vor Bang' und Grau'n"*). Again as in *The Longest Journey*, Wagnerian imagery is fraught with contradictions: Valhalla has been purchased through violence and treachery with the stolen gold of the Rhine, and the radiance of its bridge is an illusion of the trickster Loge, who foretells the fall of the gods at their moment of greatest strength.[40] "They hasten to their end," he cries, "though they think themselves enduring." Although the image bathes Margaret's vision of connection in all its radiance, the reader cannot stop his ears to the wails of the Rhine-maidens below. The power to bridge the opposing forces of the novel is challenged by this powerfully fraught symbol, prefigured by the disingenuous "Only" of the epigraph. No sooner does Margaret propose the glorious call to "live in fragments no longer" than the narrator counters with a flat: "But she failed" (168).

It is Helen's goblins that prevail, and with them her visionary way of listening to music. Their returns are heralded by the drumbeat that Tibby has more than once reminded the reader to "look out for" (45, 49). Two examples: After the concert, Leonard's artsy chat with Margaret is troubled by worries about his lost umbrella, which "persisted with the steady beat of a drum" (51). When he flees their Wickham Place drawing room without his tea, Leonard leaves behind a "goblin footfall" that remains "as a hint that all is not for the best in the best of all possible worlds" (55). As if to reinforce Helen's reading of the Fifth, the "goblins" appear forthwith in Chapter 6 in Leonard's squalid basement flat teetering above the "abyss" of poverty (55–63). Two years later, as Helen and Margaret face their impending homelessness to the mechanical "heartbeat" of London (105), Leonard's rumpled wife Jacky comes looking for him at Wickham Place, trailing behind her the "faint smell" of the "abyss," like a "goblin footfall" (110). The next day when Leonard comes to apologize for his wife's bizarre behavior, he uses the Queen's Hall "performance of the Fifth Symphony of Beethoven" (111) to remind them of his identity. The sisters' unexpected enthusiasm for his overnight "adventure" becomes for

Leonard a "permanent joy" (118), echoing the "superhuman joy" of Helen's Fifth. A "new light dawned" for him as he walked home, to the beat of "the heart of a man ticking fast in his chest" (119). The sisters' admiration leads to thoughts of philanthropy: they consult Henry Wilcox (126) and pass on his bad financial advice to Leonard (130), who loses his job. The Basts plunge over the edge of the abyss.

The most powerful allusions to Helen's mythology of the Fifth come in the second half of the novel, situated at Howards End. Again the drumbeat serves as marker. Margaret, now engaged to Henry, visits the house for the first time; thinking herself alone, she is startled by the "heart of the house beating, faintly at first, then loudly, martially." Finally their noise "seemed to deafen her" (180), in pointed reference to Beethoven's timpani transition to the triumphant finale. The theme of Margaret's finale, however, is provided by the house with its comradely wych-elm: "Their message was not of eternity, but of hope on this side of the grave. As she stood in the one, gazing at the other, truer relationships had gleamed" (183). Her symphony falls short of resolution, however, when the hope that Henry will eventually learn to connect (185) and "set his soul in order" (194) is dashed by her goblins. Helen brings the Basts uninvited to Oniton; Henry's earlier sexual relationship with Jacky is revealed (203), unmasking the "panic and emptiness" at his core (206). The morning afterward, a deflated Henry sweeps away from his estate to ironic chimes of Handel's choral march from *Judas Maccabaeus*, "See, the Conquering Hero Comes" (218). Nevertheless, the "hero and heroine" are wed, though "without the aid of music" (224).

Both heroism and music are momentarily discredited. Thus it is not a Beethovenian hero or a German symphony, but a modest English farmhouse that dominates the finale of *Howards End* and holds out the promise of salvation. There, Margaret discovers the love of place and of England, and glimpses a union of the "joys of the flesh" with "the inconceivable" (182). On her second visit, the spirit of the house teaches her to "see life steadily and see it whole, group in one vision its transitoriness and its eternal youth, connect—connect without bitterness until all men are brothers" (233). Margaret makes a temporary home for her pregnant sister there. The tools of high culture are absent: the art books remain packed away and the piano is banished to a London warehouse (254–5). Music is provided by the house itself, its "song was of the moment" and "the peace of the present" (269). It is a "gust" of feminine "splendour" from which Henry Wilcox is banished; a promised cadence, but not the end of Forster's symphony.

The goblins return for one final attack, this one couched in a knot of reminiscences comparable to the return of the scherzo in the finale of the Fifth or the close of *The Longest Journey.* In Chapter 41, Leonard approaches Howards End and his death, his diseased heart beating erratically, to a blended reprise of the Beethoven and Brahms: "Again and again must the drums tap and the goblins stalk over the universe before joy can be purged of the superficial. . . . Death destroys a man, but the idea of death saves him. . . . Squalor and tragedy can beckon to all that is great in us, and strengthen the wings of love" (276). Memory meets prophecy: yet the outcome of this moment of connection is neither splendor, nor love, nor "vast roarings of a superhuman joy," but death—a death both "trivial and hideous" at the hands of Charles Wilcox. Its meaninglessness belies the consolation of Brahms's third song: "O death, acceptable is thy sentence unto the needy, and unto him whose strength faileth." In the aftermath, logic takes on the arbitrariness of a card game (280).

Margaret assumes the role of a female Beethoven at this point, healing the chaos of their lives. Helen calls her sister "'heroic'" for having "'picked up the pieces, and made us a home'" (288). Yet the resolution of the novel is no more permanent than that of Beethoven's Fifth in Helen's interpretation. The pastoral tranquility is surface-thin, its costs high. Leonard is dead, Charles destroyed, and Jacky discarded; both Helen and Henry declare themselves "'ended'" (284, 286); even "baby" is nameless and almost genderless, his future uncertain in this house of overpowering women. A faint aura of death hangs over the pastoral idyll of Howards End, its fields studded with "red poppies" and yielding to the "scyth" (285). Henry is sealed in the house with the other Wilcoxes, preparing his will and discussing his death as if it were imminent. The still-young Margaret too has prepared her will in the knowledge that her "permanent home" is threatened by every "westerly gale" that "might blow the wych-elm down and bring the end of all things" (285). Their domestic peace rests on "the weakness of logic" (288). The final words are left to Helen, as they were in the concert. "'London's creeping,'" she observes, as she points to the "red rust" on the horizon, the goblins of urbanization advancing on their pastoral retreat.[41] To this the narrator replies: "Were they possibly the earth beating time?" In this moment, the drumbeat of Beethoven's Fifth foretells something that "has never actually been played" in symphony or novel (*AN,* 168), a new tune that will be more terrible than the present can predict. Its "difficult rhythm" touches the very future of England, its countryside and the lives of people attached to the living earth, whose time is running out. It is a close such as that of *Das Rheingold,* which contains in its triumphant procession over the Rainbow Bridge the seeds of future destruction.

"There is so often an ambiguity at the heart of Mr. Forster's novels," wrote Virginia Woolf.[42] *Howards End* ends in irresolution whichever way one defines its oppositions: as Woolf's vision and realism; as city and country, public and private (Born); masculine and feminine (Langland); liberal humanism and modernist doubt (Widdowson and Medalie). Helen and her family have not solved the dilemma of liberalism, but have withdrawn from it to a rural retreat that cannot survive the onslaught of the modern. "The bathos of the ending," as David Medalie has observed, "lies in the fact that the Schlegel sisters and their charmed circle are hiding *from* England in the house that was meant to *represent* England."[43] The novel's epigraph proves itself incapable of completion. The question that has dogged critics is whether the fog of uncertainty hanging over the conclusion of *Howards End* was intentional on Forster's part or the result of muddled nostalgia for a lost past. There are arguments on both sides, but I would agree with Medalie's cautious attribution of modernist intent to the conclusion,[44] on the basis of Forster's purposeful use of Beethoven's music in the novel. As early as Chapter 5, Helen's hostile forces of the Fifth had opened its visionary world to instability and to modernist uncertainty. In this Helen agrees with Hoffmann, for whom the closing chords of the symphony leave the listener in a state of "haunted yearning," like a "fire that is thought to have been put out but repeatedly bursts forth again in bright tongues of flame."[45] The failure of both sisters to hear the message of overpowering love in Brahms's last Serious Song also presages the emotional pallor of their family life. Although the last words of *Howards End* promise the "infectious joy" of a "crop of hay as never" (291), their future is unclear. Forster's intentional failure to connect at the Queen's Hall prepares the even frailer hope of connecting in the life that is *Howards End.*

6

Tchaikovsky and the Deflowering of Masculine Love in *Maurice*

Sometimes I feel an insane anguish, but not that kind of anguish which is the herald of a new tide of love for life: rather something hopeless, final, and—like every finale—a little commonplace.

—Peter Ilyich Tchaikovsky, 1890

By 1911 with *Howards End* newly published, Forster entered a long period of disillusion related to his increasing "weariness" with heterosexual love as the "only subject that I both can and may treat" (LD, 16 June 1911). His new novel *Arctic Summer* foundered in 1912 out of fear that it "might have ended with the two [male protagonists] as companions in defeat."[1] In May 1912 Forster picked up Modeste Tchaikovsky's biography of his brother, the composer Peter Ilyich Tchaikovsky, reading from Rosa Newmarch's abridged translation published in London in 1906.[2] He devoured it with passionate interest, finding in the composer a kindred spirit: "Tchaikovsky's life better & better. Except his petulance under criticism, there is nothing to which my heart does not go out," Forster entered in his Locked Diary on May 12. By then he had reached the account of the composer's ill-fated 1876 marriage to Antonina Milyukova in a desperate move to conceal his homosexuality: "Am come to the illness in which he longed for intimacy, felt he had known no one intimately, and so tried marriage."[3] He later returned to transcribe meaningful excerpts from letters of the composer on the blank *verso* page of the Locked Diary, facing the entries for May 4–July 21, 1912:

> I am passing through a very enigmatic stage on my road to the grave. Something strange, which I cannot understand, is going on within me. A kind of life weariness has come over me. Sometimes I feel an insane anguish, but not

> that kind of anguish which is the herald of a new tide of love for life: rather something hopeless, final, and—like every finale—a little commonplace.
>
> —Tchaikovsky, aet. 50

> My malady is misanthropy, but a peculiar form of misanthropy which certainly does not spring from hatred or contempt of mankind. People who suffer from this complaint do not fear the evil which others may bring on them, so much as the disillusionment which follows upon every intimacy.
>
> —Idem[4]

Tchaikovsky's biography and its outcries of despair and loneliness entered Forster's creative imagination in 1912, to lay in wait for apologist of "homogenic love" Edward Carpenter to set *Maurice* on its exuberant course a year later.

In September 1913, finding himself in the vicinity of Millthorpe, Forster paid several long-planned visits to Carpenter and his working-class companion, George Merrill, in their rural retreat.[5] As an advocate of Walt Whitman's "love of comrades" and the author of *Love's Coming-of-Age* (1896) and *The Intermediate Sex: A Study of Some Transitional Types of Men and Women* (1908; 3rd edition, 1912), Carpenter promoted the rugged Whitmanesque ideal of healthy masculine love in the out-of-doors.[6] Forster had read Carpenter no later than 1907 during the completion of *A Room with a View*,[7] and probably revisited *The Intermediate Sex* with absorption in conjunction with his Millthorpe visit. The latter would have provided Forster with a vigorous overview of Continental research on same-sex love in German, French, and Italian, including extensive quotations from the works of Albert Moll, Richard von Krafft-Ebing, Paul Moreau, Cesare Lombroso, K. H. Ulrichs, and others.[8] Forster also likely renewed acquaintance at this time with the writings of Carpenter's English associates in the field of sexology, John Addington Symonds (his two major inquiries into the "phenomenon of sexual inversion," *A Problem in Greek Ethics* and *A Problem in Modern Ethics*)[9] and Havelock Ellis (*Sexual Inversion*, coauthored with Symonds in its first edition of 1897).[10] Palpable echoes of Symonds and Ellis in the details and language of *Maurice* suggest more than passing influence on Forster, while the novel as a whole reads somewhat like extended psychiatric case studies of Maurice and Clive, modeled perhaps on the anonymous case study provided by Symonds himself for *Sexual Inversion*.[11]

Carpenter's personal charisma coupled with Merrill's famous touch on Forster's "backside" proved cathartic. By Forster's admission in his 1960 "Notes on Maurice," the novel was "born" then and there. But as demonstrated in Philip Gardner's documentation of the genesis of *Maurice* its labor was protracted, notwithstanding Forster's claims to the contrary.[12] The novel underwent numerous waves of revision from the first draft of 1913–14 until its completion in 1959, with posthumous publication only in 1971. These include a host of changes and additions in 1914–15 (with a new "Epilogue" added by February 1915 and removed by 1932),[13] and two fresh typescripts in 1932 and 1959, separated by additional layers of revision (the most extensive in 1920, 1952, and 1958). The closeting of *Maurice* had complex reasons—personal, legal, and artistic—but as documented repeatedly in Forster's correspondence with Christopher Isherwood between 1933 and 1952,[14] the decisive cause may have been his inability to find a satisfactory "happy ending" for the novel. "I was always determined not to end sadly," he wrote Isherwood in August 1938, but how that was to be achieved in the repressive context of England in the years before World War I eluded Forster.

Maurice is Forster's only novel to treat homosexuality openly. Maurice Hall is an "average" middle-class man unlike the author in almost every way except his exclusive sexual preference for men. He is "handsome, healthy, bodily attractive, mentally torpid, not a bad business man and rather a snob."[15] He is also utterly unmusical and compares classical music with golf (*MAU*, 105). His sheer ordinariness suited Forster's aims perfectly—to show that love and sexual fulfillment are within the reach of even the most unremarkable man if he is true to himself.[16] But Maurice's search for self-knowledge and a lifelong friend is hampered by ignorance of his sexual nature. As Alan Sinfield puts it, Maurice's difficulty is "not in coming to terms with his sexuality, but in finding out what it is."[17]

Maurice's quest for identity and community as a homosexual man nearly founders in the culture of silence and persecution surrounding the "nameless vice" in Edwardian England. Behind the novel looms the infamous Labouchere Amendment to the Criminal Law Amendment Act of 1885, which had upheld the centuries-old prohibition against all consensual sexual acts between men in public or private.[18] It was under this legislation that Oscar Wilde had been convicted in 1895 to two years of imprisonment for conspiracy to commit an "act of gross indecency with another male person."[19] The sensational press coverage of the Wilde trials and the banning of Ellis and Symonds's *Sexual Inversion* in 1898 on grounds of obscenity promoted a stranglehold on public discussion and scientific study of masculine love in England until after the First World War.[20] According to Carpenter, the resounding silence around the topic of homosexuality brought considerable suffering and even physical illness to many young "inverts" bereft of any "hint of guidance," thus "leading to the most painful misunderstandings, and perversions and confusions of mind."[21] *Maurice* provides a vivid literary illustration of Carpenter's impassioned appeal for broad-minded education concerning all manifestations of human sexuality.[22]

Although a Cambridge graduate, Maurice is a spotty reader, and lacks the social contacts and intellectual sophistication that could have exposed him to the growing body of Continental and American research in the emerging field of sexology. His thoughts and actions in the novel betray not the slightest evidence of contact with the writings of the English sexologists Carpenter, Symonds, and Ellis, or with the poetry of Walt Whitman that had inspired all three (especially his "Calamus" poems). Unlike his well-read creator, Maurice sails through his young manhood with Plato's *Symposium* and Howard Pyle's *The Merry Adventures of Robin Hood* as his sole literary guides to masculine love. He accordingly appeals to a series of unreliable authorities on sexual behavior: a Hellenic aesthete, a Wildean dandy, a crusty old family doctor, and an American-trained psychoanalyst. His greatest help comes from an unlikely source—a biography of a composer and known homosexual, Peter Ilyich Tchaikovsky, following a concert featuring his Sixth Symphony in B minor of 1893, the "Pathétique." The specific details of the account in Chapter 32 leave no doubt that the volume in question can be none other than Modeste Tchaikovsky's biography of his brother.

For Robert K. Martin, *Maurice* is a rite of passage through three stages to homosexual enlightenment: the Victorian ideal of platonic restraint promoted by Symonds; physical gratification and lust; and the higher truth of healthy, rustic "masculine love" as represented by Whitman and Carpenter.[23] I would argue rather that the novel strives to transcend these turn-of-century homosexual ideologies for a modern, realistic connection of two "ordinary affectionate men" on which the happy ending essential to Forster would depend.[24] To this end, Tchaikovsky and his Pathétique Symphony served Forster as *negative* models of masculine love and emblems of old ways to be rejected before Maurice can attain emotional and sexual maturity. That the ending of the novel defies easy resolution owes much to the "difficult rhythm" of its Tchaikovskian symbolism and the problematic reception of his Sixth Symphony in Edwardian England.

As superbly documented by Philip Gardner in *MAU-A*, the Tchaikovsky references in *Maurice* stem without exception from the earliest stage of the novel (1913–14) and were retained without further revision. They serve to date this layer to the pre-1914 period—the apex of Tchaikovsky's posthumous fame in England. By that time the composer's homosexuality was public knowledge. Russia ranked with England as one of the most homophobic cultures at the time. The rumors about Tchaikovsky's sexual life that had been circulating in his homeland by the mid-1870s had likely reached the London homosexual community as early as the composer's widely publicized two-week tour to London and Cambridge in 1893.[25] Contemporary English biographies of the composer tread gingerly around the issue of his sexuality, resorting at most to encoded hints—none more pernicious than James Huneker's characterization of the composer's "psychopathic temperament" and the selective "pathological" nature of his music in his 1899 essay on Tchaikovsky.[26] Carpenter himself had identified the composer as a "thorough-going Uranian" in *The Intermediate Sex* (111). Yet Newmarch's translation of Modeste Tchaikovsky's biography would be the first published source to bring candid information on the composer's sexuality and his relationship with his nephew "Bob" to the English-speaking reader.[27]

On artistic grounds the Pathétique Symphony was an obvious choice for the background music to *Maurice*. Within several years of the composer's sudden death in 1893, mere days after the premiere of his Pathétique Symphony, Tchaikovsky's reputation in London had skyrocketed from a secondary artist of moderate interest to the third most performed composer after Beethoven and Wagner. His Sixth Symphony bore the brunt of this posthumous fame. Acknowledged as his masterpiece, glamorized by the mystery of its unspecified program and the rumors of its composer's lifestyle and death, the Pathétique was played into the ground in the decade following its sensational London premiere in February 1894. It was featured there several times a season, and became a centerpiece for resident and visiting conductors. By 1898 the London critics were already decrying the "barbarous doing to death of this splendid *opus summum* of the great Russian, and the consequent utter neglect of so many other masterpieces."[28]

Forster would have had ample opportunity to hear this immensely popular symphony in concert. Pertinent to the novel, however, is the performance that he attended in Manchester on February 21, 1907 (L: F414). It was conducted by one of its most acclaimed interpreters, Hans Richter, whose Pathétique was celebrated for its "barbaric splendour and passion."[29] At the time Forster was visiting his friend and fellow Kingsman H. O. (Hugh) Meredith, who had accepted an academic position in Manchester in 1905 and had married Christabel Iles the following year. Meredith is widely acknowledged as the inspiration for Clive Durham. He and Forster had shared a similar romance at Cambridge beginning in winter 1902–3. As Forster later recounted to P. N. Furbank, "it was not a physical relationship, or at least went no further than kisses and embraces. This was by mutual agreement." The connection with Meredith had been momentous for Forster, who felt "as if all the 'greatness' of the world had been opened up to him."[30] The further parallels with the novel extend to Meredith's subsequent marriage and his disappointing transformation into a "jolly old boy" who adamantly rejected Forster's novel when shown an early draft in 1914.[31] The Manchester performance may provide a personal key to Forster's association of the Pathétique Symphony with Maurice's failed platonic relationship with Clive Durham.

In the first part of the novel, the Pathétique Symphony furnishes the sound image for Edwardian Cambridge and for what Robert K. Martin calls its "false vision of an idealised homosexuality."[32] There, Clive imposes on the naive and grateful Maurice a sexless union of souls modeled on the love of Socrates and Phaedo, a "love passionate but temperate, such as only finer natures can understand . . . a narrow and beautiful path, high above either abyss" (91). Clive's textbook is palpable: Symonds's *A Problem in Greek Ethics.*[33] Forster's own experience of "Greek love" as Cambridge undergraduate and Apostle gives this segment of the novel its easy conviction noted by most early readers of the manuscript (except Meredith). Dated as well is its coded metaphoric language of homosexuality associated with prewar England, with its "land through the looking-glass" peopled by Theban bands, Merry Men, Ganymedes, "children of light," and "unspeakables of the Oscar Wilde sort." One such unspeakable is Risley, an upper-class Trinity undergraduate who has perfected to the point of caricature the exaggerated speech, effeminate mannerisms, and gamboling gait of a Wildean dandy (Risley was modeled after the openly gay Lytton Strachey, who recognized himself "gleefully" on reading the novel).[34] Risley also "adored music" (32) in a context in which being "musical" was tantamount to an admission of homosexuality.[35] Yet Risley has one huge advantage over Clive and Maurice: he is informed in matters of sexuality. As Alan Sinfield observes, Risley "does know how to be queer."[36]

Wanting to see this "queer fish" again (36), Maurice calls on him at Trinity. Instead he finds Clive, who blushes at being discovered in the room of a flagrant "invert." The awkward and inhibited Clive is rooting through Risley's collection of pianola rolls looking for the "Pathetic Symphony," and exploits its covert symbolism to disclose his sexual interest and sound out Maurice, but to no avail. The symphony and its unidentified composer mean "nothing" to Maurice, who does not even know its popular "March" movement. Clive accordingly downplays his musical knowledge in a gesture of intimacy:

> "So you like this style of music." [Maurice says]
> "I do."
> "A good waltz is more my style."
> "Mine too," said Durham, meeting his eye (38).

Forster's revision of the original "walk" to "waltz" in the 1914 typescript (*MAU-A*, 230) prepares a meaningful detail in the next scene.

Maurice overcomes his indifference to classical music to attend a late-night gathering with Clive, toting the pianola rolls of the Tchaikovsky—minus its March, missing from Risley's collection.[37] Clive's friends are surprised to find Maurice in the artsy group around Fetherstonhaugh's pianola back at King's. The sole reported conversational topic—music—and the valuable player-piano place them in the upper-class aesthetic set, in contrast to the awkward, sexually naive, and suburban Maurice. It also dates the scene to the prewar period, the heyday of pianola culture. *Pianola* was a trademark of the Aeolian Company, a London subsidiary of the New York–based firm that specialized in self-playing pianos.[38] Forster may well have had in mind an upright *Orchestrelle* of the type illustrated in a lavish spread in the London *Graphic* in January 1914[39] (see Fig. 7). This illustration places the instrument at the center of a gay tableau of social privilege, rife with innuendo aimed at readers of varied sexual persuasion. The roll mechanism is in action, while an elegant female player sits at the expression bar, locking eyes with a rapt woman at her feet. Her left finger is poised on the sustaining pedal slider, while thumb and index finger of that hand operate the split treble-bass levers that adjust volume. Her unseen right hand would be activating the slider controlling tempo nuance.[40] Piano virtuosity is a common tool of seduction in turn-of-century English homoerotic novels.[41] In this light, Clive's courtship at a mechanical instrument for a musical novice is superbly ironic.

Clive is positioned at the keyboard, while Maurice kneels at his side in a position favoring the amatory over the acoustic. Clive chooses a movement (the first?), but then shifts to "the 5/4" second movement to please Maurice ("'It's nearer waltzes,'" Clive observes, in response to Forster's revision to the previous scene). Maurice listens carefully, and finds that he "rather liked it" (39). Bret Keeling aptly observes that the waltzlike second movement, "played out of sequence, becomes a means for Clive to teach Maurice not about the aesthetics of musical appreciation but about the ritual of cloaked homosexual courtship."[42] Yet Keeling's interpretation of the 5/4 movement as a cockeyed waltz for "two left feet" that reflects Maurice's physical awkwardness and Clive's sexual clumsiness overlooks its sophisticated metrical process. The

Fig. 7. Around the Pianola, published in *The Graphic* [London], 10 January 1914, p. 75 (McPherson Library, University of Victoria)

consummate grace in motion of this *Allegro con grazia* is the result of balanced two-measure pairs (see Ex. 11). The triplet turn on beat three of each alternate measure creates a rhythmic center of gravity that reverses the melodic incline, while the liberal articulation markings and dynamics enhance the flow. The effect is that of a Viennese waltz with two upbeats in each measure (and-and-ONE-two-three) and all the tempo hesitations written in. The metrical instability of the movement (the implied 2/4 + 3/4 meter in

Ex. 11. Tchaikovsky, Symphony No. 6/ii, *Allegro con grazia* (London: Eulenburg, n.d.), mm. 1–4

each measure) poses a subtle challenge to social harmony concealed under a polished surface—creating a symmetry of asymmetry.

When Clive refuses to repeat the "jolly" second movement at Maurice's request, he argues that "'a movement isn't like a separate piece—you can't repeat it.'" Instead of returning to the first movement, however, Clive skips—in the absence of the March—to the "Largo" finale [*Adagio lamentoso*]. The scene in Risley's room had emphasized the absence of the populist and militaristic March, which in early recorded performances closes with a grand *rallentando* that evokes a staid colonial majesty.[43] This hypermasculine movement would have been no calling card for a pallid aesthete such as Clive, and its aura of king (or tsar) and empire would be ill suited to a clandestine—and illegal—tryst. Yet Clive's choice of the symphony's finale as a courtship ploy is curious.

It seems to have displeased Maurice as well, being "far from jolly." The first movement would have been a more fitting signifier of erotic intent: it would have afforded several hearings of the "tender, singing, and expansive" *Andante* second theme, the soaring lyricism, suggestive hesitations, and throbbing dynamic shifts of which make it the most erotically loaded segment of the symphony (see Ex. 12). Forster's musical readers would have remembered the sensuous string slides (or *portamentos*) and languorous tempo fluctuations common to early orchestral interpretations of this theme by conductors such as Oskar Fried and Willem Mengelberg.

By contrast, the "Pathétique" finale had consistently been overlaid with programs of morbidity and death from the time of its premiere, including a reading of it as a "suicide" to the "stroke of tam tam" and a burial "with much growling of double-basses" in an 1899 London review.[44] Newmarch's memorable words in her 1910 *Grove's Dictionary* article (47) interpret it as "'une lamentation large et souffrance inconnue'" that "ponders one of the great preoccupations of all ages—the impenetrable mystery of death and futility of all human speculation." Its coda creates one of the most effective *morendo* closes in the symphonic literature, dying away to a whisper to the faltering pulse of the contrabass (iv, mm. 147–71). Clive appears not to have considered its morbid symbolism, which also escapes the unmusical Maurice. The latter leaves the evening heart aglow, "never to be quenched again" (41). The musical reader, however, is forewarned: the finale of the Pathétique predicts the failure of Clive's asceticism for its denial of the life force.

Their romance founders in Part Two of the novel, when Clive suppresses homosexual desire for a sterile marriage. The pathway of idealized "Greek love" comes to a dead end for both. Clive's faulty sexual education, ostensibly limited to Plato, Symonds's *A Problem in Greek Ethics*, and a smattering of Whitman,[45] leaves him ignorant of the anguish depicted in Ellis's case

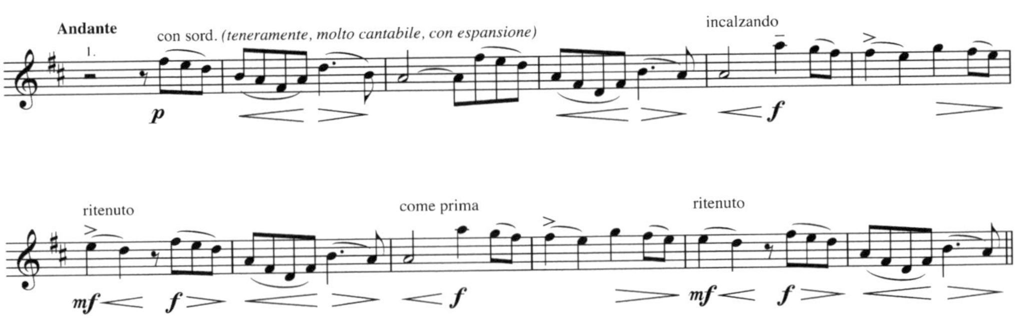

Ex. 12. Tchaikovsky, Symphony No. 6/i, mm. 89–100 (violin 1)

studies of "disastrous" marriages of convenience among homosexual men in *Sexual Inversion,* most notably that of Symonds himself.[46] Had he read Carpenter, Clive would have encountered Krafft-Ebing's warning that such marriages often remain "a cause of suffering to the end."[47] Had he read Tchaikovsky's biography, Clive would have encountered the dire consequences of the composer's marriage that had so impressed Forster. Clive's neurasthenic fit of sobbing and fainting on taking leave of Maurice (94–6) also reveals Forster's likely acquaintance with psychiatric accounts, although both Clive and Maurice remain clueless as to its import.

Part Three finds Maurice abandoned by a newlywed Clive and prey to the demons of lust and loneliness. He explores the routes to physical gratification open to him in 1914: pederasty, masturbation, and a marriage of convenience. His flirtation with pederasty occurs when he comes close to seducing Dr. Barry's young nephew, Dickie, in the novel's closest brush with pornography.[48] When he becomes suicidal, Maurice seeks medical help for his still nameless condition ("'I'm an unspeakable of the Oscar Wilde sort,'" he cries [139]). Forster's account of the meetings with Drs. Jowitt, Barry, and Lasker Jones is based in accurate medical information probably culled from Ellis and Carpenter. Young Jowitt's recent medical training had exposed him to the "degeneration theory" of Krafft-Ebing's *Psychopathia Sexualis,* which had reduced homosexuality to a mental illness relegated to the "asylum."[49] Old Dr. Barry has predictably "read no scientific works on Maurice's subject" because none existed in England when he was trained, "and any published since were in German, and therefore suspect" (140). He dispenses the standard prescription of Victorian doctors in such cases: marry and forget the whole "rubbish."[50]

So Maurice sets out to woo Violet Tonks at a concert date (141). The program conspires against them, for it features the Pathétique Symphony that "Clive had taught him to like." Afterward in the lobby he meets Risley, who "gaily" informs "his young friend that Tchaikovsky had fallen in love with his own nephew, and dedicated his masterpiece to him" (141). Risley had come to the concert primarily to see "'all respectable London'" flocking to a work memorializing a pederastic love: "'Isn't it *supreme!*'" Maurice affects shock at Risley's "'Symphonie Incestueuse et Pathique'" ("pathic" refers to a "man or a boy . . . upon whom sodomy is practised"[51]). He nonetheless follows up "at once" on Risley's recommendation of a biography of the composer.

The symphony had provided Maurice sensual enjoyment, but the Tchaikovsky-Newmarch biography reveals a kindred spirit. Maurice, like Forster, is arrested by the account of the composer's marriage, which "conveys little to the normal reader, who vaguely assumes incompatibility, but it thrilled Maurice. He knew what the disaster meant and how near Dr Barry had dragged him to it." What he would have gleaned from Modeste's description of the marriage as an "insane step" and a "terrible crisis which nearly proved fatal to [my brother's] existence"[52] temporarily deters Maurice from marriage-as-escape. He shifts his attention to the love of the composer for his adolescent nephew: "Reading on, he made the acquaintance of 'Bob', the wonderful nephew to whom Tchaikovsky turns after the breakdown, and in whom is his spiritual and musical resurrection." Modeste's description of his brother's relationship with Vladimir ("Bob") Davydov, though circumspect, suggests a shared "Greek" affection: "Tchaikovsky preferred the companionship of his nephew; was always grieved to part with him; confided to him his innermost thoughts." Modeste also cites correspondence that betrays greater warmth, none more than these words in Peter Ilyich's letter from Berlin of 8 (20) March 1891: "Bob, I idolise you! Do you remember how I once told you that the happiness your presence gave me was nothing compared to all I suffered in your absence? Away from home, with the prospect of long weeks and months apart, I feel the full meaning of my affection for you."[53] English readers may have shared Risley's detection of more than familial ties.

Maurice's appreciation of Bob seems to prescribe a similar course: the Uranian love of beautiful adolescents such as Dickie Barry. Yet again he is repelled by the Tchaikovskian solution. Forster explained in a letter of March 1915 to Forrest Reid: "Boys—you'll have seen by now why these get ruled out by me. No permanent relation to them, except as a memory, is possible, and Maurice can't live on memories" (L: R87). While the biography proves "the one literary work that had ever helped him" (141), in the end it only exacerbates his "despair." He accepts an invitation to Penge, where Clive's stale crumbs send him running to a psychiatrist.

Lasker Jones diagnoses his condition as "'congenital homosexuality'" (158), condemning Maurice to the pathology of illness current in prewar scientific discourse on sexual inversion. Lasker Jones was modeled perhaps on Dr. C. Lloyd Tuckey, an advocate of hypnosis as a "cure" for homosexuality whose *Psycho Therapeutics, or Treatment by Hypnotism and Suggestion* had reached a 4th edition in London in 1900.[54] His failure to alter Maurice's sexual inclinations, in spite of his exaggerated claims of a fifty percent success rate in cases of his type, reflects the poor prognosis for this procedure documented in many medical studies of the time. Havelock Ellis for one had rejected the efficacy of hypnosis in the treatment of homosexuality in the second edition of his *Sexual Inversion* (Philadelphia, 1901).[55] In his despair, Maurice announces his determination to marry the first woman who will have him, in spite of the desperate example of Tchaikovsky and Antonina Milyukova.

Maurice's terrified regression following the Tchaikovsky concert is disproportionate to the events of Chapter 32. Nor can it be explained by anything he might have read in Modeste Tchaikovsky's biography, which closes with the traditional account of his brother's death of cholera days after the premiere of his Sixth Symphony.[56] The underlying cause for alarm may have been the rumors of Tchaikovsky's suicide that had begun circulating in Russia and abroad almost immediately after his death, and the popular association of the Pathétique Symphony—and homosexuality—with his demise. Forster may have also heard of Bob Davydov's suicide in 1906.[57] Even the reticent Newmarch refers obliquely to the rumors about Tchaikovsky's death in her 1910 *Grove's* article.[58] The recent debate over how Tchaikovsky died is not at issue,[59] but rather the widespread rumors of suicide connected with the composer's homosexuality. By 1914 the web of homophobic supposition may have deterred Forster from elevating Tchaikovsky's symphony and his relationship with his nephew into a viable path for Maurice.

The resolution comes in the final part of the novel, where sexual "restlessness" and the symphony associated with it help propel Maurice into the arms of Alec Scudder, a gamekeeper on Clive's estate of Penge. Alec is a noble savage at home in the out-of-doors, far from the university rooms, business offices, and concert halls of Maurice's experience. Musical metaphors are abandoned in the direct, unadorned prose of their love scenes, completed for the most part in the 1950s following work on the *Billy Budd* libretto. By then the world of the English homosexual was changing, although it would not be until 1967 that the Sexual Offences Act would lift the injunction on private homosexual acts between consulting adults. The evolving drafts of the Alec-Maurice scenes across the forty-six-year genesis of the novel reveal a progressive loosening of the bygone ideologies of Whitman, Symonds, and Carpenter in favor of a natural, realistic connection of two "ordinary affectionate men." Forster's own life experience surely left its mark on the rough tenderness of the Alec-Maurice dialogue in the hotel room of Chapter 44, drafted in January-February 1952 (*MAU-A*, xli). If influence is at work, it may be that of Britten's 1950 revisions to the dialogue between Vere and Billy in the Cabin scene of *Billy Budd* (Act 3, scene 2, as discussed in Chapter 8). As if to bolster the *Budd* connection, the same chapter includes a veiled quotation from Claggart's Act 1 apostrophe to Billy ("A find in a thousand, your honour, a beauty, a jewel, the pearl of great price"), now applied to Alec ("a treasure, a charmer, a find in a thousand, the longed-for dream" [200]). Moreover, the short coda to Chapter 45 in which Maurice and Alec meet back at the Penge boathouse, written in 1958, convinces by its prosaic flatness where high-flying ideology and musical metaphor would not. Forster's last-written words of the chapter—and of the writing process of *Maurice*—are given to Alec: "'And now we shan't be parted no more, and that's finished.'"[60] This would have made a stirring close for the novel, with its heroic echo of Whitman's "I will go with him I love, It is to be enough for us that we are together—We never separate again."[61]

Yet by 1932 Forster had decided firmly that the novel must end, not here with the lovers, but with Maurice's bitter farewell to Clive. With minor revisions, the text of the final Chapter 46 reverts to the primal 1914 layer, with its echoes of past ideologies (*MAU-A*, 308). Maurice himself accuses Clive of belonging "to the past" (214). Their confrontation is heavy with the scent of the evening primrose, the "quintessentially Uranian flower."[62] By now Maurice has come to associate this night-bloomer, with its willowy stalks, bright yellow flowers, and strong fragrance, with Clive and the experiences that began in "Risley's room" (161, 180). The music of that room—the Pathétique without its March—is thus suggestively intertwined with each recurrence of this floral motif. Maurice takes his final leave of Clive while plucking off their petals to leave them as a memento of a lifeless connection. They "mourned from the ground like an expiring fire" (215). It is a *morendo* close "without twilight or compromise," pathetic with distant echoes of Tchaikovsky's finale. The "rare and beautiful flower of humanity" that Carpenter ascribed to masculine love at its best[63] is tainted with the scent of death.

Maurice abandons family, work, financial assets, social position, every piece of his past identity; Alec sacrifices his dreams of a new start and his steamer ticket to Argentina. Instead of forging a new kind of social bond comparable to that of Carpenter and Merrill, they simply disappear in a form of social suicide.[64] Maurice and Alec may seek out the "paths untrodden" of the *Calamus* poems,[65] but the mood of their departure falls short of Whitman's lusty optimism or Carpenter's rousing faith in the "love of comrades." Such is the "happy ending" that Forster observed in 1960: "I was determined that in fiction anyway two men should fall in love and remain in it for the ever and ever *that fiction allows* [my italics]" (*MAU*, 218). Forster's final, deprecating stinger is echoed in almost every other statement that he made about the conclusion of the novel. Even the suppressed Epilogue of 1914, which projects the still-devoted pair five years later as woodcutters in Yorkshire, is tainted by the encroaching "rust" on the hedges, "announcing the earth's extinction."[66] The excision of the Epilogue enhances the uncertainty facing the pair. Forster himself remained unconvinced that their love would prevail against the combined threats of class difference, the normal "vagaries, fears, illnesses, distractions, fraying out at its edges" of any relationship,[67] and the impending Great War, in which countless young men would perish. Above all he would remain wary of Alec's ability to commit permanently to Maurice, partly owing to his bisexuality ("I have sometimes thought of Alec marrying," Forster admitted to Isherwood[68]), and doubted their compatibility ("I am not quite sure whether [Alec] would have fulfilled Maurice's wishes," he admitted to Stephen Spender. "Clive would have."[69]). In this context, the narrator's bright assurance that "England belonged to them. That, besides companionship, was their reward" (209) must be read as ironic rather than triumphant.[70] Whatever consolation this statement might have held in 1914 weakens considerably with recognition that these words were added in 1952 (*MAU-A*, 294), in the shadows of two world wars, creeping urbanization, and forty years of continued legal repression of homosexuality. For all Forster's determination to end the novel happily, there is an aura of sadness about the pair, setting out against daunting odds into a fictional "greenwood" that was shrinking fast, and like the symphony, fading into silence. Mirroring Tchaikovsky's words in Forster's Locked Diary, their fate may in fact herald, not so much "a new tide of love for life: rather something hopeless, final, and—like every finale—a little commonplace."

We may never know which part of the Pathétique Symphony that Forster played on the piano in the 1917 Montazah concert at the beginning of his love affair with Mohammed el Adl. I would bet it was not the finale.

7

"Beethoven's Piano Sonatas" (1939–40) and the Twilight of the Hero

> Creativeness [is] scrapped as soon
> as the drums beat and the bombers hum.
> "What I Believe," 1939

In May 1939 Forster published "What I Believe," in which the drumbeat of fate from Beethoven's Fifth Symphony intensifies into the gathering drums of war. This polemical essay was a valiant attempt to shore up the tenets of his old-world liberal humanism, with its faith in personal relationships, in a world poised on the brink of possible annihilation. Whatever hope for mankind remained, Forster claimed, lay in private acts of generosity and pluck, and in the determination to continue "behaving creatively under the shadow of the sword" (*TCD*, 72). The latter had become a formidable task for the sixty-year-old writer, now fifteen years from his last completed novel. Although he remained active as a journalist, military pamphleteer, and tireless critic of Fascism during World War II, creative fiction eluded him. He withdrew increasingly into friendship, reading, and music during the war years. Yet even the London blackouts offered flashes of beauty and the wish to write about them in November 1939: "the searchlights from the roof of my flat: the ultraviolet light at the bottom of the Haymarket, hanging in the void like a tiny freschia [i.e., freesia] and calling out the white on the sandbags: . . . the freedom from aeroplanes, the balloons. . . . Oh yes, and the N.G. [National Gallery] concerts. I would rather notice all this than contemplate Heroism" (LD, 72).

Forster's growing distrust of the "heroic" and the cult of "Great Men" in "What I Believe" (*TCD*, 72–3) portends his shifting attitude toward Beethoven.

Once a symbol of collective heroism, Beethoven's music was increasingly becoming for him a personal call to confront "the sublime rhythm of destruction" by whatever means at hand.[1] Forster deplored the exploitation of Beethoven for wartime propaganda (refashioning the Morse code association of the rhythm of the Fifth into "V . . . for vulgarity" [LD, 80]). The touchstones of his wartime Beethoven were his Blüthner piano, the private genre of the piano sonata, and an unfinished project begun in September 1939 to annotate all of Beethoven's piano sonatas. The autograph manuscript of "Beethoven's Piano Sonatas" in King's College Cambridge is little known and has never been published: a first full edition is provided at the close of this chapter.[2] Although it would fall far short of completion, "Beethoven's Piano Sonatas" charts Forster's evolving aesthetics as well as his rising disillusion with the critical process itself. It was a project doomed from the start by its underlying contradictions and conflicts, its "difficult rhythm" owing as much to its aesthetic and musical challenges as to the political dilemma that undermined it.

"In my youth," Forster stated in a 1959 *New Yorker* interview, "we were brought up to reverence every note Beethoven ever wrote."[3] Donald Francis Tovey had captured the attitude of Forster's generation in 1910, in his "conviction that Beethoven, whether in range, depth and truth of thought, perfect sense of beauty, or absolute conscientiousness of execution, is the greatest musician, perhaps the greatest artist, that ever lived."[4] Throughout his life, Forster had played the Beethoven sonatas from his 1891 Augener edition, edited by Sigismund Lebert, which he had received as a gift from Maimie Aylward.[5] In 1969, Britten observed: "Forster knows his Beethoven sonatas (which I have heard him play with spirit)." According to Britten, Forster warmed to music dependent on "striking themes, dramatic happenings, and strong immediate moods, rather than on classical control and balance, beautiful melodies and perfection of detail."[6] He had always preferred the "middle, romantic Beethoven" and the "Beethoven tragic" of the C-minor mode.[7] His favorite Beethoven included the violin sonatas in C minor, Op. 30/2, and the "Kreutzer," Op. 47, the Third and Seventh Symphonies, the Violin Concerto, and the *Coriolan* Overture. Piano music dominated his affections, with the Third and Fourth Piano Concertos and the most popular piano sonatas (the "Moonlight," "Appassionata," "Waldstein," and "Les Adieux") garnering special comment. He played the sonatas Op. 90 and 111 for others, and had read through the five piano concertos.[8] Charles Mauron observed that Forster played the piano "well, skipping freely from page to page, excusing himself when Beethoven goes a bit too much like the wind, but striking aright the gaiety, tenderness or heroism."[9] By 1939, Beethoven dominated his private piano playing (*TCD*, 130).

His knowledge of the scholarly Beethoven literature was spotty at best. Forster considered himself "a head untrained musically" (*TCD*, 123), and admitted to musicologist E. H. W. Meyerstein in 1944 to having read "scarcely anything" about Beethoven (L: M421). Yet the young Forster had certainly encountered the Beethoven criticism by George Grove and Edward Dannreuther. More recently, he had read selected *Essays in Musical Analysis* by Tovey, including those dealing with the Ninth Symphony and the *Coriolan* Overture, as well as the latter's commentaries to the Beethoven sonatas in the 1931 Associated Board edition, which he borrowed in 1939 for the "Sonatas" project (L: I46). He also knew J. W. N. Sullivan, the author of *Beethoven: His Spiritual Development* (1927), at least well enough to have lunched with him in September 1924 (the talk was of Beethoven's "inner light" and questionable business practices).[10]

Beethoven had taken center stage in Forster's aesthetic essays since 1935, beginning with "Word-Making and Sound-Taking" (*AH*, 102–6) and culminating in "Not Listening to Music" of January 1939 (*TCD*, 127–30). At issue in both essays was the tension between the word and the musical sound, and with it the very value of musical criticism to the listening and interpretive process. In the 1935 essay Forster had argued that the "release of one's fancy" in much writing on music can obscure the "composer's intention." "These capricious insertions of words, parallels, images, jokes, and ideas, make listening to music a rocky and romantic affair," he wrote, "and I am very glad that there are also times when I seem to be alone with the sounds" (*AH*, 105). In "Not Listening to Music," Beethoven's *Coriolan* Overture serves as the battle zone. Tovey's "destruction of the Volscii" program[11] to this otherwise independent instrumental work had hardened its "exquisite sounds" for Forster, "like a road that has been tarred for traffic" (*TCD*, 129). Forster's opinion of "Tovey the ever tiresome" (*CB*, 111) had always been torn between grudging admiration for his musical commentaries and fear that they separated the reader from the "music itself." In a parallel journal entry on the *Coriolan* Overture in 1938, Forster went even further in observing that "non-programme music moves me more deeply. . . . Not to comment is the best" (*CB*, 111–2).

It is curious therefore that in September 1939 Forster embarked on a project to annotate all of Beethoven's piano sonatas, a pursuit for which he lacked both the formal music-theoretical training and the necessary confidence in the analytical process. Its timing was of the essence. Its first trace comes in a letter of September 1 to Christopher Isherwood; having just wept at the news of Hitler's invasion of Poland, Forster announced his intention to "write some notes on Beethoven's Sonatas" and begin a war journal.[12] On September 3 he took to his piano, "depressed and weepy," to twice play the yearning slow movement of the Sonata Op. 101 when news of England's declaration of war on Germany reached him (LD, 71). By September 8 the projected war journal had been abandoned, the blue-covered lined notebook purchased for its purpose now deflected to the project "to play and make notes on Beethoven's Sonatas."[13] The Sonata Op. 101 is fittingly the first entry (fol. 3–5). The project was well underway by September 30, when Forster reported to William Plomer that he had been "studying Beethoven a bit, and writing detailed notes of his sonatas into a large book which I bought to keep a war-diary in" (L: P130). The journal was to provide "a vision of Beethoven," he wrote to Forrest Reid in September 1940, "reached through playing him as well as listening to him, and based upon details" (*SL2,* 182).

The prime instigator and dedicatee of "Beethoven's Piano Sonatas" was French critic Charles Mauron, one of Forster's closest friends and the translator into French of *A Passage to India* and other Forster fiction and prose. They shared an enthusiasm for the piano and the piano sonatas of Beethoven in their letters and during Forster's periodic visits to the Maurons' farmhouse in Provence. They also shared a common concern for the tension between formalism and subjective values in art and music criticism that distinguished them from formalist critic Roger Fry.[14] The project provided a tenuous connection with Mauron, poignantly reflected in Forster's outcry on fol. 26*v,* written shortly after the fall of Paris and the French armistice with Germany on June 22, 1940, that had separated them. Forster takes refuge from the tragic news in "strumming the allegretto of the 7th symphony" at the piano, "particularly the rich gratifying section in A major [see Ex. 13], when the listener is ravished and then doubly ravished in the course of a few bars: laid on a couch amongst angels. Music like that can never be stopped. It moves through tanks and guns to its own close. Yet men continue to fight and lecture although there is such music" (fol. 26*v*).

The table of contents (fol. 2) lists all thirty-two sonatas by opus number, with spaces left for page references to be added later (the notebook is large enough to have accommodated them). The random ordering of sonatas in the manuscript itself attests to its serendipitous work plan. Forster used the Associated Board edition with analytical commentary by Tovey (L: I46), which included the numbered measures essential to the project, touching down on individual works as his fancy and playing beckoned. Once he had begun annotating a single movement of a sonata, he entered the tempo indications for each of its movements on separate pages of the notebook, reserving a full double page for each (with the intention of returning to complete them at a

Ex. 13. Beethoven, Trio from the Allegretto of Symphony No. 7, arr. Franz Liszt (Leipzig: Breitkopf & Härtel, 1871)

later date); most of these pages remained blank. In the end, he would annotate isolated movements from nine sonatas, with only the two-movement Op. 90 considered in its entirety (see Contents of "Beethoven's Piano Sonatas"). The "Hammerklavier" Sonata, Op. 106, is an exception; all its tempo indications are entered in the notebook (fol. 32–6), but *without* annotations.

Given Forster's musical taste, the selections are odd. Absent entirely are the large, heroic sonatas such as the "Waldstein," Op. 53, and the "Appassionata," Op. 57, both of which he had discussed elsewhere; there is not a single movement in the admired key of C minor, the key of the last Sonata Op. 111, which Forster himself played; and his beloved "Moonlight" and "Les Adieux" Sonatas are curiously overlooked. Included instead are some of Beethoven's more traditionally "classical" sonatas of his first decade in Vienna (including movements from Op. 7, 10/2, and 22), in which wit, craft, and brilliance prevail over grand sentiments and dramatic gestures. One would surmise that Forster's separation from his gramophone (which remained in his London flat for the duration of the war) had dictated the choices, were it not for the presence of several difficult late sonatas beginning with Op. 90 of 1814.

Forster's music-theoretical mind was narrow by comparison to that of a Grove or a Tovey; his authority as a music critic rested in his own playing of the sonatas, which gave him "a physical approach to Beethoven which cannot be gained through the slough of 'appreciation'" (*TCD,* 130). Yet despite Mauron's urgings to avoid "littérature" (fol. 1*v*) and Forster's own mistrust of the "rocky and romantic" course of poetic musical exegesis, the entries in "Beethoven's Piano Sonatas" are unabashedly programmatic. Forster's preference for dreamy "wool-gathering" over formalist analysis is evident in his metaphors, which supplant traditional musical terminology: whether whimsical, earnest, or poetic, they are often uncannily faithful to the music. At the right-hand trill in Op. 101/ii (mm. 76–8), "an electric bell is pressed upstairs." A process of developing variation clothes the notes in "bright new coats" in Op. 7/i, while a cadential affirmation in Op. 31/3 becomes "a little smile, which irradiates backwards." The sequential-contrapuntal framework of the opening theme of the much-admired Op. 109/i (mm. 1–4) becomes the "scaffolding for a dream." The fitful rising and falling motion of the "Tempest" finale, Op. 31/2/iii (mm. 1–8) suggests "a fish [that] swims against the stream," and in one of the manuscript's most poignant moments, its second theme (mm. 43–87) "loses the fish" just as the notebook trails off into silence. Forster's ironic images for established formal processes foster an aura of creative whimsy in marked contrast to the emphasis on formalist architecture in much British Beethoven criticism of the time.[15]

Contents of "Beethoven's Piano Sonatas"

Op. 101, [mvts.] i–iii (fol. 3–5)
Op. 7, i (fol. 7)
Op. 31/3, ii (fol. 12)
Op. 110, i (fol. 15)
Op. 10/2, i (fol. 20)
Op. 22, i (fol. 23) and iv (fol. 26)
Op. 90, complete (fol. 27–8)
Op. 109, i (fol. 29)
Op. 106, with no annotations (fol. 32–6)
Op. 31/2, iii (fol. 39)

Forster's prime musical value in "Beethoven's Piano Sonatas" is organic coherence. This is not surprising, given his later encomium to art as the sole earthly repository of "internal order" in "Art for Art's Sake" (1949): it possesses "an internal stability, a vital harmony," which "in the social and political category has never existed except for the convenience of historians" (*TCD,* 90). In "Beethoven's Piano Sonatas," Forster favors those sonatas that are conceived "consistently and harmoniously," such as the first movements of Op. 90 and 106 and "most earlier work" (fol. 15). By contrast, he finds himself unable to follow works composed of fragmentary or dissociated "assemblages of scraps" (fol. 15)—hence his criticism of the innovative late sonatas Op. 101 and 110. He found it impossible to hear the Sonata Op. 101

as "a single flow of inspiration," and was bewildered by the fragmentary pre-finale return of its opening theme (fol. 3). The 32nd-note arpeggios in the first theme of Op. 110/i (mm. 11–20) are dismissed as brooms that "rush up and down . . . until all sense of continuity is swept away," a vivid image for what he perceived as a disappointingly fragmentary first theme area. He also rejected movements such as the finale of Op. 90, which he found "too long" and "too trustful of [a lyrical] opening tune—the trustfulness which is so tedious in Schubert" (fol. 28). Here he evoked one of the most common critical caveats raised against Schubert's sonata-rondo finales as lacking in formal coherence. Forster's highest praise is accorded the first movement of the Sonata in E, Op. 109, which despite its fantasia-like freedom possesses the ultimate mark of organic unity—"difficult rhythm": "If it is possible to hear a whole movement as a single sound, this should be so heard, for its progress is not in time" (fol. 29).

Forster's only music-theoretical enthusiasm—and that because of its connection with poetic referentialism—had to do with key association. His frequent comments on keys (including an accurate analysis of the harmonic strategy of the development section of Op. 10/2/i, and his interesting comments on the A-flat fixation of the first group of Op. 110/i) suggest competence in the rudiments of classical tonality (fol. 20 and 15). His observations on the color associations of specific keys in the related essay, "The C Minor of That Life" (1941), likewise suggest that he possessed selective relative pitch and considerable sensitivity to the timbre of certain keys. The special character of C minor as "the wildest and most wonderful land of his empire" elicits an insightful annotation on the finale of Beethoven's Op. 2/1 in the 1941 essay. The latter also includes a critical gem addressing the structural role of repeats in Beethoven's sonatas—a recurrent point in "Beethoven's Piano Sonatas": "This knack of turning dullish stuff into great stuff is characteristic of Beethoven, and incidentally one of the reasons why one ought never to skip the repeats when playing him—for only at the repeat does one hear what the dullish stuff means" (*TCD*, 126). That this annotation appears in "The C Minor of That Life," first published in *Abinger Chronicle* in June 1941, rather than in "Beethoven's Piano Sonatas," suggests that he had abandoned his notebook by that time.

Forster was undoubtedly frustrated by his inability to transcend the metaphorical approach of most of these entries, which revert to Helen Schlegel's referential position that he had tried to vanquish in "Not Listening to Music." In turn, "Beethoven's Piano Sonatas" paves the ways for Forster's indictment of criticism and its limited value to the reader, listener, and creative artist in his 1947 Harvard address, "The Raison d'Être of Criticism in the Arts" (*TCD*,

107–23). He would choose the lofty podium of American academia to deliver a stunning blow to training in the arts, which risked the danger of sterilizing "the sensitiveness that is being trained." The work of art, he declared there, resides in a world of unconscious dreams, and is thus "recalcitrant to criticism" (*TCD*, 118). "Beethoven's Piano Sonatas" evades the social platform of the critic for the private musings of an amateur pianist. It finally succumbs to the breakdown of the word and its failure to touch on the ineffable core of music.

Yet the project appears to have been doomed from the start on other, more mysterious grounds that seem to augur a changing attitude to Beethoven's music. The "reverence" to Beethoven in which Forster had been schooled as a youth has here, from the very first entry, slipped into a prevailing mood of crabbed ill humor. For all his trumpeting of the project in letters to friends, there is a dispiriting lassitude in much of the writing, as if Forster's heart and mind were engaged elsewhere. By steering clear of his most beloved sonatas, Forster had paved the way for constant carping at the details of his selections. This is "unsatisfying," "vexing," or "dull" and that is "commonplace" or "boring"; "inspiration" flags in Op. 101, while the first movement of Op. 22 falls asleep and is all "washed out." If Forster's purpose in deflecting his war journal to aesthetic ends had been to find haven from the madness of war, the project had backfired.

The final stumbling block may have been the "Hammerklavier" Sonata, Op. 106, the fugal finale of which had remained "*absolutely* incomprehensible" as recently as a 1937 letter to Mauron (L: M242). In a letter of September 1940 he had finally come around to its previously "harsh and senseless" fugue finale, which had finally revealed itself as "a gigantic beauty, tearing down veil after veil away from the night as it gathers strength" (*SL2*, 182), probably in preparation to begin writing about it. This formidable sonata would certainly have laid bare Forster's inadequate analytical skills and his inability to rise to Mauron's challenge to write "pour le plus intelligent et le plus sensible de vos amis" (fol. 1). Its daunting musical dissociation and ongoing derailing of expectation would have posed a dilemma to Forster's aesthetic of "internal order," no section more so than the Sphinxlike introduction to the finale (mm. 1–10). In a mere ten measures Beethoven touches on every key of the chromatic scale in a range of tempos veering from *Largo* to *Prestissimo*, and in a modernist sequence of apparently disjointed fragments that juxtapose the freedom of the fantasia with the strictness of Baroque contrapuntal styles. Forster would have been in no position to uncover the deep internal logic below its haphazard surface or its subtle grounding in the musical argument of this hugely difficult sonata.[16] Certainly the entry of the movement titles of the "Hammerklavier" Sonata without annotation in the last segment of the manuscript (fol. 32–6), followed only by the disappearing fish, suggests a sudden loss of purpose.

The course of the war may have further paralyzed the project. Withdrawal into great art of the past could have provided little comfort in a world in which Forster's liberal-humanistic values were "crumbling beneath him."[17] Every aspect of his beliefs—the "importance of personal relations, art, the inner life, the traditions of rural life, the individual"[18]—was endangered by the global spread of Fascism. In the series of essays written in the months before the start of war and his Beethoven project, Forster explored the political situation from his perspective at what he would later call the "fag-end of Victorian liberalism" (*TCD*, 56). In "Post Munich," first published in June 1939 in *New Statesman and Nation,* Forster grappled with the "hideous dilemma" of the political situation, "the facts" of which "lie in opposite directions, and no exhortation will group them into a single field." The effect on any thinking person is a terrible impotence: "they drop their hands, break off in the middle with a shriek, smash physical or spiritual crockery . . . or they could shut themselves up with their culture and try to hatch something out in isolation." Art offers "a positive hope," but only for the future. For the present, "the only satisfactory release is to be found in the direction of complexity" (*TCD*, 23–5).

In this context Beethoven's sonatas, with their proposed dialectical connection of complex procedures and contradictory emotional states, may have proffered a beacon in a world that was falling apart. Indeed, a century of Beethoven criticism resonates with the social program of liberal-humanism as described in 1933 by its spokesman J. A. Hobson: "That same power of reason which brought the diverse and sometimes conflicting passions of the individual into an ordered personality, seeking its welfare as an organic and progressive whole, would perform the same service for humanity by bringing its individual members and its nations, or other groups, into finding their common good, their community, in ordered and mutually beneficial intercourse."[19] If so, "Beethoven's Piano Sonatas" was bound to meet with frustration. There, Forster reveals himself as no more able to articulate and control Beethoven than to control the events of his time. Rather than providing him with an artistic refuge of traditional liberal values of "moderation, reason and restraint,"[20] Beethoven's sonatas may have brought him full face with the "hideous dilemma" of the war years.

By 1939 his fascination with heroism was waning. As he had observed in

"What I Believe," hero-worship had been chillingly unmasked in the rise of Fascism; the drumbeats of the Fifth had accelerated into the hum of bombers; and the "Great Man" was susceptible to turning tyrant. "Hero-worship," he concluded, "is a dangerous vice" (*TCD*, 72–3). In this context, Beethoven's "power," especially his tendency to conceal "how he uses it," could prove suspect (fol. 15). Thus the classically poised Rondo Op. 22 elicits a remarkable double-edged metaphor when the "lusciousness" of its chorale texture (mm. 182–6) is "unexpectedly raped by a hero" (fol. 26*r*). Forster immediately extends the aggressive metaphor to the "Appassionata" Sonata, the first-movement coda of which injects an ominous note of premeditation to the act (it is a "very different rape . . . which has been planned from the opening bar; a thorough and thoroughly serious act of sex").[21] By February 1940 Forster's hope for victory in the war was slim, at stake the very freedom of the writer and artist threatened by the "constant fear of censorship or internment" in a letter to R. A. Rendall (*SL2*, 170). His 1945 memorial essay on "Romain Rolland and the Hero" confirms the decay of heroism. In this commentary on Rolland's novel *Jean-Christophe* (1904–12), with its theme of the Beethovenian "hero as musician," Forster compares the "easily held hopes" of those prewar years with the reality of 1945. "Today we are all of us tougher, and though we still cherish hopes they are protected by a very necessary crust of cynicism" (*TCD*, 234–5). Thereafter Beethoven remained for Forster an object of cautious love, but no longer a subject for criticism.

Beethoven's Piano Sonatas

Source: autograph manuscript, King's College, Cambridge University: EMF/15/3
Cover: Notebook with dark blue paper cover and crimson morocco spine, made by H. J. Ryman Ltd., London–Watford–Harrow; white paper label affixed, with the title in Forster's hand.

NOTES ON THE TRANSCRIPTION

Foliation is *recto* alone, unless specified. In the manuscript, Forster's original foliation is cancelled and replaced by a revised foliation in another hand; the revised foliation is used in this edition. The spelling of the original is retained. Cancellations in the manuscript are enclosed in < >, while inserted words are enclosed in \ /. Obvious missing words or significant punctuation markings and the occasional editorial addition are enclosed in square brackets.

Forster's measure numbers refer to the Associated Board edition of the complete *Beethoven Pianoforte Sonatas* (London, 1931), with commentary by

Donald Francis Tovey. Forster surrounded these references in little boxes in his manuscript; in the transcription they appear as unhighlighted numbers.

EDITION

[Title page, fol. 1] *Beethoven's Piano Sonatas.* /To be sent if I die to / Charles Mauron / Mas d'Angirany / St Remy, B. d. R. [Bouches du Rhône, Provence]

[Epigraph, fol. 1*v*] Je suis bien content que vous <ecrivez> ecriviez sur les sonates.—Je suis sur que vous le faites comme il faut, sans aucune "litterature" et en imaginant que vous ecrivez pour le plus intelligent et le plus sensible de vos amis.—Ce ne sera pas moi, malheureusement, mais un homme (ou plusieurs hommes) que vous me [*sic*] connaitrez sans doute jamais et à qui vous ferez cadeau d'années de plaisir. – Car je crois nullement que la catatrophe [*sic*] va tout ruiner. Evidemment elle va detruire beaucoup, mais dans l'ensemble je crois à la constance humaine, avec peut être une sorte de montée très lente de l'esprit, à cause de l'elargissement <tres> incessant de l'univers contemplé. / C. M. [Charles Mauron] 28–10–39[22]

[I am very happy that you are writing on the sonatas.—I am certain that you are doing it properly, without recourse to "literature" and with the most intelligent and sensitive of your friends in mind.—Unfortunately, it will not be myself, but a man (or several men) whom you will doubtless never meet and to whom you will give a gift of years of enjoyment.—For in no way do I believe that the catastrophe will ruin everything. Certainly, it will destroy much, but all in all I believe in human perseverance, with perhaps a sort of very slow ascendance of spirit, due to the unending expansion of the universe of the mind.]

Sonata in A, Op. 101

[fol. 3] Allegretto ma non troppo: Lovely but unsatisfying movement. Easy singing up to [m.] 14 where it should stop, but the teasing starts next bar with a tip into the minor. Reassurement enters. Teasing reenters with the syncopation of [m.] 29, and though we get to a nice close at last we're in for a superior and difficult piece of music. 35 has another tease (change of rhythm in the bass), and the opening song comes back middle first, bobbing up happily in its own blue sea. 55–58 must be wonderful writing, but I don't find the bob-up quite graceful. Then 94 starts a final tease, and does not allow the obvious beauty of the opening to be balanced by an obviously beautiful ending. The movement slides away, holds itself up, slides again, very superior indeed. (cf. ending of Franck's violin sonata. 1st movement?)

Then the key. First [it] pretends to be E. Then it *is* E. There's not an honest A major until about 63—i.e. more than half way through.

Don't believe movement is a single flow of inspiration.

Don't understand its return after the Adagio.

[fol. 4] Vivace alla Marcia: March goes too quick for me to get any idea of it from my own playing, but the trio 55 seq[.] gets more interesting, especially if its first section is repeated. Quiet spiky stuff, which starts pretending to be smooth, and pretends again while an electric bell is pressed upstairs in 76–78. The initial pair of semi-quavers become in 87 orchestral (double bass?), and boom away in a transition which leads back to the march.

[fol. 5] Adagio, ma non troppo: First eight bars sound like a theme for variations. 9 restarts, but then the triplet from 1 takes charge, and sends everything falling about in a lovely way, and shows that the movement is an episode, a very soft, very slow flourish.—cf. the Adagio of Op. 110, which breaks up after a couple of bars[.]

Sonata in E flat, Op. 7

[fol. 7] Allegro molto e con brio:
Does not warm up before 93. Then brilliancy and fireworks till 136, so that when the repeat starts one is in great excitement and everything sounds different through anticipation. The corresponding fireworks 273—passes into a further display at 313 which increases the whizz of the whole movement. Several little bits which had seemed merely tuneful come to the front with bright new coats on, and—most brilliant of all—the solid opening theme is at 355 hurried step up step into the air and bursts. I also very much enjoy the quiet bit 167–188 which has \the/ duty of getting back to the opening theme but performs a great deal more: with touching richness it twice sings a new little song which is never wanted again.

Sonata in E flat, Op. 31, no. 3

[fol. 12] Scherzo: Have just seen that 8–9 is an echo. I had stuck it on to the beginning of the following theme as a sort of jumping-off. Now it brings distinction where it was rather needed, for 1–8 is a bit commonplace.

90–95—a pocket storm; as in the last movement of the Moonlight, and I think elsewhere, cf. the two big storms—bigger each time—in the first movement of the Appassionata, and the smaller one in its third movement.

Talking of the App[assionata], 43–48 here find a parallel in its 3rd movet—N.B. the danger of making these discoveries is that they remove me from B[eethoven]'s state when he was writing.

The last bars 169–171 are a little smile, which irradiates backwards. Must also notice the skipping graciousness of 50–58[.]

Sonata in A flat, Op. 110

[fol. 15] Moderato cantabile: Unenjoyable, because in scraps. 1–4 sings in a second-movement way, and 4–11 can be forced to continue the song. But the effort is misdirected: the arpeggios 11–20 rush up and down like brooms until all sense of continuity is swept away.—These three scraps are in the same key, and it is a singing key—A flat: wouldn't a change of key help?—The brooms having been put away and their swing lost, the music turns to force 25 but its sudden working up only reminds us that B[eethoven] has power, does not show us how he uses it: all dies down by 32, and the noble calm of the high E flat in 39 is after a storm which has never taken place.

—These assemblages of scraps (they worry me also in the Sonatas of Hayden [*sic*]) may be a type of inspiration which I don't understand, but B[eethoven] (i) uses them[;] (ii) writes freely and fantasiastically, as in the first movement of Op 109[;] (iii) writes consistently and harmoniously [as in the first movement of][23] Op 106—the Hammerclavier—and in most earlier work. I enjoy, or anyhow follow, methods (ii) and (iii): not this method (i), of which the first movement of Op 101 is a less vexing example.

Sonata in F, Op. 10, no. 2

[fol. 20] Allegro: The piano-piece air of the start leads to such surprises that it is forgotten by the time the movement ends. The big surprise is 77–94 where Bee[thoven] turns on so much heat that none of the notes played after it sound as calm as their equivalents preceding. (The repetition of this passage, as of all exciting passages, is therefore important.) The second surprise is the reentry of the start, in D 118; not a piano-piece any more, but a song; several little changes in the scoring help the changes in key and in position; and make it the most ravishing passage in the movement, so far as sounds go; am amazed as it begins getting home, and sad when it dims back to F.

The big surprise of eighteen bars is thus organised: four bars in D minor, <four> two of transition into <in> G minor, four in that, four of transition into B flat major, and four in that. It is the longer transition that does the trick and works one up so. The bars which follow the surprise 95 seq[.] are the same as those which preceded it 69–76 and are not played more stormily, yet now their groups of triplets-plus-quarters rap and ramp about instead of turning somersaults quietly by themselves. I still find the first 54 bars <boring, or rather> faintish, and don't want *them* repeated; 38–39 with its bumping echo 42–43, doesn't work.

Sonata in B flat, Op. 22

[fol. 23] Allegro con brio: Perhaps brilliant playing would make 26–29 and 157–160 acceptable. I get them very harsh, and assume that they mustn't be softened. The rest of the movement is dull, and the long transition 91–126 more than dull; a bad habit (shared by Bach) of falling asleep is carried here to greater lengths than I remember elsewhere. After op. 31.1, the sonata I enjoy least. "Die Sonate hat sich gewaschen" = "is washed out."

[fol. 26*r*] Rondo: Compare and prefer the last movement of Op 7, which starting with similar charm and lusciousness keeps it up. Still there is one great bit here—182–194—where lusciousness is unexpectedly raped by a hero[.] The brilliancy of this leaves one in a good mood, and perhaps so left Beethoven. Up to that moment, progress sometimes flags, and the reentries of the opening theme—it comes four times in all I think and twice in each time—don't work up our excitement. Contrast the very different rape which concludes the first movement of the Appassionata, which has been planned from the opening bar; a thorough and thoroughly serious act of sex. Here the idea of sex mustn't be pressed; is indeed merely one of those guides which doesn't point in a wrong direction[.]

[fol. 26*v*] It occurs to me, before trying to annotate the sonata opposite [Op. 90], that Charles, who suggested the scheme, will now never see it. France has collapsed (to use a word of little meaning) and I write to the noise of tanks or other vehicles in the valley: not an unpleasant noise yet: crunching and poppy. Perhaps France will soon "declare war" on England and Europe's imbecillity [*sic*] increase. I wonder whether Charles keeps his wisdom. I should expect so, since I keep mine, but of course he is under Hitler now, I not yet. My heart that cared for civilisation is broken and will never be mended. My heart that cares for my friends can never break[.]

Shan't annotate to day. Have been strumming the allegretto of the 7th symphony, particularly the rich gratifying section in A major, when the listener is ravished and then doubly ravished in the course of a few bars: laid on a couch amongst angels. Music like that can never be stopped. It moves through tanks and guns to its own close. Yet men continue to fight and lecture although there is such music.

I will go on writing on these left-hand pages when what seems to be the spirit of Charles fills me.

Sonata in E minor/major, Op. 90

[fol. 27] Mit Lebhaftigkeit etc.: 1–81 a single gigantic gesture, although there are pauses in it and changes of theme. Lyric emotion until 65 when there is a good little growl, repeated in 71, which *might* introduce a fiercer mood. It doesn't, the gesture dies, the hand falls in peace. Though the actual sounds are less delicious than those in the 1st movement of Op. 101, the general effect is sweeter, because the flow isn't interrupted or in spurts. I find lovely the continuation: the bars 82–84 echoing 79–81, minims echoing crochets; I feel sure they belong to what comes after, not to what has gone, though I don't know how to prove this. The original motive returns in 84, but pricked with quavers; it becomes a little scholarly-harsh, and I don't enjoy myself quite so much until 108, when it has done its stuff, and the first motive—or rather the second theme in it: 8 originally—comes in at 108, and itself turns very scholarly in the bass.

Movement almost in the front rank. So exciting and touching that I am always surprised to get to the end. One of the many Beethoven pieces that couldn't be any other piece.

[fol. 28] Nicht zu geschwind etc.: Alas, you are boring. Such a gay rich tune—one would prophecy [*sic*] up to 24 that you *must* be a success. Suspension of judgment then starts: expectation of something gayer, richer, overwhelmingly so. This never comes and I always find you too long, though you are not much longer than the first movement, which always seems too short. Goldie [Dickinson]—the last time I saw him listening to music, in Gerald Heard's flat, felt the same.

This general judgment must be modified in particulars—e.g. how gracious is the new theme at 60[.] But Beethoven has been too trustful of his opening tune—the trustfulness which is so tedious in Schubert. Years ago, at Mrs Hope Wedgwoods at Idlerocks, the same criticism was brought against the 1st movement of the Moonlight, but undeservedly, because *there* the tune has dignity and can naturally meander; *there* it can bear the whole burden of the movement by itself.

Sonata in E, Op. 109

[fol. 29] Vivace ma non troppo: Not pianistic on my piano and with my playing, which can only get the architecture, not recapture the sensuousness heard in the concert-room two years ago. The scaffolding for a dream. Also the opening tune 1–8 is very difficult musically—it sounds as if it begins a bar instead of on a half—and its recurrences are worse and keep shifting their stresses. On the other hand, the adagios 9–15 [&] 57–65, difficult to play, are easy to follow[.]

A fantasy with—form. Not one grand effect; but occasional sweetnesses point the way and pierce the heart; chords in 9 [&] 10, and the subsidence to B major in 11 which can send one gasping; and the ravishing chord before the close 85. All the end 75–100 is a concession: B[eethoven] consents to say 'I am not elusive after all[']; says it first by a series of obvious almost juicy chords, and then by stroking the jibbing opening \tune/ the right way and wafting it out of the picture. If it is possible to hear a whole movement as a single sound, this should be so heard, for its progress is not in time. The astonishment and admiration with which I first heard it were appropriate to the raising of a curtain.—Have often failed to write about it, but the above might be worse.

Sonata in B flat, Op. 106 (Für das Hammerclavier)

[fol. 32–36] [Only the headings for all movements are entered, but otherwise blank]

Sonata in D minor, Op. 31, no. 2

[fol. 39] Allegretto: A fish swims against the stream 1–30 in D minor. A minor 43–87 loses the fish

Author's Note: Here Forster abandoned the project; the remainder of the notebook (to fol. 121) is foliated, but otherwise empty. That the frugal writer did not put it to further use suggests a hope to return to it in brighter times.

8

Claggart's Monologue and the Art of Collaboration in *Billy Budd*

> You and I have both put into [*Billy Budd*] something which lies deeper than artistic creation, and which we both understand. It could never have got there but for both of us.
>
> —EMF to Britten, December 1951

In June 1948, composer Benjamin Britten approached Forster with a proposal to furnish the libretto for his next opera. The project could not have come at a better time for the almost seventy-year-old author, battling ill health and writer's block. By October of that year, the depression of his post-war years had reached despondency: "I cannot speak to others of my worst truth, which is that I have got tired of people and personal relationships. . . . Unless I can manage to settle down to some work this year, I may go wrong in my head."[1] Based on Herman Melville's last novella, Forster's libretto to *Billy Budd* was drafted in 1948–50 with co-librettist Eric Crozier. The opera, which premiered at Covent Garden on December 1, 1951, jump-started Forster's faltering creativity and restored his self-confidence as a writer. It called into play all the resources of his lifelong experience of opera and his exploration in prose of its word-music dialectic. It also provided Forster with his first experience of interactive writing, and with it "a new sensation," he would write to friend Joe Ackerley in August 1949, "that of having more work to do than one can do, and of wanting to do it. Comes through collaboration, I suppose" (L: A597).

In the early stages of the collaboration, Forster and Crozier worked together with minimal input from Britten. The pair quickly arrived at "a state of agreement in which we can guess how the other's mind is working," Crozier wrote in March 1949. "Morgan is in charge of the drama, I am in command of the ship, and we share matters out between us."[2] By August 1949, the process had become a vigorous threesome with Britten, as confirmed by Crozier: "We are all thrilled by the work, the ideas that come seem to have a life of their own and to present themselves for testing by each of us in turn, and each one may add a little contribution to the subject under discussion, and gradually the whole scene is built up from hints that have been floating in the air among us."[3] The most intense phase of the Forster-Britten interaction began after the August meeting, when Crozier's approaching marriage to soprano Nancy Evans and his widening rift with the composer led him to step back from the project. This left Forster and Britten alone to slog out the final revisions to the libretto in December 1949; the two continued to work together or in close communication for repeated periods in 1950–51 during Britten's composition of the score. The competing claims of word and music that had troubled Forster since "Beethoven's Piano Sonatas," the fear that his fine words would not be audible (L: C320), and the inevitable friction between a sensitive composer and a prickly, aging author led to repeated border skirmishes.

One episode nearly brought the collaboration to a halt: the debacle over Claggart's Act 2, scene 2 monologue "O beauty, o handsomeness, goodness,"[4] deservedly one of the most admired segments of the opera. The outcome of their disagreement was a fully revised second version of Claggart's monologue, the genesis of which can be traced in the multiple libretto drafts and Britten's musical sketches and compositional draft of *Billy Budd* at the Britten-Pears Library, Aldeburgh.[5] As a focal point in the dramatic characterization of the opera, Claggart's monologue provides a case study of the complex creative interaction between a musical writer and a literary composer.

The idea of writing an opera on Melville's *Billy Budd* may have been Britten's.[6] It was an unlikely operatic subject, with its stammering hero, evasive narrator, claustrophobic setting, and all-male cast. Moreover, Melville had left his novella unfinished at his death in 1891, its final text undetermined when it was first published in England in 1924. *Billy Budd* was still relatively unknown three years later when Forster discussed it in *Aspects of the Novel* (142) as a "song not without words"—already he had sensed its musical potential. He immediately singled out Melville's villainous Master-at-Arms John Claggart for his "Natural Depravity," an essential, inborn propensity to evil wrapped in what Melville called "the mantle of respectability."[7] Depravity fuels Claggart's crusade to destroy the beautiful foretopman Billy Budd. In Forster's words: "He accuses Billy of trying to foment a mutiny. The charge is ridiculous, no one believes it, and yet it proves fatal. For when the boy is summoned to declare his innocence, he is so horrified that he cannot speak, his ludicrous stammer seizes him, the power within him explodes, and he knocks down his traducer, kills him, and has to be hanged" (*AN*, 142). Forster's fascination with the manly figure of Billy, coupled with the relevance of Melville's parable to the dilemmas of postwar life, may have overcome his initial scruples regarding its operatic potential.

Britten's selection of a novice in the specialized field of libretto writing was as unlikely as the subject itself. Ronald Duncan, the librettist of Britten's *The Rape of Lucretia* (1946), found the choice of Forster baffling.[8] Forster himself repeatedly expressed self-doubt owing to his inexperience in drama and poetry, which necessitated the *prose* format that would have a major impact on Britten's musical decisions. Unquestionable, however, was the breadth of Forster's operatic experience over fifty years (see Appendix B) and his commitment to Britten's music. Forster also shared the composer's enthusiasm for the later operas of Verdi and the music dramas of Wagner and Richard Strauss. Britten may have been less aware of Forster's longstanding antipathy to English music and his relative ignorance of modern music. There is little mention of twentieth-century repertoire in Forster's earlier letters and diaries, and the rare exceptions (Mahler, Shostakovitch, Stravinsky, and Berg) are often cautious at best. Yet by 1949, Forster was thirsty to hear "more new things" (LD, 90) and had considerable experience with Britten's recent music, including the operas *Peter Grimes, The Rape of Lucretia,* and *Albert Herring* (the last of which, with libretto by Crozier, had been dedicated "To E. M. Forster—in admiration"). Forster would derive great pleasure from contact with Britten's colleagues, especially Michael Tippett, and prided himself on the musical adventures of his old age (with some smugness toward those such as Florence Barger, for whom music had ended "at the death of Brahms" [L: B867]).

Claggart's central role in the opera was assured from the earliest collaborative stages. By late November 1948 when the trio met for their first planning session at the composer's Crag House on the Aldeburgh coast, they began their earliest sketches of the libretto on "three rather grubby little sheets."[9] Claggart's eventual monologue is assured a space in their terse outline-synopsis of the plot: "Soup spilling—Natural depravity of Claggart."[10] Their next meeting in mid-January 1949 saw the completion of a rough prose synopsis of the action in five scenes,[11] in which the soup-spilling scene has been excised in favor of a "monologue" for a "furtive and sinister" Claggart that "expresses his hatred of Billy and his determination to destroy him" (fol. 19). On March 2, 1949 the three again assembled for what Forster would call "sixteen remarkable Billy Budd days at Aldeburgh" (LD, 91). This intense session would produce the handwritten preliminary "Draft-Libretto in Three Acts."[12] It is almost entirely in the hand of Forster, scribbled with palpable energy on smallish sheets of cheap, woody paper with the same dark blue ink common to his correspondence of the time. Unmistakable as well is the ring of Forster's prose style throughout.

Claggart is already a well-rounded character in the March "Draft-Libretto," which includes a first version of his monologue (as "O handsomeness, o beauty o goodness!") in near-final form. Drafted entirely in Forster's hand on two separate pages (fol. 47–8), the March 1949 working copy of the monologue text reveals that he had conceived it with ease, and in a single sweep of inspiration.[13] The soliloquy captures Claggart just as his depravity is about to explode into action. Forster's text seethes with repressed longing for the handsome Billy, which may have had something to do with Britten's passing "revulsion" for the nascent project early in the March 1949 meeting.[14] So pleased was Forster with the results, however, that he highlighted his "big monologue for Claggart" on March 10 in a letter to William Plomer (L: P243), and would later prize it as "*my* most important piece of writing" in the libretto (*SL2*, 242). Although Forster continued to tinker with minor details of its text during the August and December 1949 sessions in Aldeburgh, his first vision of "O handsomeness" remained largely intact until Britten began working on its musical setting in early November 1950.

On November 23, 1950, Britten and Crozier visited Forster in Cambridge. The rising tensions among them erupted into conflict when Britten arrived an hour late and Forster berated the composer outrageously, "like some low-class servant who deserved to be whipped."[15] The next day when Britten played them parts of the newly completed Act 2, Forster voiced disappointment in Claggart's monologue. On his return to Aldeburgh, Britten received "a very deflating letter" from Forster, "full of sharply-pointed darts" about Britten's music for the monologue.[16] "I want *passion*," Forster argued, "love constricted, perverted[,] poisoned, but nevertheless *flowing* down its agonising channel; a sexual discharge gone evil. Not soggy depression or growling remorse. I seemed turning from one musical discomfort to another, and was dissatisfied. I looked for an aria perhaps, for a more recognisable form. I liked the last section best, and if it is extended so that it dominates, my vague objections may vanish. 'A longer line, a firmer melody'—exactly" (*SL2*, 242).

This had not been Forster's first attempt to meddle in Britten's musical process: the previous April had seen their first "difference of opinion" over the Novice's dirge in Act 1.[17] "He has done dry contrapuntal stuff," Forster had complained to Bob Buckingham, "no doubt original and excellent from the musician's point of view, but not at all appropriate from mine" (L: B2176). Britten had apparently taken Forster's comments in good spirit (but wisely spared the ravishing counterpoint for alto saxophone, bass clarinet, and cello that has proved one of the most admired moments in the opera). By contrast, Forster's frontal attack on Claggart's monologue, framed in an explicitly sexual program that Britten would surely have found repugnant, wounded the composer and momentarily brought his work to a standstill. He felt understandably harassed at having to "consult and seek approval [from Forster] for every phrase he writes," and appealed to Crozier, Peter Pears, and Erwin Stein before continuing with the music.[18] Crozier intervened. Forster, it seems, had been oblivious to the extent of the damage: "I did not realise that I was here touching him on the raw" (*SL2*, 243). He resolved to go easier on Britten in the future, writing in his customary year-end diary entry for 1950: "I am rather a fierce old man at the moment, and he is rather a spoilt boy, and certainly a busy one" (LD, 91).

In hindsight Britten's irritation is understandable, for Forster had put his finger squarely on the substantial musical and dramatic problems of Britten's first version of Claggart's monologue. It had been composed with Forster's December 1949 libretto-text as base, which Britten had lightly revised in November 1950 by tightening the language, improving the rhythm, and reshuffling a key phrase to improve the dramatic logic.[19] This earlier libretto version with Britten's revisions is shown in the sidebar, "Forster's Final Libretto to Claggart's Monologue [December 1949], with First-Stage Revisions by Britten [November 1950?]," with my numbered cues inserted for later reference.

The first musical setting of this text (November 1950) can be reconstructed from Britten's holograph Compositional Draft of *Billy Budd* at the Britten-Pears Library and an additional rejected fragment now in the National Library, Vienna.[20] On comparing Britten's two versions of Claggart's monologue, it becomes evident that his 1951 final version would follow Forster's advice almost to the letter. It recasts most of the opening of the aria (corresponding to sections 1 and 3–5 of the 1949–50 libretto), making this the most heavily reworked segment of the entire Compositional Draft of the opera. He would, however, retain unchanged the peroration (section 6), Claggart's vow of vengeance, which had garnered the writer's praise. The most substantial musical revisions involve the introductory 31 measures, corresponding to section (1) of the 1949–50 libretto in the sidebar on page 130. Britten's two musical settings of this segment are compared in Ex. 14.[21]

Britten's earlier setting merits every point in Forster's critique. Its theme (1950, mm. 1–3) suggests B minor, the key of "confusion" in the opera, which

105
cantabile
1951
O beau - ty, O hand - some-ness, good - - ness,
[46v]
d4
1950
O hand - some-ness, O beau - ty, O good - ness,
3
would ___ that I nev - er_en - coun - tered you! Would ___ that I lived in my
4
[47r]
Would that I ne - ver_en - coun - tered you! Would that I li - ved in my
6
own world al - ways, in that de-prav - i - ty ___ to which I was born. ___
7
own world al - ways In that de - pra - - - vi - ty in which I was
9
cresc.
There I found peace of a
10
born. ___ There ___ I found peace ___ of a
11
sort. ___ There I es - tab-lished an or - der such as reigns ___ in
13
sort. ___ There I es - tab-lished an or - der such as reigns ___ in

Ex. 14. Britten, *Billy Budd,* from Claggart's Act 2, sc. 2 monologue: "O beauty" [1951 published version], mm. 1–29; "O handsomeness" [1950 draft], mm. 1–31 (courtesy of Boosey & Hawkes, Inc., BPL, and *A*–Wn)

Forster's Final Libretto to Claggart's Monologue [December 1949], with First-Stage Revisions by Britten [November 1950?]

(1) O handsomeness, o beauty, o goodness! Would that I never encountered you! ~~That is my torment.~~ Would that I lived in my own world always, in that depravity ~~to~~ \in/ which I was born. There I found peace of a sort, there I established an order, such as reigns in Hell. But alas, alas the light shines in the darkness, and the darkness comprehends it and suffers. \Alas, alas!/ O handsomeness o beauty o goodness! Would that ~~I had~~ \I'd/ never seen you!

(2) Having seen you, what choice remains to me? None, none! I am doomed to annihilate you, I am vowed to your destruction. ~~It shall be as if you have never been.~~ I will wipe you off the face of the earth, off this ~~little~~ \tiny/ floating fragment of ~~the~~ earth, off this ship where fortune has led you. ~~You cannot escape because I have hatred on my side, and envy, and they are stronger than love.~~ First I will trouble your happiness, I will mutilate and silence the body where you dwell, it shall hang from the yard arm, it shall fall ~~with dishonour~~ into the depths of the sea, and all shall be as if nothing had been. \No, you cannot escape! With hate and envy I am stronger than love./

(3) So may it be!

(4) For what hope remains if love can escape? If love, after hatred and envy have destroyed it, still lives and grows strong in a land they cannot enter, what hope is in my own \dark/ world for me? I cannot believe it. That were torment too keen.

(5) O handsomeness, o beauty, o goodness, you are surely in my power to night. Nothing can defend you.

(6) I, John Claggart, Master at Arms upon the Indomitable, have you in my power, and I will destroy you.

places the voice in a "growling" lower register; the singer's delivery is also cramped by the unwieldy opening noun "handsomeness." Its interval of a falling *diminished* 4th (d4) on "beau-ty" (m. 2) will recur repeatedly throughout this excerpt, imparting a certain "soggy depression" to the entire exordium. By contrast, Britten's 1951 *cantabile* theme, with its opening line recast as "O beauty, o handsomeness, goodness," gives the singer a "firmer melody" both dramatically and vocally (mm. 1–2). Its key of F# minor makes for a resonant range, while the voice can blossom on the grateful sonority of the word "*beau*-ty" (mm. 1–2)—Billy's nickname. Its incisive opening on a rising perfect 4th is memorable, and will become Claggart's clarion call throughout the opera. The continuation of the 1951 version (mm. 3–15) thoroughly develops the perfect-fourth motive in an incremental ascent to the ringing d-flat^{1} climax on "hell" (m. 15).[22] Conversely, the 1950 version has difficulty breaking free of the depressive hold of its opening theme, with its confined five-note range (A#-e) and multiple diminished fourth droops. The line only briefly escapes to the pitch of a on "*es*-ta-blished" (m. 13) before falling back to an e-cadence on "hell" (m. 16). It again flares to life in mm. 17–8, only to regress to a falling sequence of diminished fourths, ending with the "growling remorse" of an interpolated "Alas" pair (mm. 22–3). Both versions then circle back to restate their opening theme (mm. 23/24), but only in the 1951 version is this reprise welcome. The limp twofold cadence at "Would that I'd never seen you" in the 1950 version (mm. 26–31) is a "musical discomfort," devoid of the heat of frustrated passion. By contrast, the powerful setting in the later version, with its terminal rising fourths on "seen you" (mm. 26 and 28), unfolds into a new tonal area that motivates the next section.

Section (2) of the 1949–50 libretto (in the sidebar on page 130) presented few difficulties: Britten held to its 1950 musical setting with only minor retouching in the later version. His struggle with the middle of the aria, however, was also considerable.[23] The root of his problems seems to have been the order of events in sections (3)–(5) of the earlier libretto, specifically the delayed reprise of "O handsomeness" in section (5), too late for a musical recapitulation. Britten would wisely delete his earlier setting of this passage (fol. 50*r*), seen in Ex. 15. Its first nine measures replicate the "O handsomeness" opening theme before shifting into an A-flat intonation (on "Nothing!"). The limitations of the original opening theme are revisited at this climactic

Ex. 15. "O handsomeness" [1950 draft, fol. 51*r*], lead-in to the peroration (courtesy BPL)

point, while the transition to the closing oath in F minor ("I, John Claggart") is abrupt and tonally ambiguous.

In the revised version, Britten moved this text segment (now recast as "O beauty") to a position following libretto section (3) ("So may it be!"), and rewrote the rest of the large middle section of the aria on a replacement bifolio (fol. 49–50) to create a "longer line." The revision solves the structural weakness of the first version by organizing the midsection around a menacingly *cantabile* false reprise of the new "O beauty" theme in E flat minor (m. 71, at rehearsal #109). The musical recapitulation in the home key (m. 101, at #110) now corresponds with Claggart's momentary glimpse of the blessed land from which he has been excluded ("If love still lives and grows strong"). When that vision provokes a "torment too keen," it is forcefully rejected with the emphatic "No! No!" (seen in Ex. 16). In contrast to the awkward transition to the peroration in the 1950 version, this new phrase, with its rising chain of signature perfect fourths, seamlessly connects the recapitulation to the distant F minor of Claggart's vow, giving it the effect of inevitability.

Claggart's monologue gives a unique glimpse into his twisted inner world. Without it he would be a cardboard villain rather than the opera's tragic catalyst. Forster had surely recognized that a powerful arialike setting of Claggart's monologue would be essential to the success of the opera. Although initially resistant, Britten capitulated in the end to Forster's musical advice to produce what Philip Reed describes as "the finely wrought, almost Verdian, set-piece aria that Forster was evidently seeking."[24] In the process, Britten also substantially improved the language and rhetorical argument of its libretto, to Forster's enthusiastic approval.[25] In the end, Claggart's monologue acquired its dark luster only when composer and librettist intruded on the other's territory.

Ex. 16. From "O beauty" [1951 published version], lead-in to the peroration, mm. 110–7 (courtesy of Boosey & Hawkes, Inc.)

In death Claggart and his monologue continue to haunt Vere, with major implications for Britten's score. In the libretto of the trial scene (Act 3, scene 2), the ghostly presence of Claggart is signaled by textual allusions to his monologue in Vere's dialogue. It was almost certainly Forster who had planted among Vere's ramblings in the March 1949 handwritten "Draft-Libretto" of its trial scene (fol. 65–75) two quotations from Claggart's monologue text. The first comes as Vere explains to the jury: "Even if the motives were foul, even if [Claggart] did desire to destroy handsomeness beauty and goodness, we must ignore them. There is a mystery here, whose veil no one can lift" (fol. 69). Later in an excised sketch for a possible epilogue, Vere again quotes Claggart, now in reference to himself: "O beauty, o handsomeness o goodness, how will you ~~ever~~ pardon me? I too have betrayed you" (fol. 74). Its revised ordering of the refrain line beginning with the later "O beauty" is striking, but even more so is Vere's guilt-ridden appropriation of Claggart's private thoughts.

During the August 1949 meeting in Aldeburgh, Britten first assumed an active role in the revision of the libretto into a text suitable for musical treatment. Crozier's typescript of the "Complete Draft-Libretto in Three Acts, March 1949" served as the primary text for their work (confirmed in the famous photographs by Kurt Hutton for the *Picture Post,* showing it on Forster's desk and Britten's lap).[26] Forster's copy (fol. 100–84) is heavily annotated, with numerous autograph foolscap insertion pages that reflect the intense collaborative work. Among them is the first draft in Forster's hand of Vere's big posttrial solo "I accept your [sic] verdict," which includes the following: "Beauty, handsomeness, goodness, it is for me to destroy you. Poor lad, poor lad, may God grant him strength! . . . No. No. God grant *me* strength, me, Edward Fairfax Vere, Captain of the Indomitable, lost with all aboard upon the infinite sea" (fol. 177 ins.). New here is Vere's appropriation of Claggart's closing oath.[27]

In mid-December 1949 Forster and Britten hunkered down together for ten days in Aldeburgh—without Crozier—to hammer out the final major revisions to the libretto. The meeting witnessed their closest collaboration to date. Some of the finer points in the symbolism and dialogue emerged; the relationship between Vere and Billy gained in intimacy and emotional warmth;[28] and the intricate system of recurring leitmotifs was enhanced. They entered their joint efforts onto their typescripts of the August draft. The pencil additions in Britten's copy are rather messy, suggesting that he first recorded their decisions as they hashed them out. Forster's ink notations of the same revisions in his typescript are mostly in fair copy. There are also several spots where one mistakenly reached for the other's copy to make an addition. As is the case with truly collaborative work, it is unclear who originated what.

Among the significant additions is a new arietta for Vere, the magnificent "Scylla and Charybdis," situated immediately after Claggart's murder. Here the impetus apparently came from Britten; his typescript contains a rough first draft of the text with a telling pencil insertion in his hand: "Beauty, handsomeness goodness." These words appear in fair copy in Forster's typescript (fol. 35*v*) to create the following: "Scylla and Charybdis and the straits of Hell. I sight them too late; I see all that the mists concealed. Beauty, handsomeness goodness is coming to trial; how can I condemn him, how can I save him?" Vere's echoes of Claggart's signature phrase in both "Scylla and Charybdis" and "I accept their verdict," which survived into the final libretto,[29] were thus a joint effort.

When Britten set Vere's Act 3 solos to music in late February and early March 1951, he intensified by musical means this process of "convergence of identity" between Vere and his Master-at-Arms.[30] Significantly, most of these musical quotations refer to Britten's revised 1951 music for the monologue.[31] Apparently its revision was already underway. Those reminiscences that appear in the orchestra alone function in the manner of the Wagnerian leitmotif, and serve to reveal the dead Claggart's continued agency during the trial scene.[32] They include orchestral statements of his later "O beauty, o handsomeness, goodness" theme as Billy is admitted before the court; as Mr. Redburn accuses him of having killed the Master-at-Arms; and as Billy is led back to the stateroom to await judgment.[33] The latter, in G flat, is the enharmonic equivalent of Claggart's key for the revised monologue (F sharp), and ends with a recollection of the music associated with Claggart's oath of destruction.

Vere's vocal lines in "Scylla and Charybdis" and "I accept their verdict" also feature musical quotations from Claggart's monologue, the narrative purpose of which is to signal his merging identity with his depraved Master-at-Arms and his complicity in Billy's death, perhaps out of a shared attraction to the Handsome Sailor. For Rupprecht, "Scylla and Charybdis" marks the climax of this psychological convergence. Its quotation of the "Beauty, handsomeness, goodness" theme unleashes a massive chain of intervals of the fourth in voice and orchestra that outplays Claggart at his own musical game.[34] For me, Claggart's musical presence reaches its high point in Vere's closing soliloquy, "I accept their verdict."[35] Reference to Claggart's monologue is unmistakable in the orchestration for low brass and strings with percussion ensemble of this solemn funeral cortege in F minor (the very timbre, key, and affective mood of Claggart's peroration). The dead Master-at-Arms makes a chilling appearance midway through the aria, as Vere's voice takes lyrical flight at "But I have seen the divine judgment of heaven" (see Ex. 17). Forster, it seems, had anticipated the musical potential of these textual quotations from Claggart's monologue as early as December 1950, in a letter to Britten: "Has [Claggart's monologue] any inverted relationship to Vere's music when he moves towards the inner cabin, end of Act III?" (*SL2*, 242). The "O beauty" theme emerges as both orchestral leitmotif (at A) and vocal quotation (at B). Yet, the falling *diminished* fourths associated with images of guilt and punishment (at X) reveal that Britten's rejected 1950 version of "O handsomeness" still haunted his memories—and Vere's persona—throughout the composition of this aria. Present as well is the theme of two rising fourths in sequence (at C), first associated with Claggart's "depravity to which I was born" in the revised version of his monologue (cf. Ex. 14, 1951, mm. 7–8). The fixation on intervals of the fourth climaxes at "it is for me to destroy you" (Ex. 17, at C), which inverts Claggart's similar outburst at the close of his peroration (at D). Vere's own peroration ("I, Edward Fairfax Vere," at E) reenacts Claggart's, likewise in F minor if a fourth higher (cf. Ex. 16, m. 117).

Vere's purposeful appropriation of Claggart's solitary monologue, which he could not have overheard from his cabin,[36] occasions one of the great mysteries of the opera. Several commentators have gone to considerable lengths to explain how these private words and musical themes could have found their way into Vere's consciousness. For Donald Mitchell, these points of convergence suggest narrative irony on Britten's part, while for Philip Rupprecht, they display the "logic of a dream" and the "collapse of Vere as an autonomous character."[37] For Lloyd Whitesell, the audience has mysteriously transferred its knowledge to Vere.[38] There is another possibility that goes back to the role that Forster's Prologue had assigned Vere as the old and fallible narrator of the entire opera. Britten's designer of the first production, John Piper, spoke for the composer in emphasizing that the entire opera "is taking place in Vere's mind," while Erwin Stein, who was in close contact with Britten during its composition, corroborated this point.[39] If this is so, it is *Vere's* voice that we are hearing throughout the opera. Its much-discussed web of verbal and musical motives and key associations,[40] his moments of convergence with Claggart's identity, and even the monologue itself, become Vere's fictive creations, the hard-won by-products of his lifelong replaying of *Billy Budd* in his mind. Depending on one's interpretation of the Epilogue, in which Vere's achievement of a "love that passes understanding" is undercut by Claggart's theme in a phantom whistle (see Ex. 18), the opera is either a persuasive moral document or a stunning feat of self-deception. Forster appears to have leaned toward the latter view, his outcome for Vere a "temporary salvation" (*AN*, 143) that is compromised in all the drafts of

Ex. 17. From Vere's "I accept their verdict" (Act 3, sc. 2) [reduced] (courtesy of Boosey & Hawkes, Inc.)

Ex. 18. From Vere's Epilogue to *Billy Budd* (courtesy of Boosey & Hawkes, Inc.)

his Epilogue by a terminal ellipsis into uncertainty. The result is one of the several epistemological gaps that Barry Emslie has detected at the heart of the plot of Britten's *Billy Budd.*[41]

The collaborative efforts of Forster and Britten in the creation of Claggart's monologue and its unfolding throughout the opera thus enhanced immeasurably the already significant narrative ambiguity of Melville's tale. With Eric Crozier as their indispensable aide, they created together what Britten would call "incomparably the finest libretto ever. For wisdom, tenderness, & dignity of language it has no equals."[42] It would inspire Britten to embark on a new stage in his operatic oeuvre, one that combines rigorous motivic and architectural integration with a degree of modernist ambiguity unprecedented in his earlier operas.

9

Conclusion

Difficult Rhythm, Prophetic Song

Over? But is the concert over? Here was the end, had anything an end, but experience proves that strange filaments cling to us after we have been with music, that the feet of the birds have, as it were become entangled in snares of heaven, that while we swooped hither and thither so aimlessly we were gathering something, and carrying it away for future use. Schumann—or was it Brahms?—sings against the gas and obliterates the squalor, or, sinking deeper till he reaches the soundless, promotes that enlargement of the spirit which is our birthright. The concert is not over when the sweet voices die. It vibrates elsewhere.

—EMF, "From the Audience"

"Wool-gathering," that homely phrase for daydreaming at a concert in "Not Listening to Music" (*TCD*, 127), takes on unexpected meaning in Forster's 1945 essay "From the Audience." After the music ends the writer takes away its filaments of beauty for use elsewhere; its "difficult rhythm" sinks into the quiet of the creative act. This is the process repeated in ever-changing guises in Forster's novels, and then deconstructed in the critical writings beginning with *Aspects of the Novel*. The divided response to Forster's novels across a century of critical opinion reflects the very real challenges of infusing music, with its indeterminacy, vagueness, and tendency to slip off into the visionary, into the postrealist novel. Yet the moments of poetic vision that cling to the music of his novels—Caroline's enveloping smoke ring, the downward course of Alpine waters into the Mediterranean, singing of Lucy's "love more mysterious," the ashes of the evening primrose at

Penge—obscure though they may be, vibrate in the reader's memory after the book is over.

The role of music in Forster's fiction is richly varied. At a basic level, music making provides realistic incidents that adorn the novel and fix its culture of time and place. When Leonard Bast goes to the Queen's Hall, it is as much to rub shoulders with his social "betters" as to hear Beethoven's music; enthusiasm for Tchaikovsky's biography and his "Pathétique" Symphony places Risley in the upper-class decadent culture of post-Wildean London; and Lucy's piano-playing charts the conflicting paths open to the Edwardian woman. The musical attitudes and sociopolitical tensions of prewar England are reflected in the collision of Elgar, Beethoven, Brahms, and Wagner in *Howards End.* On a deeper level, however, music illuminates the psychology of Forster's characters, the tangle of subconscious motives and desires concealed behind their words and deeds. In this sense, music mediates the gap between the external events of the novel and the flawed commentary of the conventional narrator. As a *wordless* narrator, its message can be obscure or downright arcane and relies heavily on the knowledge and interpretation of the reader; once decoded, however, Forster's musical narration is trustworthy. Among his most telling uses of music are those that serve the unspeakable, erotic zones, such as Lucy's playing of the magic garden music by Gluck and Wagner, Clive's rendition of Tchaikovsky's symphony, Rickie's decadent rehearing of Wagner's *Rheingold* Prelude, or Caroline's assumption of the madness of Donizetti's *Lucia.* The musical incidents in *Where Angels Fear to Tread* and *A Room with a View* largely hold to these two functions—cultural-historical context and psychological revelation. Were Forster's use of music to have ended here, it would have remained within the nineteenth-century tradition epitomized in George Eliot's *The Mill on the Floss, Middlemarch,* or *Daniel Deronda,*[1] or even in John Galsworthy's *Indian Summer of a Forsyte* (1917) from *The Forsyte Saga.* Here is where rhythm enters.

Foster always mistrusted novelists who had capitulated to the aesthetic doctrine of "pattern": when in the hands of a master technician such as Henry James, he claimed, absolute unity promotes a lifeless beauty that can chill the blood of any novel (*AN,* 152–64). "Rhythm" provided Forster with a more vital pathway, one borrowed directly from music. His "easy rhythm" is the literary equivalent of the Wagnerian leitmotif, and develops in a process of "repetition plus variation" throughout the novel, lessening "our need of an external form" (*AN,* 168). Although there are isolated examples in *Where Angels Fear to Tread* (notably Harriet's inlaid box), Forster's most extreme use of this technique occurs in his most Wagnerian novel, *The Longest Journey,* in which Wagner's music dramas furnish an intertwining web of motifs throughout the novel. The novelty of Forster's literary leitmotifs lies in their capacity for development and their extension to *nonmusical* themes in the life of an individual or a society.

The literary leitmotif is of course not unique to Forster at this time. Thomas Mann, for example, had been using the device for several years when Forster took up *The Longest Journey.* There is a difference, however: Gabriele Klöterjahn's ominous blue vein in Mann's "Tristan" (1902) or Siegmund Aarenhold's little crease at the bridge of his nose in "The Blood of the Walsungs" (1905) remain fixed in their signification, and function as what Forster called "banners" (*AN,* 167). By contrast Forster's motifs develop new meaning with each recurrence, just as Sieglinde's theme, first used to herald the birth of her child of sorrow in Wagner's *Die Walküre* ("O hehrstes Wunder!"), will evolve into Brünnhilde's theme of world redemption that brings *Götterdämmerung* to a glorious close. Forster's Wiltshire train in *The Longest Journey* is one such motif: at first a neutral detail in the landscape around Cadover, it becomes an omen of death for Rickie; in the epilogue, its whistle recalls the sacrifice on which Stephen's survival depends. A more focused use of the device occurs in *Howards End,* in which the drumbeat of Beethoven's Fifth swells to become the very heartbeat of the novel. Forster's own image for this process (*AN,* 165–7) is Vinteuil's Sonata as used in Proust's *Swann's Way* (1913) and *Within a Budding Grove* (1918–19) from *Remembrance of Things Past,* which antedate Forster's procedures by a decade.

Forster's mixture of realism, social comedy, and "prophecy" has elicited considerable critical comment. His great if vexing visionary moments are almost exclusively associated with the musical subtext of each novel. Even the male romp in the Sacred Pond in *A Room with a View* cannot avoid comparison with the "nymphs in *Götterdämmerung*" (*RV,* 149). Most provocative, however, are Forster's deflections into prophetic song at the close of each of his novels, just as the plot may appear to be winding down to a conventional resolution. The effect is to destabilize the close: the louder the background music, the more troublesome the issues it is trying to conceal. The radiance of the Mystic Rose scene in *The Longest Journey* deflects the reader from the dismal death that awaits Rickie only hours later. Both the ashes of the evening primrose in *Maurice* and the "love more mysterious" of *A Room with a View* mitigate the psychosexual fissures in Forster's "happy ending." His esoteric musical codas prove one of the chief sources of the originality and incipient modernism of E. M. Forster's novels.

The most grandiose instance of difficult rhythm occurs in *A Passage to India.* The structural use of Western music as the foundation for its pattern of recurring motifs is no different from the procedures of *The Longest Journey* or *Howards End,* though less prominent. Its social and symbolic use of music, however, is unique among Forster's novels, and contributes to the unequivocal modernism of *A Passage to India.* Western art-music has no role in the debased lives of its resident English colonials, who lack the character and breeding to appreciate Beethoven, Brahms, and Wagner, and for whom all serious art is "bad form" (*PI,* 60). Shallow popular dances played by an amateur band provide the novel's rare snippets of Europeanized music: the incidental music to H. H. Davies's romantic comedy *Cousin Kate* (43) or Charles Ancliffe's waltz "Nights of Gladness" (283), a hit of the Palm-Court circuit. Heard from a distance, these British imports disrupt the quiet of the Mosque (41) and compete with the din of the Temple (284). Hindu classical music, represented by Professor Godbole's evening raga (95–6) and the Gokul Ashtami Festival at the Palace of Mau (281–7), fares no better. It is experienced from the equally uncomprehending perspectives of Islamic India (Aziz) and colonial Britain (Fielding, Mrs. Moore, and Miss Quested). Godbole's "song of an unknown bird" (95), proffered to bring pleasure to the English guests at Fielding's tea party, merely irritates: it comes at the wrong time (as everyone is leaving), ends at the wrong place (on the subdominant), and infects Mrs. Moore and Miss Quested with a fatal "apathy" that foretells the disaster of the Marabar Caves (145). Whether from East or West, traditional music divides people in Forster's India, as befits a novel that heralds the decay of the "personal relationships" at the core of his troubled liberalism.

The stifling "silence" of primeval India (152) provides the backdrop for the spectacular auditory world of *A Passage to India.* The novel bristles with random noise, with an uncanny Babel of sound that disrupts at every turn. Owls hoot, the jackals "bayed their desires and mingled with the percussion of drums" (55), a mangy squirrel squeaks "in tune with the infinite" to the "ponk ponk" of a coppersmith (126), and the "sound of spitting" emerges from "dark corners" (142). Even the piano produces only a "remarkable noise" when an angry Aziz strikes its swollen keys at thoughts of the English "closing their broken ranks against the alien" (302). The threatening drums of Mohurram; the competing jangle of bells from Hindu temple, Christian church, marriage chapel, and Chandrapore train station; the dull "pomper, pomper, pomper" of the train wheels; and a primitive band of itinerant sweepers, banging on sieves—all pound out a bewildering collective rhythm that bespeaks the essential otherness of India to the uncomprehending Westerner. The climax of this sound-world takes place at the festival in Mau, a spectacular concatenation of "music . . . from so many sources that the sum total was untrammelled. The braying banging crooning melted into a single mass which trailed round the palace before joining the thunder" (282). There, Godbole's choir, with clashing cymbals and drums, competes with a loud European band in the courtyard and the thumping of an electric power generator. As midnight strikes, "the rending note of the conch broke forth, followed by the trumpeting of elephants," shrieks and laughter, the popping of fireworks, a full gun salute, "and drowning all an immense peal of thunder" that "cracked like a mallet on the dome" (285, 310). This splendid auditory 'happening' transcends reason and the capacity of the word to comprehend it: "How can it be expressed in anything but itself? Not only from the unbeliever are mysteries hid, but the adept himself cannot retain them" (285).

At the heart of the uncanny music of *A Passage to India* is the voice of the Marabar Caves, each a stifling, silent granite tomb with a "terrifying echo" that resounds through the novel (158–9). Their "Bou-oum" is a great leveler that reduces all human sounds—the words of love and poetry, religion and music, vileness and "hope, politeness, the blowing of a nose, the squeak of a boot"—to the same dull roar. The horror of its message lies in its imperviousness to human understanding, its denigration of Western ideals of form and grandeur, and its dogged proclamation that "nothing has value" (160). For Fielding, the novel's *honnête homme,* the Marabar Caves are the sound-image for modern life: "'Everything echoes now; there's no stopping the echo. The original sound may be harmless, but the echo is always evil'" (272). Its lingering vibration proclaims the present impossibility of connecting East and West, man and woman, and man and man. Beyond the final "No, not yet" and "No, not there" (316) echoes the difficult rhythm of the Marabar Caves.

The tension of word and music continued to haunt Forster in the 1930s and 1940s, with "Beethoven's Piano Sonatas" as the gauge of his struggle. It is fitting that his last major project would bring him to the genre of opera in the circle around Benjamin Britten. Forster's earlier characterization of Herman Melville's tale as a "song not without words" seems to foretell the renewed connection of music and literature that he would achieve in collaboration with Britten and Crozier. The vaunted ambiguity of Melville's incomplete tale was tailor-made to Forster's visionary inclinations and facilitated those intermittent bursts of poetic heightening conducive to aria treatment. The opera's most stunning example of difficult rhythm, Britten's famous episode of thirty-four chords connecting Acts 3 and 4, was made possible by the librettists' decision to overlay the interview between Vere and the condemned

Billy with verbal silence. In the opera, their offstage love scene defers to pure music to express what may have been inexpressible publicly in the England of 1951. The numerous attempts to interpret Britten's arresting orchestral interlude speak to its holding power for the listener beyond the final measures of the opera.[2]

Billy Budd has barely made it onto the screen of Forster criticism. Mary Lago is alone among Forster biographers in recognizing that the libretto was "the high plateau of his later years."[3] The opera brought his experience of dramatic music to bear on a project that probed some of his deepest concerns—the struggle between civic duty and private conscience, the contest of goodness and depravity, and the possibility of masculine love in a repressive society. It also brought him head-on with the tension between word and music in the genre of opera, which had been created on this very premise. It dismissed him "peacefully" into his seventies and convinced him—at a stage of his life wracked with self-doubt as a writer and a man—that "I have achieved" (*SL2*, 246). To borrow a phrase from the aged Captain Vere, *Billy Budd* is E. M. Forster's "far-shining sail" in a life devoted to word and music.

APPENDIX A

Forster's Known *Ballets Russes* Attendance

Ballet Title	Music	Choreogr	EMF Attendance	Sources
L'Après-midi d'un faune	Debussy	Nijinsky	23.7.1913	L: D69; LD, 32
La Boutique fantasque	Rossini (o/Respighi)	Massine	1.7.1919 30.7.1919(M)	L: L305 L: L306
Le Carnaval	Schumann (o/Glazunov, Liadov, R-Korsakov, N.Tcherepnin)	Fokine	20.7.1911 20.6.1912 May 1919 (or *Papillons?*) 30.7.1919(M)	Stape,42 *SL1*, 136; LD, 29 EMF to Ludolf (17.5.1919) L: L306
Cléopatre	Arensky (and others)	Fokine	30.7.1919(M)	L: L306
The Firebird	Stravinsky	Fokine	18.6.1912 20.6.1912	L: D53 *SL1*, 136; LD, 29
The Good-Humoured Ladies	D.Scarlatti (o/Tommasini)	Massine	May 1919 1.7.1919	EMF to Ludolf (17.5.1919) L: L305
Le Pavillon d'Armide	Tcherepnin	Fokine	20.7.1911 28.7.1911(M)	Stape, 42 *SL1*, 122
Petrouchka	Stravinsky	Fokine	May 1919	EMF to Ludolf (17.5.1919)
Polovtsian Dances from Prince Igor	Borodin	Fokine	11.7.1913 23.7.1913	L: D69; LD, 32
Le Sacre du printemps	Stravinsky	Nijinsky	11.7.1913 23.7.1913	L: D69 LD, 32
Schéhérazade	Rimsky-Korsakov	Fokine	20.7.1911 28.7.1911(M)	Stape, 42 *SL1*, 122
Le Spectre de la rose	Weber (o/Berlioz)	Fokine	11.7.1913	EMF, "Shrine for Diaghilev" L: D69
Les Sylphides	Chopin (o/Glazunov, Stravinsky, Tanayev)	Fokine	28.7.1911(M) 18.6.1912 20.6.1912 11.7.1913 1.7.1919	*SL1*, 122 L: D53 *SL1*, 136; LD, 29 L: D69 L: L305
Thamar	Balakirev	Fokine	18.6.1912	L: D53

o/ = orchestration (M) = matinee

APPENDIX B

Forster's Known Opera Attendance

Composer	Title	Date/Venue	Performance Data	Comments
Berg, A.	*Wozzeck*	13.2.1952/CG	C: E. Kleiber	Forster's 2nd hearing
Berlin, I.	*Annie Get Your Gun*	4.1947/NY, Imperial Th	S: Ethel Merman	
Bernstein, L.	*West Side Story*	3.1959/London, Her Majesty's Th	S: Chita Rivera George Chakiris	
Bliss, A.	*The Olympians*	Fall 1949/CG	D: Peter Brook	EMF: "much better than the critics suggested"
Britten, B.	*Albert Herring*	10.1947	English Opera Group	
		7.6.1948/Aldeburgh Festival		EMF review, *Listener* (24.6. 1948)
	Billy Budd	1.12.1951/CG		World premiere
		13.5.1952/CG		EMF: "probably going"
		9.1.1964/CG	C: G. Solti	Premiere of 2-act version
	Gloriana	8.6.1953/CG	C: J. Pritchard S: Joan Cross Peter Pears	world premiere; "Coronation Gala" for Queen Elizabeth II
		2.7.1953/CG		
		22.11.1963/London, Royal Festival Hall		Britten's 50th birthday; announcement of Kennedy assassination postponed until afterward
	Peter Grimes	6.1945/Sadler's Wells	C: R. Goodall S: Joan Cross Peter Pears	EMF attended 2nd performance
		7(?).1.1949/CG		
		24.11.1953/CG		EMF: "very fine"

Appendix B: Forster's Known Opera Attendance (cont'd.)

Composer	Title	Date/Venue	Performance Data	Comments
	The Turn of the Screw	6(?).10.1955/ Sadler's Wells	English Opera Group	London premiere
Charpentier, G.	*Louise*	5.1911/CG	C: C. Campanini	
		7.1913/CG		EMF: "with Mother"
Debussy, C.	*Pelléas et Mélisande*	21.5.1909/CG	C: Campanini S: Rose Féart Edmond Warnery	London premiere; lead singers selected by Debussy (HR, 341)
		9.5.1911/CG	C: Campanini	
Donizetti, G.	*Lucia di Lammermoor*	12.5.1903/Florence, Teatro Verdi	S: Tetrazzini	Attended with Dent
		20.7.1908/CG	C: Campanini S: Tetrazzini	
		10.4.1959/CG		Joan Sutherland on medical leave
Gluck, C. W.	*Armide*	7.1906 (?)	C: A. Messager	Sung in French
		6.6.1908/CG	C: H. Richter S: Emmy Destinn	Sung in German EMF: "most beautiful"
		10.5.1909/CG	C: P. Pitt	Sung in French
	Iphigenia in Aulis	4.1959/London, Morley College		Amateur production
	Iphigenia in Tauris	17.12.1950/n.p.		May have been a radio production
		9.1962/Cambridge		EMF: Gluck is "a novelist's opera composer" (L: M284)
	Orfeo	7.1965/Cambridge?		Lago identifies the composer as Gluck (L: F278)
Menotti, G. C.	*The Telephone* *The Medium*	7.1947/NY, Ethel Barrymore Th		
Musorgsky, M.	*Boris Godunov*	6/7.1913/London, Drury Lane Russian Season	S: Fyodor Chaliapin D: S. Diaghilev	EMF: "with Mother"; Chaliapin's first London role
		19.6.1931/London, Lyceum Th	S: Chaliapin	A largely Russian cast
		19.11.1949/CG	S: Boris Christoff D: Peter Brook	Christoff's first performance of this rolc

Appendix B: Forster's Known Opera Attendance (cont'd.)

Composer	Title	Date/Venue	Performance Data	Comments
Mozart, W. A.	*Don Giovanni*	Early 1920/n.p.		Turning point in EMF's appreciation of Mozart
		6.1957/Vienna, Staatsoper		
	Idomeneo	20.2.1955/KCC, Cambridge	Touring company	EMF: "a lovely opera" (L: B2370)
		29.1.1964/London, Sadler's Wells		
	The Marriage of Figaro	16.5.1904/York		Sung in English; "Mozart is topsy-turvy" (NJ,12)
	Die Zauberflöte	14.9.1902/Munich		
		6(?).1943/Sadler's Wells (?)		Sung in English; EMF: "largely piffle" (L: P164)
Offenbach, J.	*La Belle Hélène*	4.1926(?)/Bordeaux		
		2.1960/n.p.		EMF: "charming light stuff" (L: B1044)
	Les Contes d'Hoffmann	5.10.1910/CG		Attended with Masood
Puccini, G.	*Girl of the Golden West*	1.1963/Sadler's Wells		Sung in English
	Madama Butterfly	16.11.1907/CG		EMF: "with Mother"
Purcell, H.	*Dido and Aeneas*	5.1951/n.p.	S: Nancy Evans	Concert version
Rodgers & Hammerstein	*Carousel*	5.6.1947/Chicago		EMF: "a long dull Musical Comedy" (LD)
Rossini, G.	*La Cenerentola*	11.1901/Florence, Teatro Verdi		
Saint-Saëns, C.	*Samson et Dalila*	25.5.1909/CG		First London run of this work; sung in French
Strauss, R.	*Elektra*	12.3.1910 & 15.3.1910/CG	C: R. Strauss	First London run of this work
		10(?).5.1938/CG	C: T. Beecham S: Rose Pauly Kerstin Thorborg	

Appendix B: Forster's Known Opera Attendance (cont'd.)

Composer	Title	Date/Venue	Performance Data	Comments
	Der Rosenkavalier	–9.6.1924/CG	C: B. Walter S: Lotte Lehmann Elisabeth Schumann, Delia Reinhardt	One of the classic productions of this work (HR, 427)
		3.6.1936/CG	C: F. Reiner S: Elis. Rethberg	
	The Rosencavalier	26.5.1959/ Glyndebourne		May have been dress rehearsal; sung in English
	Salome	28.12.1910/CG	C: Beecham	EMF: "disappointing"; attended with Masood and declared his love afterward
		3.11.1953/CG	C: R. Kempe S: Ljuba Welitsch	
Tchaikovsky, P. I.	*The Queen of Spades*	21.12.1950/CG	C: E. Kleiber S: Edith Coates	
Verdi, G.	*Aida*	7.6(?).1933/CG	C: J. Barbirolli S: Eva Turner	EMF: "absolutely ravished" (L: R203)
	Falstaff	6(?).1960/Munich		EMF: "not very good" (L: B661)
	La forza del destino	12.6.1931	C: T. Serafin S: Rosa Ponselle	EMF also owned Ponselle's recording
	Otello	26.11.1956/CG	C: R. Kubelik	
	La traviata	5(?).1962		Plans to go
Wagner, R.	*Lohengrin*	8.1954/Bayreuth	D: Wolfgang Wagner S: Birgit Nilsson	
	Die Meistersinger	1.1902/Rome		Sung in Italian; opened 26.12.1901
	Parsifal	17.5(?).1927/CG	S: Lauritz Melchior	
		30.4.1930/CG	S: Melchior	EMF: "with mother"
		7.8.1954/Bayreuth	D: Wieland Wagner S: Hans Hotter Martha Mödl	
	Der Ring des Nibelungen	28.3–3.4.1905/ Dresden Court Opera		

Appendix B: Forster's Known Opera Attendance (cont'd.)

Composer	Title	Date/Venue	Performance Data	Comments
		8.1954/Bayreuth	D: Wieland Wagner S: Hans Hotter Martha Mödl	
	Das Rheingold	27.5.1954/CG	C: F. Stiedry	Opening night of this new minimalist staging of *Ring*
	Götterdämmerung	8.2.1908/CG	C: H. Richter	Sung in English (Jameson)
		8.5.1912/CG		Sung in German
		–9.6.1924/CG	C: B. Walter (?)	
		28.5.1955/CG	C: R. Kempe	With May Buckingham
	Tristan und Isolde	3.6.1898/CG	S: Milka Ternina Jean de Reszke	Forster's first opera
		Spring 1908/CG	C: H. Richter	
		5/6.1926/CG	C: B. Walter(?)	
		9.12(?).1954/CG	C: R. Kempe S: Wolfgang Windgassen	Windgassen's CG début
Walton, W.	*Troilus and Cressida*	4.1955	S: Peter Pears	

C = Conductor D = Director HR = Rosenthal, *Two Centuries* S = Singer(s)
CG = Covent Garden Th = Theatre

Notes

Preface

Epigraph to Preface: *AN,* 168.

1. Proust, *Within a Budding Grove,* in *Remembrance,* 1: 575.
2. EMF, "From the Audience," 7.
3. "Novels of E. M. Forster" (1934), in Stape, *Critical Assessments,* 2: 54.
4. *Billy Budd,* Op. 50, by Benjamin Britten, Eric Crozier, and Edward Morgan Forster (London: Hawkes and Son, 1951).

Chapter 1: E. M. Forster's Life in Music

Epigraph to Chap. 1: Jones, "Forster on His Life" (1959), 11.

1. Ashby, *Forster Country*; Beauman, *Forster: A Biography*; Furbank, *A Life*; Lago and Furbank, *Selected Letters* [*SL1* and *SL2*]; King, *Forster and His World*; Stape, *Chronology*; Stone, *Cave and the Mountain.*
2. Undated letter from ACF to Mary Aylward (KCC: EMF/18/188/2).
3. *SL1,* 10; the beating of the other boy is reported in L: F311.
4. Smith, *Five Centuries of Cambridge Musicians,* 47–55; Brooke, *History of the University of Cambridge,* 4: 457–9.
5. Brooke, ibid., 4: 458; *SL1,* 43.
6. *As We Were* (1930), quoted in Fowler, *Cambridge Commemorated,* 270.
7. Browning, *Memories of Sixty Years,* 185–7, 229–30, 308.
8. Radcliffe, *Dent,* 5–30.
9. Furbank, *A Life,* 1: 58; *SL1,* 40, n. 2; Venn, *Alumni Cantabrigienses,* Part 2, 4: 554.
10. Woolf, *Sowing,* quoted in Fowler, *Cambridge Commemorated,* 267.

11. Clive Carey's correspondence with Dent reports these topics at an evening at Cyril Rootham's in May 1903 (Carey, *Duet for Two Voices,* 21).

12. EMF, *Goldsworthy Lowes Dickinson,* 83; Stone, *Cave and the Mountain,* 72–98, provides an introduction to Dickinson.

13. EMF, "Magic Flute;" *Goldsworthy Lowes Dickinson,* 177–80.

14. EMF, "My First Opera," 373–4.

15. *Musical Times* 39 (1898): 463.

16. Dent, "Donizetti: An Italian Romantic," 100; on his earlier appreciation of Donizetti, see his letter of May 1903 to Clive Carey, in Carey, *Duet for Two Voices,* 9–10.

17. Diary of E. J. Dent, vol. 7 (ms. KCC: Dent Box 1).

18. ACF to Louisa Whichelo, 8 January [?] 1902 (KCC: EMF/18/188/11).

19. Ibid.

20. NJ, 16 (31 December 1904). Clive Durham will identify "books and music" as the retreats from sexual activity of the homosexual aesthete (*MAU,* 62).

21. NJ, 19 (1 April 1905). Forster retained the program from this performance, purchased and signed on 27 March 1905, in his library until his death (EMF, "List of the Books," #162).

22. EMF, "My First Opera," 374.

23. Howes, "Cecil Sharp," *NG2,* 23: 219–20.

24. Heine, notes to *Arctic Summer,* 332 (the song occurs on p. 183).

25. On the novel's genesis, see Stallybrass, introduction to *PI,* 11–9; on the Indian trips, see Furbank, *A Life,* 1: 220–54; 2: 68–104.

26. EMF, *Hill of Devi,* 203.

27. Ibid., 45–6.

28. Garafola, *Diaghilev's Ballets Russes,* 314–25; Garafola's Diaghilev chronology in Garafola and Baer, *Ballets Russes and Its World,* 320–34, was helpful in assembling my Appendix A.

29. Garafola, *Diaghilev's Ballets Russes,* 63.

30. "Sunday Music" (2 September 1917), in EMF, *Prince's Tale,* 184–7; "A Musician in Egypt" (21 October 1917) and "Handel in Egypt" (6 January 1918), in EMF, *Uncollected Egyptian Essays,* 37–40, 47–50.

31. EMF to S. R. Masood (29 July 1916), quoted in Furbank, *A Life,* 2: 28.

32. Beauman, *Forster: A Biography,* 301–2.

33. Furbank, *A Life,* 2: 24–5.

34. "A Musician in Egypt," in EMF, *Uncollected Egyptian Essays,* 37–40, contains an overview of Terni's recent music.

35. Hyden, *Pavlova.*

36. EMF, *Alexandria,* 137.

37. EMF to F. Barger, 10 December 1917 (L: B81): "I never get to a piano now and fear the power to learn anything new may permanently leave me: all I can accomplish are washy reminiscences of the old."

38. The then-popular "Serenade" from Riccardo Drigo's ballet *Arlekinada.*

39. Although mention of Chopin is infrequent in Forster's papers, he had gone through a wave of interest in Chopin's piano music in 1905, when he was working on the large Polonaise in A flat, Op. 53 (L: T212).

40. EMF to ACF, 17 February 1917 (L: F529); EMF to G. L. Dickinson, 13 April 1918 (L: D319).

41. *Diary of Virginia Woolf* (12 March 1922), rpt. in Stape, *Interviews and Recollections,* 47.

42. EMF to ACF, 3 March 1924 (L: F650); the letter is dated 1923; Lago corrected the year to 1924.

43. Read and Welch, *From Tin Foil to Stereo,* 257–8.

44. Ferguson, "Forster at the National Gallery Concerts," 63.

45. Hess, "Great Adventure," 5.

46. EMF, "From the Audience," 6–7.

47. Roerick, "Forster and America," 61–2.

48. EMF to Merritt, 1 April 1947.

49. In October 1961 he again referred with satisfaction to the Harvard talk in an ill-fated conversation with Robert Craft at King's (Craft, "Tea in Cambridge," rpt. in Stape, *Interviews and Recollections,* 25).

50. Forbes, *History of Music at Harvard,* 103–10; Pollack, *Aaron Copland,* 421.

51. Patrick Wilkinson, "The Later Years," in Stape, *Interviews and Recollections,* 167.

52. Ibid., 179; Glenway Wescott, "A Dinner, a Talk, a Walk with Forster," in Stape, *Interviews and Recollections,* 110–11.

53. May Buckingham, "Some Reminiscences of E. M. Forster," in Stape, *Critical Assessments,* 1: 75.

54. Diogenes, "Some Musical Fashions," 148–9.

55. Dibble, "Dannreuther," 286–97.

56. Ibid., 295–6.

57. "The Lost Guide" (17 June 1956), in EMF, *Alexandria,* 355.

58. Radcliffe, *Dent,* 10.

59. EMF to Bob Buckingham, 20 August 1937 (L: B1498), and 18 February 1938 (L: B1550).

60. Kermode, *Concerning E. M. Forster,* 33.

61. Stape, *Chronology,* lists a number of these performances, including several for which I was unable to locate the primary references. Rosenthal, *Two Centuries,* greatly assisted in dating and identifying these productions.

62. This was the first English-language *Ring* cycle in London, and was immensely successful; see Rosenthal, *Two Centuries,* 327–9.

63. "Memories of Morgan," rpt. in Stape, *Interviews and Recollections,* 209–17.

64. "Revolution at Bayreuth," rpt. in EMF, *Prince's Tale,* 172–3. Forster had been equally unsettled by the Covent Garden *Rheingold,* which he had seen a few months

earlier on its May 27 opening night; as he wrote to the Earl of Harewood, "The whole production suffered from too much driftiness, in fact my eyes went tired. I wonder what Bayreuth will do—I fear for less restraint still, there" (L: H66). On the Bayreuth productions of 1954, see Spotts, *Bayreuth,* 212–9.

65. Stape, *Chronology,* 40.

66. Rosenthal, *Two Centuries,* 535.

67. Ibid., 427.

68. Ibid., 618.

69. Ibid., 378.

70. Ibid., 473.

71. Jones, "Forster on His Life," 12.

72. Ibid., 11.

73. EMF, "From the Audience," 7.

Chapter 2: "Creating" *Lucia*

Epigraph to Chap. 2: "Three Countries," fol. 119.

1. For the early reviews, see Gardner, *Critical Heritage,* 43–64.

2. Britten to Enid Slater, 23 November 1942, in *BBLL2,* #399.

3. Gattey, *Tetrazzini,* 71–9.

4. Gattey and Thomas G. Kaufman, "Chronology of Tetrazzini's Appearances," in Gattey, *Tetrazzini,* 280–300.

5. Ibid., 300–4.

6. Gattey, *Tetrazzini,* 31.

7. As recounted by Ian Watt and Lucio Ruotolo, in Stone, *Cave and the Mountain,* 171.

8. L: H67; Forster made similar comments in a letter to Eric Fletcher on 11 April 1959 (L: F139).

9. Forster returned for a second taste of Tetrazzini's *Lucia* at Covent Garden in 1908 (see Appendix B). Over fifty years later he compared the 1959 Covent Garden production unfavorably to the Florence *Lucia* in a letter to Fletcher (L: F139). In Joan Sutherland's defense, on the night that Forster saw the opera, the diva was on medical leave according to her *Prima Donna's Progress,* 75 and 441.

10. Stone, *Cave and the Mountain,* 171. Pierre Degott's recent "Représentations d'opéra," 38–42, is the only prior study of the scene and delivers an interesting if contrasting perspective.

11. Ardis, "Hellenism and the Lure of Italy," 67–71; Buzard, *Beaten Track,* 285–331; Pemble, *Mediterranean Passion.*

12. C. L. G., "Re-emergence of the Prima Donna," 820. See also Gattey, *Tetrazzini,* 82–3; Dent, "Italian Opera in the Eighteenth Century," 500.

13. Rosenthal, *Two Centuries*; Pemble, *Mediterranean Passion,* 230–1.

14. Tetrazzini's vocal manual *How to Sing* (1923) attempted to stem this tide of

contempt against coloratura as "false, showy, superficial, unworthy, [and] dramatically unreal" (75–9).

15. Dent, "Donizetti," 100 and 107.

16. With the exception of a single performance of *Lucia* at Covent Garden in 1925, with Toti dal Monte in the title role, according to Rosenthal, *Two Centuries*, 747–74.

17. Stallybrass, *WAFT*, 10; Dent also supplied the novel's title (Furbank, *A Life*, 1: 123).

18. Loewenberg, *Annals of Opera*, 1: col. 771.

19. Ardis, "Hellenism and the Lure of Italy," 63; on English guidebook culture, see Pemble, *Mediterranean Passion*, 70–4.

20. Ellis (?), "Bayreuth Hush," 109–14.

21. Ringger, "*Lucia di Lammermoor*," 69–79; for the American literary perspective, see Solie, "Fictions of the Opera Box." Donizetti's *Lucia* also contributes to the suicide of Tolstoy's *Anna Karenina* (1875–76).

22. Smart, "Silencing of Lucia," 127, n. 18; Forster would refer to Tetrazzini as "ugly and stout" in "Three Countries," fol. 119, also quoted in *WAFT*, 10.

23. Buzard, *Beaten Track*, 295.

24. The composite aria form consisted of an opening instrumental *scena* with vocal recitative, followed by a slow, lyrical aria (*cantabile*), a middle section of varying length (*tempo di mezzo*), and a virtuoso closing aria (*cabaletta*). Both arias end with a *cadenza*, a long vocalise that was originally improvised but by the end of the nineteenth century had become a written tradition. The cadenza features *coloratura*, florid untexted singing that displays the singer's highest range and virtuosity. The first-act "entrance aria" is shorter and is traditionally called a *cavatina*.

25. Showalter, *Female Malady*; Clément, *Opera, or the Undoing of Women*, 89; McClary, *Feminine Endings*, 80–86; Smart, "Silencing of Lucia," 119–22; Sala, "Women Crazed by Love," 19–41; and Koestenbaum, "Opera and Homosexuality," 242–7.

26. Foucault, *Madness and Civilization: A History of Insanity in the Age of Reason* (1965), discussed in McClary, *Feminine Endings*, 82–4, and Smart, "Silencing of Lucia," 119–20.

27. Dijkstra, *Idols of Perversity*, 37–50.

28. Clément, *Opera, or the Undoing of Women*, 89; McClary, *Feminine Endings*, 92–9.

29. "Silencing of Lucia," 128.

30. Forster's description accurately reflects Cammarano's stage direction: "She is dressed in a flowing white gown, and her hair streams loosely down over her shoulders. She has gone mad and is quite oblivious of her surroundings."

31. Sala, "Women Crazed by Love," 31.

32. Barblan, *L'Opera di Donizetti*, 124; Smart, "Silencing of Lucia," 130.

33. Smart, ibid., 131.

34. Ibid., 128.

35. Pugliese, "Origins of *Lucia di Lammermoor*'s Cadenza," 23–42.

36. Koestenbaum, "Opera and Homosexuality," 246.

37. McClary's focus on this cabaletta (*Feminine Endings*, 93–9) is thus exceptional, as is her conclusion that its vocal extravagance is a triumphant escape for its heroine.

38. "Discography," in Gattey, *Tetrazzini*, 333, and items nos. 5 and 41 (338, 343). All are available in a recorded anthology issued by Pearl Gemm (GEMM LP 220–7).

39. Gattey, "Discography," nos. 16, 17, and 64.

40. According to Aspinall, "*Lucia* Cadenza," 16, the modern preference for the version with recall of the love duet probably owes much to the 1926 *Lucia* recording by Toti Dal Monte.

41. Clive Brown, *Classical & Romantic Performing Practice*, 415–38.

42. The Ricordi reading is shown in the lower staff of each system. The upper staves show only embellishments and deviations from the edition in the 1904, 1907, and 1911 recordings; blank measures or segments of measures indicate that the performance follows the original score without notable alterations. *Portamento* is indicated by a line connecting the affected pitches.

43. *WAFT*, 110; Forster's word choice is provocative, given his use of the term "respectability" as a covert signal for sexual continence.

44. See "The Vision of Endymion" by Sir Edward J. Poynter, or "Endymion on Mount Latmos" by John Atkinson Grimshaw. The myth is recounted in Graves, *Greek Myths*, 199–200.

Chapter 3: Wagnerism, "Decadent" Wagnerites, and Wagnerian Motives in *The Longest Journey*

Epigraph to Chap. 3: EMF, "Author's Introduction," *LJ*, lxvi.

1. Gardner, *Critical Heritage*, 65–100; Heine, *LJ*, lvii–lxii.

2. EMF, "Author's Introduction," *LJ*, lxvi–lxvii.

3. Tambling, *E. M. Forster*, 47; Kaplan, "Absent Father, Passive Son," 51.

4. Heine, "Editor's Introduction," *LJ*, vii.

5. Earlier accounts of Forster's appropriation of Wagner in *LJ* include: Burra, "Novels of Forster," 52–4; Blissett, "Wagnerian Fiction," 259–60; DiGaetani, *Wagner and the Modern British Novel*, 159; Heine, *LJ*, xiii–xiv. Recent studies by Tony Brown, "Forster's *Parsifal*," and Herz, "End of Parsival," explore its *Parsifal* references.

6. On the visual references, see Graham Smith, "Between Past and Future," 220–2; idem, "Past in the Present," 79–89.

7. Trilling, *Forster*, 67.

8. On Wagnerism, see Large, *Wagnerism in European Culture and Politics*, esp. Weber, "Wagner, Wagnerism, and Musical Idealism," 28–71; on Wagnerism in England, see Sutton, *Aubrey Beardsley and British Wagnerism*, and Sessa, *Wagner and the English*, who also addresses English Wagner reception beginning in the 1870s and 1880s (25–49).

9. Heine, *LJ,* xiii.

10. As described by Stoddard Martin, *Wagner to "The Waste Land",* 99–113.

11. Sessa, "At Wagner's Shrine," in Large, *Wagnerism in European Culture and Politics,* 246.

12. "Wagner and Wagnerism," *Nineteenth Century* 13 (March 1883): 444, quoted in Sessa, *Wagner and the English,* 48.

13. Sutton, *Aubrey Beardsley and British Wagnerism,* 25, and esp. 46–56; Sessa, *Wagner and the English,* 99–103; Morris, "Tristan's Wounds," 271–4. A significant text in the construction of pathological Wagnerism was Max Nordau's *Die Entartung* (1892), translated into English and published in 1895 as *Degeneration* (Sutton, 51).

14. For perceptive readings of Beardsley's Wagnerian illustrations, see Sutton, *Aubrey Beardsley and British Wagnerism,* 28–44, 61–5, 90–4, 175–92.

15. EMF, "My First Opera," 373–4.

16. Sutton, *Aubrey Beardsley and British Wagnerism,* 13–4, 194–6.

17. Quoted by Heine, *LJ,* xl.

18. On this likelihood, see Heine, *LJ,* x.

19. Krehbiel, *Wagnerian Drama* (1891/1901); Lavignac, *Music Dramas of Richard Wagner* (1898); Newman, *Study of Wagner* (1899); Chamberlain, *Richard Wagner* (1900); Henderson, *Richard Wagner* (1901).

20. Carpenter, "Art and Democracy: Wagner, Millet, and Whitman," in *Angels' Wings* (1898); Symons, "Ideas of Richard Wagner" (1905).

21. Stape, *Chronology,* 21; Tony Brown, "Forster's *Parsifal,*" 94–6.

22. For a transcription of the sketch, see Heine, *LJ,* xlviii–xlix.

23. EMF, "Author's Introduction," *LJ,* lxvii.

24. NJ (23 March 1906), quoted by Heine, *LJ,* xiv.

25. Heine, "The Manuscripts of *The Longest Journey,*" in *LJ-A,* Appendix C (307–95); this material was omitted in the Penguin reissue of *LJ.*

26. EMF, "Author's Introduction," *LJ,* lxvi.

27. The mournful "Sir Percival" was originally Watts's more famous painting of the heroic "Sir Galahad" in an early draft (Heine, *LJ,* 308–9); the change must be purposeful.

28. Guernemanz's aphorism from Act 1 of *Parsifal* places salvation for the Grail knights in enlightenment attained through compassion by the intercession of an innocent fool: "Durch Mitleid wißend, der reine Tor."

29. As explored in Hanns Fuchs, *Richard Wagner und die Homosexualität* (1903), discussed by Sutton, *Aubrey Beardsley and British Wagnerism,* 54, and Morris, "Tristan's Wounds," 275–8.

30. According to Philip Brett (in conversation, November 2001), who had listened to the recording of *Götterdämmerung* with Forster in the latter's Cambridge rooms.

31. *LJ,* 5. Forster revised the initial draft from "a few chords" to the later "Prelude to Rhinegold" (Heine, *LJ-A,* 313).

32. The volume control on many pianolas was located on the crossbar just under the keyboard; see Chapter 6, and esp. Fig. 7.

33. Rpt. Dover (1967); see esp. plates 125, 134, and 135.

34. I am indebted to the subtle reading of this illustration by Sutton, *Aubrey Beardsley and British Wagnerism*, 175–6.

35. Stone, *Cave and the Mountain*, 200.

36. Dickinson, *Meaning of Good*, 225–7; see Heine, *LJ*, xxxii.

37. Heine, *LJ*, xiii.

38. Forster's wording for this theme resonates with Lavignac's "Primeval Element" (*Music Dramas of Richard Wagner*, 344).

39. Heine, *LJ-A*, 316–7.

40. Forster may have been influenced by the description of the scene in Weston, *Legends of the Wagner Drama*, 92.

41. Tony Brown, "Forster's *Parsifal*," 100–1.

42. As interpreted in Herz, "End of Parsival," 147.

43. Heine, *LJ-A*, 324.

44. Ansell appears blind to more compassionate readings of Elsa as victim of male dominance, whose ignorance of her husband's name would have reduced her to a position of weakness in both the marriage and the social order of tenth-century Brabant; on this revisionist view, see Williams, *Wagner and the Romantic Hero*, 64.

45. The neutral "see life" was Forster's initial version of this Grail reference (Heine, *LJ-A*, 346).

46. EMF, "Author's Introduction," in *LJ*, lxix; and Heine, *LJ*, xiv.

47. Williams, *Wagner and the Romantic Hero*, 8–13, describes these normative characteristics of a "romantic hero."

48. Henderson, *Richard Wagner*, 403.

49. A rejected draft recalls the words of the late Mr. Failing that "such a boy must find out life for himself" (Heine, *LJ-A*, 369–70).

50. Weston, *Legends of the Wagner Drama*, 97, which describes the characteristics of the Nordic epic hero.

51. The two most extensive revisions—the excision of the "fantasy" chapter (originally Chapter 14) and the conflation of two rejected chapters into the current Chapter 31—both revolve around Stephen (the original drafts are transcribed in Heine, *LJ-A*, 332–8 and 373–85).

52. Ibid., 379–80 (fol. A63).

53. "Pessimism in Literature" (1906), rpt. in EMF, *Albergo Empedocle*, 144.

54. Ellis, *Wagner's Prose Works*, 8 vols. (1893–99); for the relevant passages from *Opera and Drama*, see *Wagner's Prose Works*, 2: 327–30, 344–50; the 1879 essay, originally published in *Bayreuther Blätter*, is found in *Wagner's Prose Works*, 6: 173–91.

55. Ellis, *Wagner's Prose Works*, 2: 328–9, 345–6.

56. "Zur Wagner-Frage," *Musikalisches Wochenblatt* (1870), quoted in Kropfinger, *Wagner and Beethoven*, 218.

57. In this broad conclusion I am in full agreement with DiGaetani, *Wagner and the Modern British Novel,* 94 and 159, and Heine, *LJ,* xiii.

58. *Opera and Drama* in Ellis, *Wagner's Prose Works,* 2: 346–8.

59. Ibid., 6: 183.

60. Kropfinger, *Wagner and Beethoven,* 218.

61. By such as Carolyn Abbate, Thomas S. Grey, and Joseph Kerman, as discussed in Grey, *Wagner's Musical Prose,* 319–26.

62. Krehbiel, *Wagnerian Drama,* 19; Henderson, *Richard Wagner,* 199; Chamberlain, *Richard Wagner,* 232; Carpenter, *Angels' Wings,* 16.

63. As Forster admitted in a 1953 Paris interview (Furbank and Haskell, "Art of Fiction," 36). Likewise the term *Leitmotiv* was popularized by Wagner disciple Hans von Wolzogen and only grudgingly tolerated by Wagner; see "On the Application of Music to the Drama" in Ellis, *Wagner's Prose Works,* 6: 184, and Breig, "Musical Works," 441–2.

64. *AN,* 164–9; Nattiez, *Proust as Musician,* 8, summarizes the Wagnerian development of Vinteuil's "petite phrase" across the novel.

65. Lavignac, *Music Dramas of Richard Wagner,* 344.

66. Henderson, *Richard Wagner,* 444–5.

Chapter 4: "New Woman" or "Piano Girl": Lucy's Music in *A Room with a View*

1. On Forster's reactions, see *RV,* 13–5. This chapter is a substantial revision of an earlier version: Fillion, "Edwardian Perspectives on Nineteenth-Century Music in E. M. Forster's *A Room with a View,*" *19th-Century Music* 25 (2002): 266–95, with permission of the University of California Press.

2. *Observer* (27 July 1958), rpt. in *RV,* 231–3.

3. Crews, *Perils of Humanism,* 83; see also Land, *Challenge and Conventionality,* 117, where music is reduced to Lucy's escape valve.

4. Unsigned review, *Observer* (8 November 1908): 4, in Gardner, *Critical Heritage,* 109.

5. Lucas, "Wagner and Forster," in Stape, *Critical Assessments,* 3: 161–2. On music as emotional signifier in *RV,* see Beer, *Achievement of E. M. Forster,* 59–60; Sullivan, "Forster's Symbolism," 219; McDowell, *E. M. Forster,* 22–3; and Beauman, *Forster: A Biography,* 206–7. Kermode, *Concerning E. M.* Forster, which appeared in 2009 after the completion of my study, provides an astute reading of Lucy's Op. 111 that complements my own (38–46).

6. Solie, *Music in Other Words,* 85–117; Da Sousa Correa, *Music and Victorian Culture,* 59–101; Lustig, "Piano's Progress"; Burgan, "Heroines at the Piano." A telling visual depiction of the "piano girl" is provided by the 1903 painting "Courtship" by Edmund Blair Leighton (1853–1922).

7. Weliver, *Women Musicians in Victorian Fiction,* 55–6.

8. This approaches Edmond de Goncourt's famous 1880 description of piano-playing as a woman's "hashish" and an outlet for her sexuality, as quoted in Pistone, *Le Piano dans la littérature française,* 128.

9. Law, "Perniciously Homosexual Art," 180–3; Burgan, "Heroines at the Piano," 59–60.

10. Forster suppressed its suggestive, clandestine midnight encounter of Mr. Beebe and George Emerson, reprinted in *LN,* 106–12.

11. Weliver, *Women Musicians in Victorian Fiction,* 114.

12. Such as Hüttner's 1829 solo arrangement, "*Adelaide en forme de nocturne,*" cited in Kinsky, *Das Werk Beethovens,* 110.

13. Rosecrance, *Forster's Narrative Vision,* 90–2.

14. Ibid., 91; Stallybrass also draws this connection in *RV,* 243.

15. On the rhythmic association of water and music in *RV,* see Crews, *Perils of Humanism,* 89.

16. Wagner, "The Composer as Listener," quoted in Kropfinger, *Wagner and Beethoven,* 55.

17. Pederson, "Beethoven and Masculinity," 313–31.

18. Lenz, *Beethoven et ses trois styles,* 257. With few exceptions, the radical nature of Lucy's repertoire choice has gone unappreciated; exceptions are Higdon, "Opus 3 or Opus 111," and Beauman, *Forster: A Biography,* 206, the latter of whom proposes this "difficult" piece as an image of Lucy's potential "greatness."

19. On the poetic and formal implications of the key of C minor to Beethoven, see Tusa, "Beethoven's 'C-Minor Mood,'" esp. 24.

20. Lenz, *Beethoven et ses trois styles,* 266.

21. Kunze, *Beethoven: Werke im Spiegel seiner Zeit,* 378.

22. Ibid., 377.

23. Dannreuther, "Beethoven and His Works," 203.

24. Pianists sometimes divide the opening gesture between the hands, opting for safety over daring.

25. *The Harmonicon* 1 (1823): 112–3, in Kunze, *Beethoven: Werke im Spiegel seiner Zeit,* 374–5.

26. Bekker, *Beethoven,* 190–1; Brendel, *Music Sounded Out,* 71; Mellers, *Beethoven and the Voice of God,* 253, 264; Kinderman, "Klaviersonate Op. 111," in Riethmüller, *Beethoven: Interpretationen seiner Werke,* 2: 181; Kinderman, *Beethoven,* 236.

27. Pederson, "Beethoven and Masculinity," 326.

28. The poem is considered a model of modern pastoral lyricism (Alpers, *What Is Pastoral?,* 295–300). The verses are quoted by Alpers (295) from Christopher Ricks, ed., *The Poems of Tennyson,* 2nd ed. (Berkeley and Los Angeles: University of California Press, 1987), 2: 286–8.

29. Daverio, *Robert Schumann,* 74–5.

30. Forster culled this phrase from a journal entry of 15 May 1905: "Art is concerned

with complete things; Life puts up with incompleted, & does not—or should not—apply the test of durability" (NJ, 21).

31. Rosen, *Romantic Generation,* 41–8.

32. Gluck's *drame héroïque* in five acts to the classic libretto by Philippe Quinault (Paris, 1777) is available in full score edited by Klaus Hortschansky in *Gluck: Sämtliche Werke,* I: 8a, 149–59. Brissler's piano-vocal arrangement, from which my Ex. 6 is excerpted to be playable as a single piece, was available in 1907 in the Peters edition (64–7).

33. This could only have been the first Covent Garden *Armide,* presented in French in July 1906. According to Rosenthal, *Two Centuries,* 317, 334, 743–4, there were four performances between July 6 and 26; the next production, in German, opened in June 6, 1908, with Forster in attendance (NJ, 52), by which time *RV* was completed.

34. This is particularly evident in the 1999 recording by Les Musiciens du Louvre, Grenoble, on period instruments, conducted by Marc Minkowski (DGG 459 616-2).

35. For a contrasting reading of this scene as a religious allegory, see Lucas, "Wagner and Forster," 174–6.

36. Tony Brown, "Forster's *Parsifal,*" 93.

37. Geck and Voss, *Richard Wagner: Sämtliche Werke,* 30: *Parsifal-Dokumente,* 47, letter of Wagner to Lehmann, Bayreuth (22 January 1881).

38. Ibid., 51, letter of Wagner to King Ludwig II, Bayreuth (19 September 1881).

39. Köhler, *Richard Wagner,* 633–4.

40. Dijkstra, *Idols of Perversity,* 240–1.

41. Da Sousa Correa, *Music and Victorian Culture,* 95–101; Weliver, *Women Musicians in Victorian Fiction,* 207–14.

42. Lucas, "Wagner and Forster," 170–2.

43. Pohl-Hadow, *Grove* (1907), 3: 304; Parry, *Grove* (1910), 5: 225.

44. Scott, *Bride of Lammermoor,* 61–4.

45. *English Music* (London, 1902), 103–4, quoted in Temperley, "Sir Henry R. Bishop," *NG2,* 3: 631. It is possible, however, that Forster may have encountered the song in an undated adaptation for alto voice and piano by Charles Wood (1866–1926), Cambridge Lecturer in Music during his undergraduate years. Originally for soprano and alto with accompaniment, an undated Boston edition by C. C. Birchard and Co. is listed in the *Music Educators Journal* 29 (1943): 46.

46. A similar scene is depicted in Edmund Blair Leighton's 1896 painting "Singing to the Reverend."

47. Lucas, "Wagner and Forster," 178; Stone, *Cave and the Mountain,* 222.

48. Stone, ibid., 226, discusses the novel's "rhythm" of opposites.

49. Herz, "*A Room with a View,*" 146–7, probes the conclusion of the novel with similar intent, but locates Forster's source for its transcendent music in Dante's *Paradiso,* which Forster was reading at the time.

50. Readers interested in a full reading of the sonata are directed to Rosen's brilliant account in *Classical Style,* 441–8.

Chapter 5: Not Listening to Beethoven and Brahms at the Queen's Hall

1. *Daily News* (7 November 1910), in Gardner, *Critical Heritage,* 135. For an earlier version of segments of this chapter, see Fillion, "Forster's Beethoven."

2. Woolf, "The Novels of E. M. Forster" (1927), in Gardner, *Critical Heritage,* 319, 323–7.

3. Peter Widdowson, *E. M. Forster's 'Howards End': Fiction as History* (London: Chatto and Windus for Sussex University Press, 1977), quoted in Bradshaw, "*Howards End,*" 151; Medalie, *Forster's Modernism,* 7–25.

4. See, for example, the rich anthology of criticism assembled in the case studies of the novel edited by Duckworth (*HE-D*) and Armstrong (*HE-NCE*), in particular Duckworth, "Critical History," Widdowson, "*Howards End:* Fiction as History" (esp. 375–7), and Langland, "Gesturing toward an Open Space," all in *HE-D*; Levenson, "Liberalism and Symbolism in *Howards End,*" and Born, "Private Gardens, Public Swamps," the two latter in *HE-NCE.*

5. Widdowson, "*Howards End:* Fiction as History," in *HE-D,* 364.

6. This and all subsequent references to the novel refer to *HE-D,* the text of which is a light revision of the Abinger Edition.

7. *HE-M,* 26. The critic is Friedrich Schlegel (1772–1829), the German idealist writer and philosopher whose concept of romantic poetry as a *Mischgattung* (a "mixed genre") melding poetry and prose, philosophy and rhetoric, good humor and criticism, high poetry and folk poetry in a dialectical process (*Athenäeum-Fragment,* 1798) underlies the novel's aesthetic program.

8. Bradshaw, "*Howards End,*" 151–7, convincingly exposes the features that *connect* the "antithetical" Schlegels and Wilcoxes. See also Widdowson, "*Howards End:* Fiction as History," 373.

9. The admission price of 1–5s. in 1908–9 was half that of the Saturday Afternoon Concerts of the Queen's Hall Orchestra and was substantially lower than other major symphonic series in London.

10. NJ, 51 (1 May 1908): "On Sunday going to the 5th Beethoven at Q's Hall." The Queen's Hall program of Sunday May 3, 1908, however, did not include the Fifth Symphony. Forster evidently had either misdated his journal entry or confused this program with that advertised for Sunday, April 26 (*Times,* 24 April 1908), which included Beethoven's Fifth Symphony along with Chopin's Funeral March, Wagner's *Rienzi* overture and Lohengrin's Farewell, two songs by Coleridge Taylor, a Morris Dance by Mackenzie, and von Suppé's *Poets and Peasants* Overture.

11. I surveyed the programs of the four seasons from Fall 1906 to Spring 1910 as announced in the *Times.*

12. Weber, *Great Transformation of Musical Taste,* 266–71. In the case of a second-

tier orchestra such as that of the Queen's Hall (Weber, 304), the tradition of the mixed program was somewhat more enduring than was the case with more distinguished English ensembles.

13. This overture was paired with Beethoven's Fifth in the Sunday Concert of 1 December 1907.

14. Forster's inspiration for the pairing of Beethoven and Elgar may have been Grove (*Beethoven and His Nine Symphonies*, 172), who had described the finale of the Fifth as "all the pomp and circumstance of earthly life. It may be victory or success of some other kind that is depicted, but success it undoubtedly is, and a glorious career." Forster's excision of the word "life" for the singular "career" in Helen's observation that the symphony summarized "all that . . . could happen in her career" (*HE-M*, 31; *HE-D*, 46) bolsters Forster's likely contact with Grove's account.

15. Crump, "Identity of English Music," 166–8.

16. Westburg, "Forster's Fifth Symphony," 359–65; Hanquart, "Divertissements et divertissement," 57–65; Weatherhead, "*Howards End:* Beethoven's *Fifth*," 247–64; Foata, "Knocking at the Door," 135–45; and Björkén-Nyberg, "Music and Gender in *Howards End*," 90–103.

17. Brahms to Fritz Simrock, 8 May 1896, in Avins, *Johannes Brahms*, 733.

18. "The Raison d'Être of Criticism in the Arts" (1947), in *TCD*, 107.

19. Dennis, *Beethoven in German Politics*, 32–57.

20. Ibid., 60–1.

21. *Vom Musikalisch-Schönen* (Leipzig, 1854), 34, quoted in Grey, "Metaphorical Modes," 93.

22. Beller-McKenna, *Brahms and the German Spirit*, 5; Dahlhaus, "Wagner's Place," 114–7. For a recent perspective on the debate, see Pederson, "Defining the Term 'Absolute Music.'"

23. Björkén-Nyberg, "Music and Gender in *Howards End*," 93–5; Burnham, *Beethoven Hero*, 81–9; Pederson, "Defining the Term 'Absolute Music,'" 258–60.

24. Grove, *Beethoven and His Nine Symphonies*, 157.

25. *Ibid.*, 163. The *Allegro* third movement is a scherzo in character if not name.

26. "Beethoven," in Ellis, *Richard Wagner's Prose Works*, 5: 61–126. On Dannreuther, see Knittel, "Wagner, Deafness, and Reception," 71–3; on Wagner and nineteenth-century Beethoven reception, see Botstein, "Search for Meaning in Beethoven," 332–3.

27. Grove, *Beethoven and His Nine Symphonies*, 165. Grove in turn had borrowed this metaphor from Hector Berlioz.

28. Firchow, "Germanic Mythology in *Howards End*," 61–8, explores the Wagnerian association. The connection with the *Ring* was more emphatic in an earlier draft of the novel, which had used the word "gnomes" [cf. *Nibelungen*] in the place of "goblins" (*HE-M*, 30).

29. On the gender implications of this scene, see Langland, "Gesturing toward an Open Space," 411, and Björkén-Nyberg, "Music and Gender in *Howards End*," 101–2.

30. MacArdle, *Beethoven as I Knew Him,* 147; Forster could have accessed the quotation via Shedlock, *Beethoven,* 40.

31. Schmalfeldt, "Form as the Process of Becoming," 70 and 83; Solie, "The Living Work," 148–51.

32. As amply demonstrated by Webster, *Haydn's "Farewell" Symphony.*

33. The 1808 first version of the scherzo had included an additional reprise of the opening sections to create an ABABA^{1} design; see Brandenburg, "Once Again," 196–8.

34. Kramer, *Music and Poetry,* 235; Burnham, *Beethoven Hero,* 54.

35. EMF, "What I Believe" (1939), in *TCD,* 71. Forster's later words give every indication that he took Helen's reading of the Fifth quite seriously; in this I part company with Kermode, *Concerning E. M. Forster* (36), for whom Helen's account is merely droll.

36. Konold, *Beethoven: 5. Sinfonie,* 55–6.

37. Charlton, *Hoffmann's Musical Writings,* 250.

38. *HE-D,* 242 (emphasis mine).

39. Björkén-Nyberg, "Music and Gender in *Howards End,*" 99, concludes this of Helen's entire interpretation of the Fifth; see Weatherhead, "*Howards End:* Beethoven's *Fifth,*" 255–7, for a similar conclusion based on interpretation of the second movement.

40. Wagner, *Rhinegold,* with libretto trans. Frederick Jameson (208–21), would probably have been available to Forster.

41. Medalie, *Forster's Modernism,* 23.

42. "The Novels of E. M. Forster," in Gardner, *Critical Heritage,* 324.

43. Medalie, *Forster's Modernism,* 23.

44. Ibid., 23–5.

45. Charlton, *Hoffmann's Musical Writings,* 250.

Chapter 6: Tchaikovsky and the Deflowering of Masculine Love in *Maurice*

Epigraph to Chap. 6: Letter to Alexander Glazounov, 30 January (February 11) 1890, in Tchaikovsky-Newmarch, 599, quoted in EMF, LD, 1912.

1. EMF, "Aldeburgh Festival" (1951), quoted in Gardner, Introduction to *MAU-A,* viii.

2. Henceforth referred to as Tchaikovsky-Newmarch. Modeste's massive three-volume biography had appeared in Russian in 1900–2 and was a landmark in composers' biographies for its extensive use of personal documents, according to Malcolm H. Brown, "Tchaikovsky in Anglo-American Criticism," 141. Of the major English-language Tchaikovsky biographies available in 1912 (Edwin Evans, *Tchaikovsky* [1906]; Newmarch, *Tchaikovsky: His Life and Works* [1900/1908]; idem, "Tchaikovsky," *Grove's Dictionary* [1910]), Tchaikovsky-Newmarch is the only one consistent with Forster's LD entries and *MAU,* Chapter 32.

3. These comments are entered on an unpaginated sheet in LD, dated 12 May 1912; they refer to Tchaikovsky-Newmarch, 170–1.

4. Letters to Alexander Glazounov, 30 January (February 11) 1890 and Nadezhda von Meck, 16 (28) March 1877, in Tchaikovsky-Newmarch, 599 and 213, resp. The spread of Forster's citations suggests that he had read the entire volume and returned later to transcribe these excerpts, which identify with precision the biography read by Forster.

5. Forster recalled the visits in his 1960 "Notes on *Maurice*," pub. 1971 as "Terminal Note" (*MAU*, 217). The biographical evidence is summarized by Gardner, Introduction to *MAU-A*, ix–xii.

6. On Carpenter, see Fone, *Road to Stonewall*, 147–55; Brady, *Masculinity and Male Homosexuality*, 194–209; and Robertson, *Worshipping Walt*, 167–88.

7. According to his year-end NJ entry for 1907, as reported by Furbank, *A Life*, 1: 159. The entry also mentions Whitman and John Addington Symonds among the reading for that year. Tony Brown, "Edward Carpenter," 279–300, argues convincingly for Carpenter's impact on *RV*.

8. Carpenter, *Intermediate Sex*, 53–69. For a survey of this literature, see Ivan Crozier, Introduction to Ellis-Symonds, *Sexual Inversion*, 18–25.

9. Although privately printed in limited editions in 1908 and 1896, resp., both essays were well known in intellectual circles such as the Cambridge Apostles and were surely to be found in Carpenter's library. Forster had read unidentified works of Symonds in 1901 and 1907 (Furbank, *A Life*, 1: 86 and 159, n. 1). On Symonds, see Fone, *Road to Stonewall*, 128–45; Brady, *Masculinity and Male Homosexuality*, 162–94; and Robertson, *Worshipping Walt*, 140–67.

10. Cf. the new critical edition by Ivan Crozier (2008).

11. Case XVIII (Ellis-Symonds, *Sexual Inversion*, 142–7), identified by Crozier as Symonds (142, n. 7).

12. EMF, "Terminal Note," in *MAU*, 217. On the genesis and sources of the novel, see Gardner, Introduction to *MAU-A*, vii–liv.

13. The first publication of Epilogue in Gardner, *MAU-A*, 221–4; on its dating, ibid., xviii.

14. Zeikowitz, *Letters between Forster and Isherwood*, esp. 27 April 1933 (21), 28 August 1938 (74–5), and letters of Jan.–Feb. 1952 (149–51).

15. EMF, "Terminal Note," in *MAU*, 218.

16. Martin, "Edward Carpenter," 108–9.

17. Sinfield, *Wilde Century*, 140.

18. For a summary of the legislation, see Cook, *London and the Culture of Homosexuality*, 42–3, and Crozier, Introduction to Ellis-Symonds, *Sexual Inversion*, 10–1.

19. For a comprehensive study of the Wilde trials, see Foldy, *Trials of Oscar Wilde*.

20. Brady, *Masculinity and Male Homosexuality*, 83, 122, 152, et passim.

21. Carpenter, *Intermediate Sex*, 26.

22. Ibid., 81–2.

23. Martin, "Edward Carpenter," 101, 108–11.

24. EMF to Forrest Reid, March 1915 (L: R87), quoted in Gardner, Introduction to *MAU-A*, xxiii; EMF, "Terminal Note," *MAU*, 218.

25. Poznansky, *Tchaikovsky*, 562–3; Malcolm H. Brown, "Tchaikovsky in Anglo-American Criticism," 138. By 1905, clear suggestions of Tchaikovsky's homosexuality were circulating in print in London (Brown, 142). The 1893 tour is chronicled in Norris, *Stanford*, 388–448.

26. *Mezzotints in Modern Music*, quoted in Malcolm H. Brown, "Tchaikovsky in Anglo-American Criticism," 143.

27. Brown, "Tchaikovsky in Anglo-American Criticism," 141–2.

28. *Musical Times* 39 (1 July 1898): 471, quoted in Norris, *Stanford*, 488. The latter is a compendium of fin de siècle English reception of Tchaikovsky and his Pathétique (449–504).

29. *Musical Times* (June 1895), quoted in Norris, *Stanford*, 482.

30. Furbank, *A Life*, 1: 98.

31. Gardner, Introduction to *MAU-A*, xv–xvi.

32. Martin, "Edward Carpenter," 103.

33. Symonds, *Problem in Greek Ethics*, 51–2.

34. EMF, "Terminal Note," in *MAU*, 220.

35. Law, "Perniciously Homosexual Art," documents the widespread connection between musicality and sexual inversion in English decadent novels beginning with Wilde's *Dorian Gray*. Leppert, *Music and Image*, 17–8, traces the link between musicality and effeminacy back to eighteenth-century England. See also Carpenter, *Intermediate Sex*, 111, and Ellis-Symonds, *Sexual Inversion*, 195.

36. Sinfield, *Wilde Century*, 140.

37. My interpretation of this scene has profited from Bret L. Keeling's "No Trace of Presence" (2003), the only prior study of Tchaikovsky and the Sixth in *Maurice*. His critical perspective from gay studies and his brilliant reading of homosexual disclosure in the novel's Tchaikovsky scenes stimulated my thinking in many ways, although our accounts and overall conclusions also differ significantly.

38. The term was often extended to all player-pianos, regardless of make; see Ord-Hume, *Pianola*, 6.

39. Vol. 89 (10 January 1914): 75; *The Graphic* is among the journals that Forster places in the English bank in Florence in *RV*, 76.

40. Ord-Hume, *Pianola*, 138 (fig. 47) depicts a cross section of the action of this instrument; on the adjusting levers, see p. 160.

41. Law, "Perniciously Homosexual Art."

42. Keeling, "No Trace of Presence," 91–2.

43. Oskar Fried's 1929 Columbia recording with London's Royal Philharmonic Orchestra interprets the movement as a jaunty march at a remarkably brisk quarter note = 168, but broadens the tempo considerably for the final *fff* entry of the main theme at m. 283 (quarter note = 132).

44. *Musical Times* 40 (1 December 1899): 819, quoted in Norris, *Stanford*, 497.

45. Clive "murmured something about Eternity in an hour. Maurice did not understand" (*MAU*, 90), in likely reference to Whitman's "One Hour to Madness and Joy" (1860) from *Children of Adam* (Moon, *Leaves of Grass*, 91).

46. Ellis-Symonds, *Sexual Inversion*, 145, 213.

47. Carpenter, *Intermediate Sex*, 59, in reference to *Psychopathia Sexualis*, 256.

48. *MAU*, 129. Maurice's vision of the sleeping youth recalls contemporary English paintings of the sleeping Endymion, as already evoked in relation to Gino in *WAFT* (see Chapter 2, pp. 37–8).

49. *MAU*, 136. On the "degeneration theory" of Krafft-Ebing and others, see Mondimore, *Natural History of Homosexuality*, 35–7, and Crozier, Introduction to Ellis-Symonds, *Sexual Inversion*, 22–3.

50. Brady, *Masculinity and Male Homosexuality in Britain*, 173.

51. Keeling, "No Trace of Presence," 85. Forster may have been aware of Marc-André Raffalovich's equation of "musicality" and "pederasty" in *Uranisme et unisexualité* (1896), as described in Law, "Perniciously Homosexual Art," 183.

52. Tchaikovsky-Newmarch, 171 and 169, resp.

53. Ibid., 471 and 625, resp.

54. Crozier, Introduction to Ellis-Symonds, *Sexual Inversion*, 51–2.

55. Ibid., 65.

56. In this sense, Keeling's observations ("No Trace of Presence," 97) on the role of the biography in informing Maurice of the "details regarding Tchaikovsky's mysterious death" and the suicide of Bob Davydov are off the mark.

57. Poznansky, *Tchaikovsky*, 610–1.

58. "Several sensational accounts of the composer's end have been widely circulated and still receive credence . . ." (44).

59. For an overview of the controversy, see Poznansky, "Tchaikovsky's Suicide," Taruskin, "Pathetic Symphonist," and David Brown, "How Did Tchaikovsky Come to Die?"

60. *MAU*, 210; *MAU-A*, xliii.

61. "Long I Thought That Knowledge Alone Would Suffice" (1860), originally published among the "Calamus" poems in the 1860 edition of *Leaves of Grass* (Moon, *Leaves of Grass*, 519–20).

62. Fone, *Road to Stonewall*, 175.

63. Carpenter, *Intermediate Sex*, 11.

64. Grant, "*Maurice* as Fantasy," 202; Da Silva, "Transvaluing Immaturity," 263–4.

65. Moon, *Leaves of Grass*, 96.

66. *MAU-A*, 223. Forster surely intended a connection with the threatening "red rust" at the close of *Howards End* (*HE-D*, 288).

67. EMF to Isherwood, 27 April 1933 (L: I7), in Zeikowitz, *Letters between Forster and Isherwood*, 21.

68. EMF to Isherwood, 28 August 1938 (L: I36), in Zeikowitz, 75.

69. L: S490 (25 August 1933), quoted in *MAU-A*, xxxv.

70. Medalie, *Forster's Modernism*, 52–4, uses this statement as a focal point for his proposed "happy" ending, which in his view weakens the modernist impulses of the novel.

Chapter 7: "Beethoven's Piano Sonatas" (1939–40) and the Twilight of the Hero

Epigraph to Chap. 7: *TCD*, 75.

1. EMF, "The C Minor of That Life" (1941), in *TCD*, 125.

2. Previous discussions of the manuscript are: Halls, "Forster Collections at King's," 156; and Hutcheon, "'Sublime Noise' for Three Friends," 91, who included liberal quotations from the manuscript and situated it in the aesthetics of Roger Fry and Charles Mauron.

3. Panter-Downes, "Kingsman," in Stape, *Interviews and Recollections*, 205.

4. Tovey, "Ludwig van Beethoven," *Encyclopaedia Britannica*, 3: 650.

5. It was still in Forster's collection at his death (see "List of the Books in E. M. Forster's Rooms," #11).

6. "Forster and Music," in Kildea, *Britten on Music*, 316 and 319.

7. Panter-Downes, "Kingsman," in Stape, *Interviews and Recollections*, 204; EMF, "The C Minor of That Life," *TCD*, 125.

8. Mauron to EMF, 2 February 1929 (KCC); EMF to Mauron, 19 May 1935 (L: M238).

9. Mauron, "Orpheus and Morgan" (1959), in Stape, *Interviews and Recollections*, 193–4.

10. LD, 57: "Sullivan to lunch. . . . He strummed Beethoven unattractively, but spoke of him interestingly. B. one who lived by an inner light, then became aware of people's behavior in an external way, thought dishonesty was the proper thing, and cheated like Hell."

11. Tovey, *Essays in Musical Analysis*, Vol. 4, 43–5.

12. L: I45, in Zeikowitz, *Letters between Forster and Isherwood*, 87.

13. L: I46, ibid., 89.

14. Hutcheon, "'Sublime Noise' for Three Friends," 97.

15. Tovey, *Companion to Beethoven's Pianoforte Sonatas* (1941) and his commentaries on those works in Tovey-Craxton, *Beethoven* (1941); for an (Austro-)American formalist perspective, see Rudolph Réti's *Thematic Patterns in Sonatas of Beethoven*, begun in the mid-1940s and published in 1951.

16. As discussed by Rosen, *Classical Style*, 407–34, esp. 426–9.

17. *TCD*, 76. On Forster's liberal-humanism, see especially Crews, *Perils of Humanism*, 19–36; Medalie, *Forster's Modernism*, 1–62; Medalie, "Bloomsbury and Other Values," 38–45; Beauman, *E. M. Forster*, 353–63.

18. Beauman, *E. M. Forster,* 368.

19. *Rationalism and Humanism,* 20, quoted in Medalie, *Forster's Modernism,* 32.

20. George L. Bernstein, *Liberalism and Liberal Politics in Edwardian England* (1986), 198, quoted in Medalie, *Forster's Modernism,* 5.

21. A distinctly different take on the Appassionata Sonata than that found in *CB* (1928), 36, which transcribes an excerpt from Lenin's letter to Gorki regarding the Sonata Op. 57: "I know nothing more beautiful than the Appassionata. . . . It is marvellous, unearthly music" and a tribute to the artist "who can create such beauty in a filthy hell."

22. Mauron to EMF, 28 October 1939 (KCC: EMF 18/365), which Forster transcribed faithfully here, including Mauron's carelessness with accents.

23. These words are indicated by ditto marks in the manuscript.

Chapter 8: Claggart's Monologue and the Art of Collaboration in *Billy Budd*

Epigraph to Chap. 8: Letter of 9 December 1951, *SL2,* 246, written following the December 1 premiere of *Billy Budd.*

1. LD (8 October 1948); Furbank, *A Life,* 2: 282 calls it "one of the acutest depressions of his life."

2. Crozier to Nancy Evans, undated [c. 9 March] 1949, in Crozier, "Writing of *Billy Budd,*" 57.

3. Crozier to Evans, third week of August 1949 (ibid., 61).

4. This chapter refers to the 1951 4-act division of *Billy Budd,* the final product of the intense collaboration with Forster. It was published in a vocal score edited by Erwin Stein (London: Boosey & Hawkes, 1952), and recorded in 1998 by Kent Nagano with the Hallé Orchestra (Erato 3984-21631-2). The 2-act version of *Billy Budd,* Op. 50 (1960–1), on which most subsequent performances and scholarly work are based, was published in full score by Boosey & Hawkes in 1985, to which edition this chapter refers. In the latter, see 204–23 (#105-111) for Claggart's monologue.

5. I am grateful to the BPL for generous access to the unpublished materials cited below, and permission to quote from them. On the compositional chronology of the libretto and music of *Billy Budd,* see Crozier, "Writing of *Billy Budd*"; Reed, *BBCOH,* 42–73; and the Forster-Britten correspondence in *SL2, BBLL2,* and *BBLL3.* On the sketches and drafts, see Reed, "Sketches for *Billy Budd,*" 231–52.

6. Crozier, "Writing an Opera" (typescript of BBC broadcast, 1 December 1951, KCC), 4. William Plomer claimed to have proposed the subject to Britten (Plomer, *Autobiography,* 438); Plomer's edition of Melville's *Billy Budd* was the primary source for the libretto project.

7. Melville, *Billy Budd,* 325.

8. Duncan, *Working with Britten,* 111–2.

9. Crozier, "Writing an Opera," 18. The traditional dating of this first meeting in

January 1949, which Crozier himself later advanced ("Opera Team," 30), is inconsistent with his earliest accounts. The inaccuracy carried over into Crozier's manuscript notes on the libretto materials that he organized in 1980 for BPL and into his "Writing of *Billy Budd*" (52–3), and has remained unquestioned to the present (cf. Reed, *BBCOH,* 47).

10. "Earliest Materials" (BPL, Box 502.1/1, fol. 3*r*), facs. in Reed, *BBCOH,* 48; cf. Melville, *Billy Budd,* 321–6.

11. "Rough Synopsis of the Action," January 1949 (BPL, Box 502.1/2, fol. 5–21).

12. BPL, Box 502.1/3, fol. 25–29, 32–76. Following the meeting, Crozier typed up the results to create the "Complete Draft-Libretto in Three Acts, March 1949" (BPL, Box 502.1/4, fol. 1–184), which provided the template for the August 1949 meeting.

13. As confirmed in a letter to Lionel Trilling (*SL2,* 237), written on Forster's return to Cambridge.

14. Crozier, "Writing of *Billy Budd,*" 56–7; Emslie, "*Billy Budd* and the Fear of Words," 47.

15. Crozier, ibid., 62.

16. Ibid., 62.

17. *Billy Budd,* full score, 87–93, beginning at #42.

18. Crozier, "Writing of *Billy Budd,*" 62.

19. Forster's December 1949 text incorporates the revisions entered in his carbon copy of the typescript "Second version—August 1949" (BPL, Box. 502.1/—), fol. 20; Britten's revisions are entered in his original typescript of the same version (BPL, Box 502.1/6), fol. 20.

20. Compositional Draft (BPL, 2–9300892); rejected draft of the eventual mm. 3–41 (*A*-Wn 38.741, fol. 7; I consulted the photocopy of the latter at BPL). On both sources, see Reed, "Sketches for *Billy Budd,*" 232–3, 242–6, who also provides a facsimile of the relevant folio of the *A*-Wn fragment (240–1) and outlines the multilayered configuration of the manuscript (242–3).

21. The opening three measures of the 1950 draft (still entitled "O handsomeness") are deleted but legible at the foot of fol. 46*v* of Britten's Compositional Draft. The continuation (mm. 4–41) covered the original fol. 47 (*r* and *v*). Britten cut this page out of the draft in 1951 (to become the *A*-Wn fragment) and replaced it with a new final version of mm. 1–41 on different paper.

22. In my account, c^1-b^1 refers to the octave above middle C; with c-b and C-B denoting one and two octaves lower, resp.

23. Britten's 1950 version is deleted but legible in his Compositional Draft, fol. 48*v* and 51*r* (systems 1–3).

24. Reed, "Sketches for *Billy Budd,*" 243.

25. EMF to Britten, 26 July 1951 (L: B609), in which he confirms that all Britten's libretto revisions had been "completely right."

26. A number of these photographs appear in Crozier, "Opera Team"; the full run of photos is available at BPL.

27. Cf. Sidebar on page 130, section 6.

28. On the emotional development of the Billy-Vere relationship at this stage, see Hindley, "Love and Salvation," 375–9.

29. For the authoritative libretto texts, see Herbert, *Operas of Britten,* 202 and 204.

30. The term originated with Rupprecht, *Britten's Musical Language,* 122, to denote the appropriation of the literary and musical motives of a character by another; see also Mitchell, "*Billy Budd* Notebook," in *BBCOH,* 122. Whitesell, "Britten's Dubious Trysts," 684, also elaborates on the topic of convergence in Britten's other operas.

31. This would place the revision of Claggart's monologue well before the July 1951 date proposed by Reed (*BBCOH,* 66). Britten may have already recognized that his original monologue theme lacked sufficient profile to transfer agency from Claggart to Vere.

32. My thinking on this scene has been both stimulated and corroborated by Rupprecht's brilliant analysis of this scene in *Britten's Musical Language,* 96–130.

33. See *Billy Budd,* full score, 437 (#81/+8); 438 (#82); 451 (#89/-3).

34. Rupprecht, *Britten's Musical Language,* 122–5.

35. *Billy Budd,* full score, 465–73 (#97).

36. Basil Coleman, the producer of the 1951 premiere supervised by Britten, was adamant that Claggart should be "isolated" for his monologue; see Coleman and Piper, "*Billy Budd* on the Stage," 24.

37. Mitchell, in *BBCOH,* 127–8; Rupprecht, *Britten's Musical Language,* 123 and 97.

38. Whitesell, "Britten's Dubious Trysts," 676.

39. Coleman and Piper, "*Billy Budd* on the Stage," 21; Stein, "*Billy Budd,*" 207.

40. Stein, *Billy Budd,* 201–9; Peter Evans, *Music of Benjamin Britten,* 168–84; Whittall, "Twisted Relations," 152–69; Cooke, *BBCOH,* 85–110.

41. Emslie, "*Billy Budd* and the Fear of Words," 51. On modernist ambiguity in Britten's *Billy Budd,* see Mitchell, "Billy Budd Notebook," 11; Whittall, "Twisted Relations," 150; Emslie, "*Billy Budd* and the Fear of Words," 43–59; Whitesell, "Britten's Dubious Trysts," 640–3. Law, "Adapters' Dialogue in *Billy Budd,*" 320–34, also explores the implications of Vere's role as narrator of the opera.

42. Britten to EMF, 7 December 1951, in *BBLL3,* 682.

Chapter 9: Conclusion: Difficult Rhythm, Prophetic Song

Epigraph to Chap. 9: EMF, "From the Audience" (1945), in *National Gallery Concerts,* 7.

1. Clapp-Itnyre, "Indecent Musical Displays"; Solie, *Music in Other Words,* 153–86; Weliver, *Women Musicians in Victorian Fiction,* 206–44; Da Sousa Correa, *George Eliot, Music and Victorian Culture.*

2. Whittall, "Twisted Relations," 152–9; Emslie, "*Billy Budd* and the Fear of Words," 53–4; Hindley, "'Interview Chords' Again," 99–126.

3. Lago, "Forster on E. M. Forster," 145.

Works Cited

Works by E. M. Forster

Abinger Harvest. San Diego: Harcourt Brace & Company [A Harvest Book], 1936.

Albergo Empedocle and Other Writings. ed. George H. Thomson. New York: Liveright, 1971.

Alexandria: A History and a Guide, and Pharos and Pharillon. ed. Miriam Allott. Abinger Edition, 16. London: André Deutsch, 2004.

Arctic Summer. ed. Elizabeth Heine. Abinger Edition, 9. London: Edward Arnold, 1980.

Aspects of the Novel. San Diego: Harcourt Brace & Company [A Harvest Book], 1927.

"Author's Introduction." Oxford World's Classics edition of *The Longest Journey,* reprinted in *LJ-A,* lxvi–lxx.

"Beethoven's Piano Sonatas." Ms. KCC (EMF/15/3).

Commonplace Book. ed. Philip Gardner. Stanford: Stanford University Press, 1985.

"From the Audience," *National Gallery Concerts in Aid of the Musicians' Benevolent Fund: 10th October 1939–10th October 1944,* 6–7. London: Printed for the Trustees, 1945.

Goldsworthy Lowes Dickinson. London: Edward Arnold Publishers Ltd., 1934; pocket edition, idem, 1962.

The Hill of Devi and Other Indian Writings. ed. Elizabeth Heine. Abinger Edition, 14. London: Edward Arnold, 1983.

Howards End. ed. Paul B. Armstrong. Norton Critical Edition. New York: Norton, 1998.

Howards End. ed. Alistair M. Duckworth. Case Studies in Contemporary Criticism. Boston: Bedford Books, 1997.

Howards End. ed. Oliver Stallybrass. Abinger Edition, 4. London: Edward Arnold, 1973.
"List of the Books in E. M. Forster's Rooms" (June 1970). Ms. KCC (EMF/31/1).
"Locked Diary" [a.k.a. "Locked Journal"]. Ms. KCC (EMF/12/8).
The Longest Journey. ed. Elizabeth Heine. Abinger Edition, 2. London: Edward Arnold, 1984.
The Longest Journey. ed. from the Abinger Edition, with introduction by Elizabeth Heine. London: Penguin, 1988.
The Lucy Novels: Early Sketches for A Room with a View. ed. Oliver Stallybrass. Abinger Edition, 3a. London: Edward Arnold, 1977.
"The Magic Flute." *The Listener* 58 (21 November 1957): 850–3.
The Manuscripts of Howards End. ed. Oliver Stallybrass. Abinger Edition, 4a. London: Edward Arnold, 1973.
Marianne Thornton. ed. Evelyne Hanquart-Turner. Abinger Edition, 15. London: André Deutsch, 2000.
Maurice. ed. P. N. Furbank. London: Edward Arnold, 1971; rpt. London: Penguin, 1972.
Maurice. ed. Philip Gardner. Abinger Edition, 5. London: André Deutsch, 1999.
"My First Opera." *Opera* 14 (1963): 373–4.
"Notebook Journal, 1903–9." Ms. KCC (EMF/12/7).
A Passage to India. ed. from the Abinger Edition, with introduction by Oliver Stallybrass. London: Penguin, 1979.
The Prince's Tale and Other Uncollected Writings. ed. P. N. Furbank. Abinger Edition, 17. London: André Deutsch, 1998.
A Room with a View. ed. from the Abinger Edition, with introduction by Oliver Stallybrass. London: Penguin, 1978.
"A Shrine for Diaghilev." *Observer* (25 December 1955): 4.
"Three Countries" (1959). Ms. KCC (EMF/6/29).
Two Cheers for Democracy. San Diego: Harcourt Brace & Company [A Harvest Book], 1951.
The Uncollected Egyptian Essays of E. M. Forster. ed. Hilda D. Spear and Abdel-Moneim Aly. N.p.: Blackness Press, 1988.
"A View without a Room." *The Observer* (27 July 1958): 15.
Where Angels Fear to Tread. ed. from the Abinger Edition, with introduction by Oliver Stallybrass. London: Penguin, 1976.

Other Works

Alpers, Paul. *What Is Pastoral?* Chicago: University of Chicago Press, 1996.
Ardis, Ann. "Hellenism and the Lure of Italy." In *The Cambridge Companion to E. M. Forster,* ed. David Bradshaw, 62–76. Cambridge: Cambridge University Press, 2007.

Ashby, Margaret. *Forster Country.* Stevenage, England: Flaunden Press, 1991.

Aspinall, Michael. "The *Lucia* Cadenza." In *Secondo Convegno Europeo di Analisi Musicale,* ed. Rossana Dalmonte and Mario Baroni, 15–20. Trento: Università degli Studi di Trento, 1992.

Avins, Styra, ed. *Johannes Brahms: Life and Letters.* Trans. Josef Eisinger and Styra Avins. Oxford: Oxford University Press, 1997.

Barblan, Guglielmo. *L'Opera di Donizetti nell'età romantica.* Bergamo: Edizione del centenario, 1948.

Beardsley, Aubrey. *The Later Work of Aubrey Beardsley.* London, 1900; rpt. New York: Dover Publications, 1967.

Beauman, Nicola. *E. M. Forster: A Biography.* New York: Alfred A. Knopf, 1994.

Beer, J. B. *The Achievement of E. M. Forster.* London: Chatto & Windus, 1963.

Bekker, Paul. *Beethoven.* Berlin: Schuster & Loeffler, 1911.

Beller-McKenna, Daniel. *Brahms and the German Spirit.* Cambridge, Mass.: Harvard University Press, 2004.

Björkén-Nyberg, Cecilia. "'Listening, Listening': Music and Gender in *Howards End, Sinister Street* and *Pilgrimage.*" In *Literature and Music,* ed. Michael J. Meyer, 89–115. Rodopi Perspectives on Modern Literature, 25. Amsterdam: Rodopi, 2002.

Blissett, William. "Wagnerian Fiction in English." *Criticism* 5 (1963): 239–60.

Born, Daniel. "Private Gardens, Public Swamps: *Howards End* and the Revaluation of Liberal Guilt." *Novel: A Forum on Fiction* 25 (1992): 141–59; excerpted in Armstrong, *HE-NCE,* 365–77.

Botstein, Leon. "The Search for Meaning in Beethoven: Popularity, Intimacy, and Politics in Historical Perspective." In *Beethoven and His World,* ed. Scott Burnham and Michael P. Steinberg, 332–66. Princeton: Princeton University Press, 2000.

Bradshaw, David. "*Howards End.*" In *The Cambridge Companion to E. M. Forster,* ed. David Bradshaw, 151–72. Cambridge: Cambridge University Press, 2007.

Brady, Sean. *Masculinity and Male Homosexuality in Britain, 1861–1913.* Basingstoke: Palgrave Macmillan, 2005.

Brandenburg, Sieghard. "Once Again: On the Question of the Repeat of the Scherzo and Trio in Beethoven's Fifth Symphony." In *Beethoven Essays: Studies in Honor of Elliot Forbes,* ed. Lewis Lockwood and Phyllis Benjamin, 146–98. Cambridge, Mass.: Harvard University Press, 1984.

Breig, Werner. "The Musical Works." Trans. Paul Knight and Horst Loeschmann. In *Wagner Handbook,* ed. Ulrich Müller and Peter Wapnewski, 397–482. Trans. and ed. John Deathridge. Cambridge, Mass.: Harvard University Press, 1992.

Brendel, Alfred. *Music Sounded Out: Essays, Lectures, Interviews, Afterthoughts.* London: Robson Books, 1990.

Britten, Benjamin. *Billy Budd,* Op. 50 [full score of the 1960–1 revised 2-act version]. London: Boosey & Hawkes, 1985.

Brooke, Christopher N. L. *A History of the University of Cambridge.* Vol. 4, *1870–1990.* Cambridge: Cambridge University Press, 1993.

Brown, Clive. *Classical & Romantic Performing Practice, 1750–1900*. New York: Oxford University Press, 1999.

Brown, David. "How Did Tchaikovsky Come to Die: And Does It Really Matter?" *Music & Letters* 78 (1997): 581–8.

Brown, Malcolm Hamrick. "Tchaikovsky and His Music in Anglo-American Criticism, 1890s-1950s." In *Queer Episodes in Music and Modern Identity*, ed. Sophie Fuller and Lloyd Whitesell, 134–49. Urbana: University of Illinois Press, 2002.

Brown, Tony. "E. M. Forster's *Parsifal*: A Reading of *The Longest Journey*." *Journal of European Studies* 12 (1982): 30–54; rpt. in Stape, *Critical Assessments*, 3: 92–114.

———. "Edward Carpenter, Forster and the Evolution of *A Room with a View*." *English Literature in Transition* 30 (1987): 279–300.

Browning, Oscar. *Memories of Sixty Years at Eton, Cambridge and Elsewhere*. 2nd ed. London: John Lane, 1910.

Burgan, Mary. "Heroines at the Piano: Women and Music in Nineteenth-Century Fiction." *Victorian Studies* 30 (1986): 51–76.

Burnham, Scott. *Beethoven Hero*. Princeton, N. J.: Princeton University Press, 1995.

Burra, Peter. "The Novels of E. M. Forster." *Nineteenth Century and After* 116 (1934): 581–94; rpt. in Stape, *Critical Assessments*, 2: 48–60.

Buzard, James. *The Beaten Track: European Tourism, Literature, and the Ways to Culture*. Oxford: Oxford University Press, 1993.

Carey, Hugh. *Duet for Two Voices: An Informal Biography of Edward Dent Compiled from His Letters to Clive Carey*. Cambridge: Cambridge University Press, 1979.

Carpenter, Edward. *Angels' Wings: A Series of Essays on Art and Its Relation to Life*. London: Swan Sonnenschein & Co., 1898.

———. *The Intermediate Sex: A Study of Some Transitional Types of Men and Women*. 3rd ed. London: George Allen, 1912.

Chamberlain, Houston Stewart. *Richard Wagner*. Trans. G. Ainslie Hight and rev. by the author. London: Dent, 1900.

Charlton, David, ed. *E. T. A. Hoffmann's Musical Writings: Kreisleriana, The Poet and the Composer, Music Criticism*. Trans. Martyn Clarke. Cambridge: Cambridge University Press, 1989.

Clapp-Itnyre, Alisa. "Indecent Musical Displays: Feminizing the Pastoral in Eliot's *The Mill on the Floss*." In *The Idea of Music in Victorian Fiction*, ed. Sophie Fuller and Nicky Losseff, 129–49. Aldershot: Ashgate, 2004.

Cleather, Alice Leighton, and Basil Crump. *Parsifal, Lohengrin, and the Legend of the Holy Grail: Described and Interpreted in Accordance with Wagner's Own Writing*. London: Methuen, 1904.

Clément, Catherine. *Opera, or the Undoing of Women*. Trans. Betsy Wing. Minneapolis: University of Minnesota Press, 1988.

C. L. G. "The Re-emergence of the Prima Donna." *The Spectator* 99 (23 November 1907): 820.

Coleman, Basil, and John Piper. "*Billy Budd* on the Stage: An Early Discussion between Producer and Designer." *Tempo* 21 (1951): 21–5.

Colls, Robert, and Philip Dodd, eds. *Englishness: Politics and Culture, 1880–1920.* London: Croom Helm, 1986.

Cook, Matt. *London and the Culture of Homosexuality, 1885–1914.* Cambridge: Cambridge University Press, 2003.

Cooke, Mervyn, and Philip Reed, eds. *Benjamin Britten: Billy Budd.* Cambridge Opera Handbooks. Cambridge: Cambridge University Press, 1993.

Crews, Frederick C. *E. M. Forster: The Perils of Humanism.* Princeton: Princeton University Press, 1962.

Crozier, Eric. "An Opera Team Sets to Work." *Picture Post* 45/3 (15 October 1949): 29–31.

———. "Writing an Opera." *Adam International Review* 20/224–6 (1952): 17–9.

———. "The Writing of *Billy Budd.*" *Opera Quarterly* 4 (1986): 11–27; rpt. in Stape, *Critical Assessments* 1: 51–65.

Crump, Jeremy. "The Identity of English Music: The Reception of Elgar, 1899–1935." In *Englishness: Politics and Culture, 1880–1920,* ed. Robert Colls and Philip Dodd, 164–90. London: Croom Helm, 1986.

Dahlhaus, Carl. "Wagner's Place in the History of Music." Trans. Alfred Clayton. In *Wagner Handbook,* ed. Ulrich Müller and Peter Wapnewski, 99–117. Trans. and ed. John Deathridge. Cambridge, Mass.: Harvard University Press, 1992.

Dannreuther, Edward. "Beethoven and His Works: A Study." *Macmillan's Magazine* 34 (July 1876): 193–209.

Da Silva, Stephen. "Transvaluing Immaturity: Reverse Discourses of Male Homosexuality in E. M. Forster's Posthumously Published Fiction." *Criticism* 40 (1998): 237–72.

Da Sousa Correa, Delia. *George Eliot, Music and Victorian Culture.* Basingstoke: Palgrave Macmillan, 2003.

Daverio, John. *Robert Schumann: Herald of a "New Poetic Age."* New York: Oxford University Press, 1997.

Degott, Pierre. "Représentations d'opéra et représentation de l'opéra dans deux romans de l'époque victorienne et édouardienne." *Cahiers victoriens et édouardiens* 59 (April 2004): 29–43.

Dennis, David B. *Beethoven in German Politics, 1870–1989.* New Haven: Yale University Press, 1996.

Dent, Edward J. "Donizetti: An Italian Romantic." In *Fanfare for Ernest Newman,* ed. Herbert van Thal, 86–107. London: Arthur Barker, 1955.

———. "Italian Opera in the Eighteenth Century, and Its Influence on the Music of the Classical Period." *Sammelbände der internationalen Musik-Gesellschaft* 14 (1912–3): 500–9.

Dibble, Jeremy. "Edward Dannreuther and the Orme Square Phenomenon." In *Mu-*

sic and British Culture, 1785–1914: Essays in Honour of Cyril Ehrlich, ed. Christina Bashford and Leanne Langley, 275–98. New York: Oxford University Press, 1970.

Dickinson, Goldsworthy Lowes. *The Meaning of Good: A Dialogue.* Glasgow: James Maclehose & Sons, 1901.

DiGaetani, John Louis. *Richard Wagner and the Modern British Novel.* Rutherford: Fairleigh Dickinson University Press, 1978.

Dijkstra, Bram. *Idols of Perversity: Fantasies of Feminine Evil in Fin-de-siècle Culture.* New York: Oxford University Press, 1986.

Diogenes [pseud.]. "Some Musical Fashions." *Monthly Musical Record* 28 (1 July 1898): 148–50.

Donizetti, Giacomo. *Lucia di Lammermoor: Partitura.* Rpt. New York: Kalmus, n.d.

Duckworth, Alistair M., ed. *Howards End* (ed. from the Abinger Edition). Case Studies in Contemporary Criticism. Boston: Bedford Books, 1997.

———. "A Critical History of *Howards End.*" In Duckworth, *HE-D,* 295–312.

Duncan, Ronald. *Working with Britten: A Personal Memoir.* Welcombe, U.K.: Rebel Press, 1981.

Ellis, Havelock, and John Addington Symonds. *Sexual Inversion: A Critical Edition.* ed. with introduction by Ivan Crozier. Basingstoke: Palgrave Macmillan, 2008.

Ellis, William Ashton, trans. *Richard Wagner's Prose Works.* 8 vols. London: Kegan Paul, 1893–99; rpt. St. Clair Shores, Mich.: Scholarly Press, 1972.

——— (?). "The Bayreuth Hush." *The Meister* 2 (1889): 109–14.

Emslie, Barry. "*Billy Budd* and the Fear of Words." *Cambridge Opera Journal* 4 (1992): 43–59.

Evans, Edwin [Jr.]. *Tchaikovsky.* The Master Musicians. London, 1906; rpt. London: J. M. Dent & Sons Ltd., 1926.

Evans, Peter. *The Music of Benjamin Britten.* Rev. ed. London: J. M. Dent & Sons Ltd., 1989 (Chapter 8: "*Billy Budd,*" 163–87).

Ferguson, Howard. "E. M. Forster at the National Gallery Concerts." *London Magazine* 22 (December 1982–January 1983): 63–70.

Fillion, Michelle. "Edwardian Perspectives on Nineteenth-Century Music in E. M. Forster's *A Room with a View.*" *19th-Century Music* 25 (2002): 266–95.

———. "E. M. Forster's Beethoven." *Beethoven Forum* 9 (2002): 171–203.

Firchow, Peter E. "Germany and Germanic Mythology in *Howards End.*" *Comparative Literature* 33 (1981): 50–68.

Foata, Anne. "The Knocking at the Door: A Fantasy on Fate, Forster and Beethoven's Fifth." *Cahiers victoriens et édouardiens* 44 (1996): 135–45.

Foldy, Michael S. *The Trials of Oscar Wilde: Deviance, Morality, and Late-Victorian Society.* New Haven: Yale University Press, 1997.

Fone, Byrne R. S. *A Road to Stonewall: Male Homosexuality and Homophobia in English and American Literature, 1750–1969.* New York: Twayne Publishers, 1995.

Forbes, Elliot. *A History of Music at Harvard to 1972.* Cambridge, Mass.: Department of Music, Harvard University, 1988.

Fowler, Laurence and Helen, eds. *Cambridge Commemorated: An Anthology of University Life.* Cambridge: Cambridge University Press, 1984.

Fuller, Sophie, and Nicky Losseff, eds. *The Idea of Music in Victorian Fiction.* Aldershot: Ashgate, 2004.

Furbank, P. N. *E. M. Forster: A Life.* 2 vols. New York: Harcourt Brace & Company, 1981.

———, and F. J. H. Haskell. "The Art of Fiction: I, E. M. Forster." *Paris Review* 1 (1953): 28–41.

Garafola, Lynn. *Diaghilev's Ballets Russes.* New York: Oxford University Press, 1989.

———, and Nancy Van Norman Baer, eds. *The Ballets Russes and Its World.* New Haven: Yale University Press, 1999.

Gardner, Philip. *E. M. Forster: The Critical Heritage.* London: Routledge & Kegan Paul, 1973.

Gattey, Charles Neilson. *Luisa Tetrazzini: The Florentine Nightingale.* Portland, Ore.: Amadeus Press, 1995.

Geck, Martin, and Egon Voss, eds. *Richard Wagner: Sämtliche Werke,* vol. 30: *Dokumente zur Entstehung und erster Aufführung des Bühnenweihfestspiels Parsifal.* Mainz: B. Schott's Söhne, 1970.

Gluck, Christoph Willibald. *Sämtliche Werke,* I, vol. 8a, *Armide.* ed. Klaus Hortschansky. Kassel, Basel: Bärenreiter, 1987.

———. *Armide.* Arr. for piano and voice by Friedrich Brissler. Leipzig: Peters, 1882(?).

Grant, Kathleen. "*Maurice* as Fantasy." In *E. M. Forster: Centenary Revaluations,* ed. Judith Scherer Herz and Robert K. Martin, 191–203. Toronto: University of Toronto Press, 1982.

Graves, Robert. *The Greek Myths.* London: The Folio Society, 1996.

Grey, Thomas S. "Metaphorical Modes in Nineteenth-Century Music Criticism: Image, Narrative, and Idea." In *Music and Text: Critical Inquiries,* ed. Steven Paul Scher, 93–117. Cambridge: Cambridge University Press, 1992.

———. *Wagner's Musical Prose: Texts and Contexts.* Cambridge: Cambridge University Press, 1995.

Grove, George. *Beethoven and His Nine Symphonies.* 3rd ed. London: Novello, Ewer and Company, 1898; rpt. New York: Dover Publications, Inc., 1962.

Halls, Michael. "The Forster Collections at King's: A Survey." *Twentieth-Century Literature* 31 (1985): 147–60.

Hanquart, Evelyne. "Divertissements et divertissement: la musique et E. M. Forster." *Cahiers victoriens et édouardiens* 19 (1984): 57–65.

Henderson, W. J. *Richard Wagner, His Life and Dramas: A Biographical Study of the Man and an Explanation of His Work.* New York: G. P. Putnam's Sons, 1901.

Herbert, David, ed. *The Operas of Benjamin Britten.* London: Hamish Hamilton, 1979.

Herz, Judith Scherer. "*A Room with a View*." In *The Cambridge Companion to E. M. Forster,* ed. David Bradshaw, 138–50. Cambridge: Cambridge University Press, 2007.

———. "'This is the End of Parsival': The Orphic and the Operatic in *The Longest Journey*." In *Queer Forster,* ed. Robert K. Martin and George Piggford, 137–50. Chicago: University of Chicago Press, 1997.

Hess, Myra. "A Great Adventure." In *National Gallery Concerts In Aid of the Musicians' Benevolent Fund: 10th October 1939–10th October 1944,* 5. London: Printed for the Trustees, 1945.

Higdon, David Leon. "Opus 3 or Opus 111 in Forster's *A Room with a View*." *English Language Notes* 28/4 (June 1991): 57–60.

Hindley, Clifford. "Britten's *Billy Budd:* The 'Interview Chords' Again." *Musical Quarterly* 78 (1994): 99–126.

———. "Love and Salvation in Britten's *Billy Budd*." *Music & Letters* 70 (1989): 363–81.

Holdsworth, R. V. *Arthur Symons: Poetry and Prose.* Cheadle, England: Carcanet Press, 1974.

Howes, Frank. "Cecil Sharp." *NG2,* 23: 219–20.

Hutcheon, Linda. "'Sublime Noise' for Three Friends: Music in the Critical Writings of E. M. Forster, Roger Fry and Charles Mauron." In *E. M. Forster: Centenary Revaluations,* ed. Judith Scherer Herz and Robert K. Martin, 84–98. Toronto: University of Toronto Press, 1982.

Hyden, Walford. *Pavlova: The Genius of Dance.* London: Constable & Co. Ltd., 1931.

Jones, David. "E. M. Forster on His Life and His Books: An Interview Recorded for Television." *Listener* (1 January 1959): 11–12.

Kaplan, Carola M. "Absent Father, Passive Son: The Dilemma of Rickie Elliot in *The Longest Journey*." *Twentieth-Century Literature* 33 (1987): 196–210; rpt. in *E. M. Forster: New Casebooks,* ed. Jeremy Tambling, 51–66. Basingstoke: Palgrave, 1995.

Keeling, Bret L. "'No Trace of Presence': Tchaikovsky and the Sixth in Forster's *Maurice*." *Mosaic: A Journal for the Interdisciplinary Study of Literature* 36 (2003): 85–101.

Kermode, Frank. *Concerning E. M. Forster.* New York: Farrar, Straus and Giroux, 2009.

Kildea, Paul. *Britten on Music.* Oxford: Oxford University Press, 2003.

Kinderman, William. *Beethoven.* Berkeley: University of California Press, 1995.

King, Francis. *E. M. Forster and His World.* London: Thames & Hudson, 1978.

Kinsky, Georg. *Das Werk Beethovens: Thematisch-Bibliographisches Verzeichnis seiner sämtlichen vollendeten Kompositionen.* ed. and completed by Hans Halm. Munich: G. Henle Verlag, 1983.

Knittel, K. M. "Wagner, Deafness, and the Reception of Beethoven's Late Style." *Journal of the American Musicological Society* 51 (1998): 49–82.

Koestenbaum, Wayne. "Opera and Homosexuality: Seven Arias." *Yale Journal of Criticism* 5 (1991): 235–54.

Köhler, Joachim. *Richard Wagner: The Last of the Titans.* Trans. Stewart Spencer. New Haven: Yale University Press, 2004.

Konold, Wulf. *Ludwig van Beethoven 5. Sinfonie: Einführung und Analyse mit Partitur.* Mainz: Schott, 1979.

Kramer, Lawrence. *Music and Poetry: The Nineteenth Century and After.* Berkeley: University of California Press, 1984.

Krehbiel, Henry Edward. *Studies in the Wagnerian Drama.* New York, 1891; rpt. New York: Harper & Brothers, 1901.

Kropfinger, Klaus. *Wagner and Beethoven: Richard Wagner's Reception of Beethoven.* Trans. Peter Palmer. Cambridge: Cambridge University Press, 1991.

Kunze, Stefan, ed. *Ludwig van Beethoven: Die Werke im Spiegel seiner Zeit: Gesammelte Konzertberichte und Rezensionen bis 1830.* Laaber: Laaber-Verlag, 1987.

Lago, Mary, comp. *Calendar of the Letters of E. M. Forster.* London: Mansell, 1985.

———. "Introduction: Forster on E. M. Forster." *Twentieth-Century Literature* 31 (1985): 137–46.

———, and P. N. Furbank, eds. *Selected Letters of E. M. Forster,* vol. 1, 1879–1920. London: Collins, 1983; idem, vol. 2, 1921–70. Cambridge, Mass.: The Belknap Press of Harvard University Press, 1985.

Land, Stephen K. *Challenge and Conventionality in the Fiction of E. M. Forster.* AMS Studies in Modern Literature, 19. New York: AMS Press, 1990.

Langland, Elizabeth. "Gesturing toward an Open Space: Gender, Form, and Language in *Howards End.*" In Duckworth, *HE-D,* 400–15.

Large, David C., and William Weber, with Anne Dzamba Sessa. *Wagnerism in European Culture and Politics.* Ithaca: Cornell University Press, 1984.

Lavignac, Albert. *Le Voyage artistique à Bayreuth.* 4th ed. Paris, 1900. Trans. Esther Singleton as *The Music Dramas of Richard Wagner and His Festival Theatre in Bayreuth.* New York, 1898; rpt. New York: Haskell House Publishers Ltd., 1969.

Law, Joe. "The 'Perniciously Homosexual Art': Music and Homoerotic Desire in *The Picture of Dorian Gray* and Other *Fin-de-siècle* Fiction." In *The Idea of Music in Victorian Fiction,* ed. Sophie Fuller and Nicky Losseff, 173–96. Aldershot: Ashgate, 2004.

———. "'We have ventured to tidy up Vere': The Adapters' Dialogue in *Billy Budd.*" *Twentieth-Century Literature* 31 (1985): 297–314; rpt. in Stape, *Critical Assessments,* 2: 320–34.

Lenz, Wilhelm von. *Beethoven et ses trois styles.* St. Petersburg, 1852. 2nd ed., ed. M. D. Calvocoressi. Paris: G. Legouix, 1909; rpt. with foreword by Joseph Kerman, New York: Da Capo, 1980.

Leppert, Richard. *Music and Image: Ideology & Socio-Cultural Formation in 18th-Century England.* Cambridge: Cambridge University Press, 1988.

Levenson, Michael. *Modernism and the Fate of Individuality: Character and Novel-*

istic Form from Conrad to Woolf. Cambridge: Cambridge University Press, 1990. Excerpt (78–93) rpt. as "Liberalism and Symbolism in *Howards End,*" in *HE-NCE,* 353–65.

Loewenberg, Alfred. *Annals of Opera, 1597–1940.* 2nd ed. Geneva: Societas Bibliographica, 1955.

Lucas, John. "Wagner and Forster: *Parsifal* and *A Room with a View.*" *English Literary History* 33 (1966): 92–117; rpt. in Stape, *Critical Assessments,* 3: 159–80.

Lustig, Jodi. "The Piano's Progress: The Piano in Play in the Victorian Novel." In *The Idea of Music in Victorian Fiction,* ed. Sophie Fuller and Nicky Losseff, 83–104. Aldershot: Ashgate, 2004.

MacArdle, Donald W., ed. *Beethoven as I Knew Him: A Biography by Anton Felix Schindler.* Trans. by Constance S. Jolly of *Biographie von Ludwig van Beethoven,* 3rd rev. ed. (1860). Mineola, N.Y.: Dover, 1996.

Martin, Robert K. "Edward Carpenter and the Double Structure of *Maurice.*" *Journal of Homosexuality* 8 (1983): 35–46; rpt. in Tambling, *E. M. Forster: New Casebooks,* 100–14.

———, and George Piggford, eds. *Queer Forster.* Chicago: University of Chicago Press, 1997.

Martin, Stoddard. *Wagner to "The Waste Land": A Study of the Relationship of Wagner to English Literature.* London: Macmillan, 1982.

McClary, Susan. *Feminine Endings: Music, Gender, and Sexuality.* Minneapolis: University of Minnesota Press, 1991.

McDowell, Frederick P. W. *E. M. Forster.* Rev. ed. Boston: Twayne Publishers, 1982.

Medalie, David. "Bloomsbury and Other Values." In *The Cambridge Companion to E. M. Forster,* ed. David Bradshaw, 32–46. Cambridge: Cambridge University Press, 2007.

———. *E. M. Forster's Modernism.* Basingstoke: Palgrave, 2002.

Mellers, Wilfrid. *Beethoven and the Voice of God.* New York: Oxford University Press, 1983.

Melville, Herman. *Billy Budd and Other Stories.* Intro. Frederick Busch. New York: Penguin Books, 1986.

Mitchell, Donald. "A *Billy Budd* Notebook." *Opera News* 43 (31 March 1979): 9–14; revised as "A *Billy Budd* Notebook (1979–1991)," in Cooke and Reed, *BBCOH,* 111–34.

———, and Philip Reed, eds. *Letters from a Life: The Selected Letters and Diaries of Benjamin Britten, 1913–1976,* vol. 2, 1939–1945. Berkeley: University of California Press, 1991.

———, Philip Reed, and Mervyn Cooke, eds. *Letters from a Life: The Selected Letters of Benjamin Britten, 1913–1976,* vol. 3, 1946–1951. Berkeley: University of California Press, 2004.

Mondimore, Francis Mark. *A Natural History of Homosexuality.* Baltimore: The Johns Hopkins University Press, 1996.

Moon, Michael, ed. *Walt Whitman: Leaves of Grass and Other Writings.* Norton Critical Edition. New York: Norton, 2002.

Morris, Mitchell. "Tristan's Wounds: On Homosexual Wagnerians at the Fin de Siècle." In *Queer Episodes in Music and Modern Identity,* ed. Sophie Fuller and Lloyd Whitesell, 271–91. Urbana: University of Illinois Press, 2002.

Müller, Ulrich, and Peter Wapnewski, ed. *Wagner Handbook.* Trans. and ed. John Deathridge. Cambridge, Mass.: Harvard University Press, 1992.

Nattiez, Jean-Jacques. *Proust as Musician.* Trans. Derrick Puffett. Cambridge: Cambridge University Press, 1989.

Newman, Ernest. *A Study of Wagner.* London: Bertram Dobell, 1899.

Newmarch, Rosa. "Peter Ilich Tchaikovsky." *Grove's Dictionary of Music and Musicians.* ed. J. A. Fuller Maitland. Vol. 5: 33–49. New York: Macmillan, 1910.

———. *Tchaikovsky: His Life and Works.* London: G. Richards, 1900; ed. and expanded by Edwin Evans, Sr. London: William Reeves, 1908.

Norris, Gerald. *Stanford, the Cambridge Jubilee and Tchaikovsky.* North Pomfret, Vt.: David & Charles, 1980.

Ord-Hume, Arthur W. J. G. *Pianola: A History of the Self-Playing Piano.* London: George Allen & Unwin, 1984.

Panter-Downes, Mollie. "Kingsman." *New Yorker* (19 September 1959): 51–80.

Parry, Sir C. Hubert H. "Variations." *Grove's Dictionary of Music and Musicians.* ed. J. A. Fuller Maitland. Vol. 5: 218–32. New York: Macmillan, 1910.

Pederson, Sanna. "Beethoven and Masculinity." In *Beethoven and His World,* ed. Scott Burnham and Michael P. Steinberg, 313–31. Princeton: Princeton University Press, 2000.

———. "Defining the Term 'Absolute Music' Historically." *Music & Letters* 90 (2009): 240–62.

Pemble, John. *The Mediterranean Passion: Victorians and Edwardians in the South.* Oxford: Oxford University Press, 1987.

Pistone, Danièle. *Le Piano dans la littérature française des origines jusqu'en 1900.* Paris: Champion, 1975.

Plomer, William. *The Autobiography of William Plomer.* Postscript Simon Nowell-Smith. London: Jonathan Cape, 1975.

Pohl, C. F., and W. H. Hadow. "Wolfgang Amadeus Mozart." *Grove's Dictionary of Music and Musicians,* 3: 284–313. London: Macmillan, 1907.

Pollack, Howard. *Aaron Copland: The Life and Work of an Uncommon Man.* New York: Henry Holt and Company, 1999.

Poznansky, Alexander. *Tchaikovsky: The Quest for the Inner Man.* New York: Schirmer Books, 1991.

———. "Tchaikovsky's Suicide: Myth and Reality." *19th-Century Music* 11 (1988): 199–220.

Proust, Marcel. *Remembrance of Things Past.* Trans. C. K. Scott Moncrieff and Terence Kilmartin. New York: Random House, 1981.

Pugliese, Romana Margherita. "The Origins of *Lucia di Lammermoor*'s Cadenza." *Cambridge Opera Journal* 16 (2004): 23–42.

Radcliffe, Philip. *E. J. Dent: A Centenary Memoir.* Rickmansworth, England: Triad Press, 1976.

Read, Oliver, and Walter L. Welch. *From Tin Foil to Stereo: Evolution of the Phonograph.* 2nd ed. Indianapolis, Ind.: Howard W. Sams & Co., 1976.

Reed, Philip. "From First Thoughts to First Night: A *Billy Budd* Chronology." In Cooke and Reed, *BBCOH,* 42–73.

———. "On the Sketches for *Billy Budd.*" In *On Mahler and Britten: Essays in Honour of Donald Mitchell on His Seventieth Birthday,* ed. Philip Reed, 231–52. Woodbridge, U.K.: Boydell Press, and Aldeburgh: The Britten-Pears Library, 1995.

Réti, Rudolph. *Thematic Patterns in Sonatas of Beethoven.* New York: Macmillan, 1951.

Riethmüller, Albrecht, Carl Dahlhaus, and Alexander L. Ringer, eds. *Beethoven: Interpretationen seiner Werke.* 2 vols. Laaber: Laaber-Verlag, 1994.

Ringger, Kurt. "*«Lucia di Lammermoor»* ou les regrets d'Emma Bovary." In *Littérature et Opéra: Colloque de Cerisy, 1985,* ed. Philippe Berthier and Kurt Ringger, 69–79. Grenoble, France: Presses universitaires de Grenoble, 1987.

Robertson, Michael. *Worshipping Walt: The Whitman Disciples.* Princeton: Princeton University Press, 2008.

Roerick, William. "Forster and America." In *Aspects of E. M. Forster: Essays and Recollections Written for His Ninetieth Birthday, 1st January 1969,* ed. Oliver Stallybrass, 61–72. London: Edward Arnold, 1969.

Rosecrance, Barbara. *Forster's Narrative Vision.* Ithaca: Cornell University Press, 1982.

Rosen, Charles. *The Classical Style: Haydn, Mozart, Beethoven.* New York: Norton, 1972.

———. *The Romantic Generation.* Cambridge, Mass.: Harvard University Press, 1995.

Rosenthal, Harold. *Two Centuries of Opera at Covent Garden.* London: Putnam, 1958.

Rupprecht, Philip. *Britten's Musical Language.* Cambridge: Cambridge University Press, 2001.

Sadie, Stanley, and John Tyrrell, eds. *The New Grove Dictionary of Music and Musicians,* 2nd ed. London: Macmillan Publishers Limited, and New York: Grove's Dictionaries, Inc., 2001.

Sala, Emilio. "Women Crazed by Love: An Aspect of Romantic Opera." *Opera Quarterly* 10 (1994): 19–41.

Schmalfeldt, Janet. "Form as the Process of Becoming: The Beethoven-Hegelian Tradition and the 'Tempest' Sonata." *Beethoven Forum* 4, 37–71. Lincoln: University of Nebraska Press, 1995.

Scott, Sir Walter. *Waverley Novels.* Melrose Edition, 1: *Bride of Lammermoor.* Boston: Houghton, Osgood and Company, 1878.

Sessa, Anne Dzamba. "At Wagner's Shrine: British and American Wagnerians." In *Wagnerism in European Culture and Politics,* ed. David C. Large and William Weber, 246–77. Ithaca: Cornell University Press, 1984.

———. *Richard Wagner and the English.* London: Associated University Presses, 1979.

Shedlock, J. S. *Beethoven.* London: George Bell & Sons, 1903.

Showalter, Elaine. *The Female Malady: Women, Madness, and English Culture, 1830–1980.* New York: Pantheon Books, 1985.

Sinfield, Alan. *The Wilde Century: Effeminacy, Oscar Wilde and the Queer Moment.* New York: Columbia University Press, 1994.

Smart, Mary Ann. "The Silencing of Lucia." *Cambridge Opera Journal* 4 (1992): 119–41.

Smith, Graham. "Between Past and Future: Portrait Photographs in the Novels of E. M. Forster." *Visual Resources* 22 (2006): 203–37.

———. "The Past in the Present: Photographs of Classical Art in the Writings of E. M. Forster." *Arion* 11 (2003): 71–102.

Smith, William James. *Five Centuries of Cambridge Musicians, 1464–1964.* Cambridge: W. Heffer & Sons, 1964.

Solie, Ruth A. "Fictions of the Opera Box." In *The Work of Opera: Genre, Nationhood, and Sexual Difference,* ed. Richard Dellamora and Daniel Fischlin, 185–208. New York: Columbia University Press, 1997.

———. "The Living Work: Organicism and Musical Analysis." *19th-Century Music* 4 (1980): 147–56.

———. *Music in Other Words: Victorian Conversations.* Berkeley: University of California Press, 2004.

Spotts, Frederic. *Bayreuth: A History of the Wagner Festival.* New Haven: Yale University Press, 1994.

Stape, J. H. *An E. M. Forster Chronology.* Basingstoke: Palgrave, 1993.

———, ed. *E. M. Forster: Critical Assessments.* 4 vols. Mountfield, England: Helm Information, 1997.

———, ed. *E. M. Forster: Interviews and Recollections.* London: St. Martin's Press, 1993.

Stein, Erwin. "*Billy Budd.*" In *Benjamin Britten: A Commentary on His Works from a Group of Specialists,* ed. Donald Mitchell and Hans Keller, 198–210. Westport, Conn.: Greenwood Press, 1952. Also issued as "The Music of 'Billy Budd.'" *Opera* 3/4 (1952): 206–14.

Stone, Wilfred. *The Cave and the Mountain: A Study of E. M. Forster.* Stanford: Stanford University Press, 1966.

Sullivan, Zohreh T. "Forster's Symbolism: *A Room with a View,* Fourth Chapter." *Journal of Narrative Technique* 6 (1976): 217–23.

Sutherland, Joan. *A Prima Donna's Progress: The Autobiography of Joan Sutherland.* Washington, D.C.: Regnery Publishing, Inc., 1997.

Sutton, Emma. *Aubrey Beardsley and British Wagnerism in the 1890s.* Oxford: Oxford University Press, 2002.

Symonds, John Addington. *A Problem in Greek Ethics: Being an Inquiry into the Phenomenon of Sexual Inversion [1873].* London: Privately Printed, 1908.

———. *A Problem in Modern Ethics: Being an Inquiry into the Phenomenon of Sexual Inversion.* London: Privately Printed, 1896.

Symons, Arthur. "The Ideas of Richard Wagner." *Quarterly Review* 203 (July 1905): 73–108. Rpt. in *Studies in Seven Arts,* 223–98. New York: E. P. Dutton and Co., 1907.

Tambling, Jeremy, ed. *E. M. Forster: New Casebooks.* Basingstoke: Palgrave, 1995.

Taruskin, Richard. "Pathetic Symphonist: Chaikovsky, Russia, Sexuality, and the Study of Music." *The New Republic* (6 February 1995): 26–40.

Tchaikovsky, Modeste. *The Life & Letters of Peter Ilich Tchaikovsky.* ed. and trans. by Rosa Newmarch. London: John Lane Company, 1906.

Temperley, Nicholas, with Bruce Carr (work-list). "Sir Henry R. Bishop." *NG2,* 3: 630–4.

Tetrazzini, Luisa. *How to Sing.* New York: G. H. Doran, 1923; rpt. New York: Da Capo, 1975.

Tovey, Donald Francis. *A Companion to Beethoven's Pianoforte Sonatas (Bar-to-bar Analysis).* London: Associated Board of the Royal Schools of Music, 1931.

———. *Essays in Musical Analysis.* London: Oxford University Press, 1935.

———. "Ludwig van Beethoven," *Encyclopaedia Britannica,* 11th ed. Vol 3: 644–51. Cambridge: Cambridge University Press, 1910.

———, with H. Craxton. *Beethoven Pianoforte Sonatas.* London: Associated Board of the Royal Schools of Music, 1931.

Trevelyan, Robert Calverley. *The Birth of Parsival.* London: Longmans, Green, and Co., 1905.

Trilling, Lionel. *E. M. Forster: A Study.* London: Hogarth Press, 1959.

Tusa, Michael C. "Beethoven's 'C-Minor Mood': Some Thoughts on the Structural Implications of Key Choice." *Beethoven Forum* 2, 1–27. Lincoln: University of Nebraska Press, 1993.

Venn, J. A., comp. *Alumni Cantabrigienses: A Biographical List of All Known Students, Graduates and Holders of Office at the University of Cambridge, from the Earliest Times to 1900.* Part 2 (6 vols.). Cambridge: Cambridge University Press, 1940–54.

Wagner, Richard. *Parsifal.* Piano arr. Karl Klindworth. Mainz: Schott, 1902.

———. *The Rhinegold* [Piano-vocal score]. Trans. Frederick Jameson. New York: Schirmer, n.d.

Weatherhead, Andrea K. "*Howards End:* Beethoven's *Fifth.*" *Twentieth-Century Literature* 31 (1985): 247–64.

Weber, William. *The Great Transformation of Musical Taste: Concert Programming from Haydn to Brahms.* Cambridge: Cambridge University Press, 2008.

———. "Wagner, Wagnerism, and Musical Idealism." In *Wagnerism in European Culture and Politics,* ed. David C. Large and William Weber, 28–71. Ithaca: Cornell University Press, 1984.

Webster, James. *Haydn's "Farewell" Symphony and the Idea of Classical Style.* Cambridge: Cambridge University Press, 1991.

Weliver, Phyllis. *Women Musicians in Victorian Fiction, 1860–1900.* Aldershot: Ashgate, 2000.

Westburg, Barry R. "Forster's Fifth Symphony: Another Aspect of *Howards End.*" *Modern Fiction Studies* 10 (1964–5): 359–65.

Weston, Jessie L. *The Legends of the Wagner Drama: Studies in Mythology and Romance.* New York: Scribner, 1900.

Whitesell, Lloyd. "Britten's Dubious Trysts." *Journal of the American Musicological Society* 56 (2003): 637–94.

Whittall, Arnold. "'Twisted Relations': Method and Meaning in Britten's *Billy Budd.*" *Cambridge Opera Journal* 2 (1990): 145–71.

Widdowson, Peter. "*Howards End:* Fiction as History." In Duckworth, *HE-D,* 364–78.

Williams, Simon. *Wagner and the Romantic Hero.* Cambridge: Cambridge University Press, 2004.

Zeikowitz, Richard E., ed. *Letters between Forster and Isherwood on Homosexuality and Literature.* Basingstoke: Palgrave, 2008.

Index

Locators for figures and musical examples are in **bold**. Musical and literary works are indexed under the composer's or author's name except in the case of the *Billy Budd* libretto, *Howards End, The Longest Journey, Maurice, A Room with a View,* and *Where Angels Fear to Tread,* which have their own entries and are alphabetized by title.

MICHELLE FILLION is professor of musicology at the University of Victoria, British Columbia, and the editor of *Early Viennese Chamber Music with Obbligato Keyboard.*

The University of Illinois Press
is a founding member of the
Association of American University Presses.

University of Illinois Press
1325 South Oak Street
Champaign, IL 61820-6903
www.press.uillinois.edu